EDMUND BLUNDEN AND JAPAN

Edmund Blunden and Japan

The History of a Relationship

Sumie Okada

Foreword by
John Bayley

M
MACMILLAN
PRESS

First published 1988

Published by
THE MACMILLAN PRESS LTD
Houndmills, Basingstoke, Hampshire RG21 2XS
and London
Companies and representatives
throughout the world

Typeset by Wessex Typesetters
(Division of The Eastern Press Ltd)
Frome, Somerset

Printed in Hong Kong

British Library Cataloguing in Publication Data
Okada, Sumie
Edmund Blunden and Japan: the history
of a relationship.
1. Blunden, Edmund—Homes and haunts—
Japan 2. Poets, English—20th century—
Homes and haunts—Japan 3. Blunden,
Edmund—Bibliography
I. Title
821′.912 PR6003.L8Z/
ISBN 0–333–44034–X

Contents

List of Plates

Plates 1 and 3 courtesy of Mr Jiro Hayashi; Plate 2 courtesy of Ms Shiotsuki; Plates 4 and 5 courtesy of Miss Yoshiko Hongo; Plate 6 courtesy of Miss Yukino Tsuboike; Plate 8 courtesy of the Imperial War Museum; Plate 9 courtesy of the National Portrait Gallery; Plates 10–13 and 15 courtesy of Mrs Claire Blunden.

Acknowledgements

I am very grateful to Mrs Claire Blunden for giving me the opportunity to work on her husband's correspondence with Aki Hayashi and for granting me permission to publish it. She has also provided much invaluable information which I have used in the course of writing this book.

I should like to thank very deeply Professor John Bayley for his priceless support, encouragement and most inspiring guidance over many years, without which this book could never have been completed.

Thanks are due to the late Professor Yoshitaka Sakai, one of Blunden's pupils, for offering most interesting and vivid memories of his tutor. I am very grateful to Professor Willem Grootaers for his help and support in Japan. My thanks are also due to Professor D. S. Brewer for inviting me to Emmanuel College, where I took the M.Litt. degree from Cambridge University, and for arranging my interview with Dr Takeshi Saito; and to Dr Carmen Blacker for her valuable comments and suggestions.

My thanks are also due to the following people and libraries for information and help: Mr H. G. Blunden; Mr A. H. Buck; Christ's Hospital Library; Mr Arthur Crook; Professor J. O. Gauntlett; Mr Nick Gill; the late Sir Hugh Greene; Guildhall Library, London; Miss Keiko Hani; Sir Rupert Hart-Davis; Dr Roger Highfield and Merton College Library, Oxford; Professor Mikio Hiramatsu; Mrs Hiroko Maruyama; Professor Peter Milward; Mr Gordon Phillips; Mr N. M. Plumley; Mrs Clare Ross; the late Dr Takeshi Saito; Professor John Stevens; the late Professor Richard Storry; Miss Yukino Tsuboike; the Humanities Research Center, Texas University; the Librarian of Tsuda College; Mr C. R. Watters; Mrs Jill Williamson and the Registry Office, Yokohama City.

I am very grateful to the Great Britain–Sasakawa Foundation for the grant given through Emmanuel College to help with the preparation of this book. I owe a deep debt of thanks to Darwin College, Emmanuel College, Robinson College and Wolfson College, Cambridge, for their kind help.

This book is dedicated to my father, who has helped me very greatly, and to the memory of my dearest mother, who always gave me her encouragement and understanding.

The author and publishers wish to thank A. D. Peters & Co. Ltd, for permission to quote the extracts from the published works of Edmund Blunden.

Foreword

JOHN BAYLEY

For some years I have followed with interest Sumie Okada's research into the remarkable story of the English poet and man of letters Edmund Blunden, and the Japanese teacher Aki Hayashi, whom he met in the 1920s while lecturing at the University of Tokyo. Their story was a strange and touching one, throwing a lot of light on both English and Japanese behaviour at the time in relation to one another's culture and customs. It was far from being a Madam Butterfly situation, because Aki Hayashi was a remarkable and determined woman who might herself have become a writer; while Blunden was in many ways the weaker of the two – a charming and warm personality, emotionally responsive and always in need of love, a fine poet who had suffered greatly from his experiences as a soldier in the trenches during the Great War of 1914–18. Their relationship, which continued from the time they first fell in love in Japan until Aki Hayashi's death in London many years later, is a human tale of profound psychological interest, which might have inspired a story by Henry James or Joseph Conrad (one remembers the latter's story 'Amy Foster' about the ill-starred marriage between an English country girl and a foreign castaway from central Europe).

Not that the relation of Blunden and Aki Hayashi was exactly ill starred. It was, on the contrary, in many ways happy for both of them, as Blunden's letters to her so movingly reveal. But though it is clear that they had much in common and enjoyed a tender and intimate time together, Okada's study also reveals how difficult it is for such a relationship to have a permanent and settled outcome. Blunden never forsook his Japanese friend, who for the rest of her life was of the greatest help and service to his books and studies, but his letters also reveal the inevitable change in their lives, and in their attitudes towards each other. Aki became more 'English' than Blunden could ever become 'Japanese', but at the same time not only his outlook and character but his poetry, too, was greatly influenced by his life in Japan, and what he had learnt there from Aki Hayashi.

Sumie Okada has produced a book that is as absorbing to read as a *nouvelle*, and will also be of great interest to readers of English poetry and of English and Japanese culture between the wars. Other poets than Blunden (notably William Empson and James Kirkup) have been influenced by Japan, and no student of the subject will be able to ignore Sumie Okada's important contribution to the history of this little-known area of English poetry and letters.

Introduction

The object of my book is to publish a selection of Edmund Blunden's letters to Aki Hayashi together with a chronological narrative of their friendship and notes. The letters, which are so far unpublished, number more than 1400 in total and date from 1925 to 1962. When I first encountered these letters they were all in disarray; and my preparatory task seemed enormous as I had to put them in chronological order, transcribe them and have them typed.

The first chapter of my narrative will be biographical, covering the relationship of Aki Hayashi and Edmund Blunden during his stay in Japan and after. The purpose of this chapter is to make it clear to the reader under what circumstances the letters were written. The second chapter will be about Blunden's relationships with Japan and Japanese academics and writers. It will also discuss his own attitudes to teaching English literature in Japan, and his poems on Japan. In Chapter 3 I discuss more fully Blunden's personal relations with Aki Hayashi and illustrate this with some quotations and commentary on Blunden's more personal poems.

Following the narrative is a selection of the most important letters referred to in the text, which I have edited and annotated. Finally, there is a chapter containing my interviews with and letters from people who remember Blunden and Aki Hayashi personally. There is also an appendix giving details of the scholarly work Aki did for Blunden on Leigh Hunt and a chronological list of other work done by her for Blunden.

It is almost sixty years since Edmund Blunden first started to 'occupy the Chair of Lafcadio Hearn' at Tokyo University, accepting the invitation arranged by Dr Takeshi Saito. In all, he made seven visits to Japan, including his first assignment during 1924–7, his return as a cultural envoy for the United Kingdom Liaison Mission during 1947–50 influencing a wider audience with 600 lectures, and short visits in 1955, 1959, 1960, 1962, and 1964.

Blunden met Aki Hayashi, a 36-year-old teacher of English, a year after his arrival, in 1925. She was seven years older than he, and a graduate of Tsuda College, which is renowned for its English teaching. Yet she was a rather commonplace woman – tiny, plain and dark-skinned (in Japan a pale complexion is a necessary feature of the traditional beautiful woman). In the eyes of Blunden's Japanese pupils she looked unlovable, and they were jealous because she gained his affection and esteem. A romance began which is not unlike something out of Lady Murasaki's tenth-century 'Tale of Genji'. Blunden, afflicted with asthma and solitude, fell in love with her, strongly touched by her 'unselfish patience and splendid courage'. He writes: 'How gentle and beautiful a love has awakened between you and I! I shall rely on it and live on it in many solitary hours' (letter dated 29 August 1925). In the summer of 1927 Blunden took her to England. Since then no one had researched this Anglo-Japanese relationship, which was regarded by his Japanese pupils as an unfortunate lapse, which cast a shadow across his time in Japan.

Blunden must have taken pity on Aki because of the problems she suffered with her health, her brothers and her excessively demanding school duties. Moreover he was moved by her frustration in a society unsympathetic to a highly educated woman with an 'acute and enquiring mind'.

Aki was attracted to Blunden through his kindness and sympathetic understanding, embodied in the 80 love-letters he sent her between 1925 and 1926. In 1925 they spent the Christmas holiday together in Ikaho, a famous hot-spring resort in the mountains of Gunma prefecture, 120 km north-west of Tokyo, and soon afterwards Aki resigned her post to join Blunden in Tokyo. Thus they started living together, although Blunden was still married to his first wife, Mary, who remained in England with their two children. From the summer of 1927 Aki lived in London, working as his literary assistant, until her lonely death in 1962. His romantic love for Aki, however, faded after their arrival in England, and his affection changed into a filial devotion, though he admits in a letter that Aki is the 'only real gain I found in Japan'. He married Sylva Norman in 1932, obtaining a divorce in 1944, and married Claire Poynting in 1945. For Aki Hayashi, however Blunden remained the most important man in her life.

In London Aki constantly suffered from poor health, which later developed into diabetes. In spite of poverty and inadequate accommodation she showed no sign of homesickness or interest in returning to Japan. Her psychological ordeal during the Second World War is painfully hinted at in her letters. She was upset to see herself labelled in her registration book as 'enemy alien', and was worried about the threat of possible internment, in addition to her fear of the air raids and food shortages. In 1949, she became a naturalised British citizen, entitled to receive the old-age pension from 1958. She writes, 'How eagerly looking forward to that year!' (3 July 1955). She hoped it would lessen the financial burden she had imposed on Blunden.

Despite Aki's naturalisation and the length of her stay in England, she never lost her characteristically Japanese qualities, her ingrained loyalty and humility. She preferred not to disclose her naturalised status to her family, in order to avoid gossip among the Japanese. As long as he was in England, Blunden never failed to reward Aki in some way for her devotion, and attempted to console her whenever he was in London. However, his appointments in Tokyo and Hong Kong in the 1950s and '60s increased her loneliness, and she badly missed his company in her old age. It seems most tragic that she was unable to love anyone other than him.

Aki devoted herself to assisting Blunden by copying old newspapers and manuscripts in the British Museum, preparing his major publications on Leigh Hunt, William Collins, Charles Lamb, Coleridge, Shelley, Keats, Tennyson, Hardy, etc. She was industrious in seeking out undiscovered literary facts and passages. For instance, Blunden praises her discovery of a letter from Woodhouse to John Clare, writing 'It is quite a discovery, and your name shall be mentioned in connection with it when I use it in a book' (27 June 1931). Blunden's minute knowledge of Shelley's friends, which once amazed Dr Saito, Professor of English at Tokyo and Blunden's closest Japanese friend, equally suggests that Aki had been at work behind the scenes. Her reliability seems to have become known in literary circles – and figures such as Graham Greene and George Orwell asked Blunden to obtain her assistance with Japanese matters.

1

Biographical

The relationship of Aki Hayashi and Edmund Blunden during his stay in Japan and after

Edmund Blunden was 28 years old when he first met the 36-year-old Aki Hayashi in Japan during the summer of 1925. He had arrived in Japan in the spring of the previous year as a Professor of English Literature at Tokyo Imperial University (Teidai), the most prestigious educational institute in the country. His teaching post in Japan was arranged by Dr Takeshi Saito, a young, yet highly respected scholar of English literature, who was on leave in London and Oxford. Dr Saito, having been asked by his senior colleague, Professor Sanki Ichikawa, to find a suitable successor to Robert Nichols, met Blunden at Siegfried Sassoon's home in London and was favourably impressed both by Blunden's attentive personality and by his recognised work as a poet. Blunden had published *The Waggoner* in 1920, and two years later was awarded the Hawthornden Prize for *The Shepherd, and Other Poems of Peace and War*.

Blunden had married Mary Daines in June 1918, and in the spring of 1920 he went back to Oxford to resume his studies, which had been interrupted by the war, but left after the summer term. He then worked on *The Athenaeum* as Middleton Murry's assistant until he left for Japan in 1924.

Dr Saito felt privileged to know such promising English poets and literary figures as Sassoon, Blunden and Ralph Hodgson – two of whom he successfully persuaded to come to teach in Japan (Blunden in Tokyo and Hodgson in Sendai, the capital of the north-eastern part of Japan). Blunden came to Japan alone, leaving his wife and children, John and Clare, behind in England.

Undoubtedly the early days of Blunden's life in Tokyo were beset with difficulties. He was not only lonely and asthmatic, but also spoke hardly any Japanese. Moreover, the humid and changeable weather, and his timber accommodation in the rather unattractive city must have contrasted sharply with the rural context to which he was accustomed, the spacious green meadows, high spires, peaceful gardens and brick houses of Yalding in Kent where he had been brought up, and Oxford where he had studied. Even his war experiences as a soldier in Belgium and France, and his brief voyage to South America, could scarcely have cushioned the 'culture-shock' of the Far East.

In fact, at the beginning of his stay, Blunden was assisted by his gardener in Stansfield, Crick, who looked after domestic matters such as shopping and cleaning in the strange new country. But Crick soon returned to England and Blunden moved into a room in Kikufuji Hotel in Hongo,[1] about five minutes' walk from the University (Teidai, as the students used to call it). Kikufuji Hotel was an inn, and a number of well-known writers and scholars, both Japanese and foreign, had rooms there as long-term lodgers. Meals were provided, which Blunden described to Aki as 'strange'. Kikufuji Hotel, which had been a haven for many famous patrons, was destroyed in bombing raids during the Second World War.

In 1925 the Local Council for Education in Nagano Prefecture organised a Summer School for Japanese teachers of English in Karuizawa, a popular summer resort much cultivated by the Western missionaries, with its cool fresh air, fields spread at the foot of the dormant volcano, Mount Asama, woods of white birches, and many waterfalls such as Senga-Taki. Many foreign missionaries had villas in this town alongside those of wealthy Japanese families escaping from the hot and humid Japanese summer.

In the summer of 1925 it was also the setting for a romance – unforeseeable and secret. Among the participants of the Summer School was Aki Hayashi, a teacher of English at a Junior High School in Anjo, near Nagoya,[2] who had enrolled in order to polish her English and enrich her teaching by attending various lectures on western cultures given by prominent scholars like Inazo Nitobe,[3] Edmund Blunden, and Takeshi Saito.

Aki Hayashi was discontented with her professional and personal life. She was plain and did not possess the pale skin thought conventionally beautiful by the Japanese. She was born on 20 August 1889 in Tokushima into a well-to-do family, but her father, who worked for a bank, died quite young. Aki was educated at Kinjo Girls' High School in Nagoya, a Protestant missionary school in the mid-eastern part of Japan with a long and respected history of instructing middle-class girls in the Christian faith and way of life.

Aki's eldest brother, Miyakitsu, had been to Sapporo Agricultural

College – now incorporated into Hokkaido University – and was greatly influenced by a famous American missionary-teacher, Dr Clark, who left an inspiring message to Japanese youth – 'Boys, be ambitious!'. Miyakitsu became a Christian, and under his influence so too did Aki. In those days in Japan being a Christian meant belonging to a special group of people – well-to-do, well-educated and well-read, even in English. But to the majority of ordinary Japanese they were self-seeking people who refused to contain themselves and their life-style within accepted Japanese norms, and were often closely acquainted with 'strange' foreign ideas and people. Under the religious influence of Confucius, Japan cultivated, and still strongly cultivates, a great deal of reverence for conformism in thought and society. Consequently in such a society, minorities tended to suffer prejudice and oppression for no good reason. People generally feared the stigma of belonging to a minority group, and tried to remain within the majority even at great cost to their own true causes or beliefs. This ethos, still detectable, must have been overwhelming about sixty years ago, at the time when Aki first met Blunden.

Sadly, in such an 'immature' society, Aki belonged, in every aspect of her life, to a non-conformist group. Her education, for instance, was an exceedingly privileged one for a woman of the Meiji and Taisho eras[4] during the early 1900s. Yet ironically, this very privilege made her life more difficult than that of the average woman who accepted the wife-and-mother cycle without any doubts or reservations.

Aki went to Tsuda College, which had been founded within the compound of the British Embassy in 1900 by Miss Umeko Tsuda. Miss Tsuda was a distinguished woman, having been one of the five women students selected for the cultural missions led by Ambassador Tomomi Iwakura,[5] whose aim was to learn the English language and acquire general western knowledge in America.[6] She was only seven years old when she was sent to Boston, the youngest member of all. After pursuing her studies at Bryn Mawr College, she founded Tsuda College in order to give women the opportuntiy to train as experts in English language and literature.

Miss Tsuda's school (as Blunden used to call it in his letters to Aki) has prospered, despite the many difficulties of its pioneering days, and still maintains its high standing in women's education in Japan. Miss Tsuda literally devoted her life to her College and the teaching of English, and remained unmarried until her death at sixty-five. As can perhaps be imagined from this degree of dedication, she was a strict perfectionist in English teaching. Aki was one of the early students, who were fortunate enough to learn directly from Umeko Tsuda – there were only about thirty students in her whole year who aimed at becoming teachers of English.

In those days it was almost impossible for women both to marry and to pursue a career. Most women had to sacrifice opportunity at the high school level, so the handful of career-minded women who proceeded to a College tended to be unfortunate with regard to marriage. Above all, the average Japanese man and indeed society as a whole much preferred docile and domesticated wives to ones of high intelligence. The marriage of one woman graduate, a contemporary of Aki, was a failure and she had to raise her two children by teaching English to wealthy families who could afford to employ a private governess. Only the wealthy and intellectual learned English; the average Japanese lived in a totally different world, detached from outside influences. Yet, even for them, the western countries had a vaguely alluring aura of civilisation and culture superior to their own. The times themselves were changing – people in the Taisho Era increasingly aspired to assimilate western notions of democracy and liberty into Japanese society. Paradoxically, however, they still retained the isolationist complex of 'the children of Heaven', as Blunden half-seriously complained in a letter to Aki.

Aki thus had many understandable grievances against the general attitude of Japanese society towards her. Personally she was independent and strong-willed, and thus may have blamed herself in part for her discontent. Disappointed in her prospects in Japan, her spirit was naturally drawn towards England and its culture – to which her Christian education had introduced her.

From a purely practical point of view, Blunden accepted his post in Japan because of the offer of a very high salary at Teidai. It was customary for the Ministry of Education to pay almost five times as much to foreign teachers as to their Japanese counterparts. The wages were paid in yen, so Blunden often complained to Aki about losses caused by fluctuations in the exchange rate. Apart from the lure of money, Blunden's interest in Japan and its traditional arts and culture had been awoken by his mother, and also by a chance encounter in his village, Yalding. He writes in his poem 'Looking Eastward':

Down our street when I was a boy I met with a friendly man
Who took me to the stone-cross steps and said to me, See Japan.

I stared at the East he pointed; never have I seen a sky so fine,
A shining height of clouds and sun-bright, and loftier hyaline.

And, See the Mountain, said my friend, and I traced the region
cloud,
With intense wish to shape that peak, which made him smile so
proud.

I nearly saw, not that alone, but as it felt to me
Cities and domes and lakes and falls and even doorway and
tree.

But just the final face of the thing came not; and I told him so,
I only knew that the man was right and that I was stupid and
slow.

He smiled, and said I should find all out, and the words he left
me were these:
I come from my shop to see Japan, and the Mountain, when I
please.[7]

Perhaps, for a young man distant from his family and rather deprived of comfort, it was natural to seek a woman companion. But it was difficult for Blunden to find a satisfactory framework for their relationship. For a time he established a *ménage à trois* with his first wife and Aki, and later hit upon the expedient of making Aki his permanent literary assistant. The thirty-seven years of their relationship reveal its seriousness; but the strains of a cross-cultural relationship are also evident. It is also apparent that without Aki's earnestness and diligence Blunden could never have been so prolific. In particular, he assimilated from Aki a wealth of knowledge of matters Japanese – from the general cultural and educational systems, to the particular discovery of reference books and *Ukiyo-ye* paintings.[8]

One of his early letters to Aki, dated 1 August 1925, was written at Karuizawa Hotel, and its tone is properly formal, beginning 'Dear Miss Hayashi' and ending 'yours sincerely Edmund Blunden'. Blunden suggests that Aki should look in at the Hotel and says that he would be delighted if she could come to have dinner with him on 3 August. He was, as usual, surrounded by 'many earnest acquaintances' and was frequently visited by them. Hence, 'I hope this time to be fairly free & at ease; my last few days were not so'.

It may well be imagined that Aki was a respected participant in the Summer School because her English was much better and more fluent than that of the male participants – one of her acquaintances remembered her speaking English more fluently than even Teidai students. Blunden himself commended her command of English, mentioning how few other Japanese were able to keep up a similar correspondence in English. Naturally, it must have been more congenial for Blunden to converse with someone who could manage more than just basic student English. With her 'keen and enquiring mind' Aki doubtless approached Blunden, perhaps after the classes or seminars, asking various questions on linguistic and literary matters. Blunden took an interest in her and invited her to dinner at the hotel where he was staying. About a fortnight later the tone of his letters had already markedly changed, beginning 'My dear' and ending 'With my love E.'. Behind the scenes, romance had begun between the two, possibly very intimate and eventually 'consummated', as hinted in the letter of 3 September 1925.

They often met at the post office or railway station; and when Aki was ill with a cold, Blunden visited her at Ichidaya[9] where she was staying (undated letter sent from 218 Karuizawa). Being in love, Blunden often saw Aki in his imagination and found that even the imagination could hurt him.

> How I see you all the time, but would much rather the reality than the imagination! Love & love again to you; your Edmund. . . . As the train carried me this way I looked round on all the faces, but they only impressed on me your absence. I can see you too, but imagination is not the life itself, and hurts as much as it pleases.
>
> (31 August 1925)

Another interesting trait of Blunden is that he was exceptionally sensitive and aware of the *location* where his beloved was. For instance, he writes:

> How beautiful it was to see you last evening & be at peace; I am still happy because of those happy hours. I woke up looking the way you are & sending you my blessings.
>
> (17 August 1925)

> This train is going in your direction – a pleasant thought, but only partly so.
>
> (29 August 1925)

Perhaps his senses of direction and location had been sharpened by his days as a soldier, always attentive to sources of danger – and it was this watchfulness which he now applied to his love. One of the sad ironies of life!

As he himself mentions, being surrounded by many earnest friends and admirers could constrain his freedom of action somewhat. He wanted to meet Aki as often and freely as possible, but his own respectability, under the scrutiny of many curious eyes (and his own inner eye, too), prevented him from behaving how he wanted: 'It's not the fear of catching your cold which keeps me here this evening, but – respectability! that curse (Monday, 7 p.m. [August 1925])'.

Meeting at the hotel or at a railway junction, dining together and going to concerts, there was no doubt that Blunden was committing adultery. Though he sent part of a Shakespearean love sonnet to Aki swearing eternal love (28 August 1925), he sensed the necessity to guard himself against criticism from his friends (let alone his wife who would learn of the affair eventually), and perhaps against the possibility of a request for marriage from Aki herself. Thus he used the tactic of mixing discouraging sentences with his sweet loving remarks.

> I have just had a letter from my friend Siegfried Sassoon, the greatest of poets in England now. He closes with the suggestion that I sh.^{d} become a Bookseller when I go back, and he will provide the capital at the beginning. Alas, my dear, I am afraid he would utterly change his mind if he knew about *us*; and yet, shall I grieve for that? Even that I could endure, if the worst came to the worst – I hold you so fast in my love and honour, you must be my refuge if ever my friends forsake me. *But it will help us, if we can keep a secret*.
>
> I don't feel like sleep; so restless and so alone. My room is untidy, I'll spend some hours in straightening things. I have here some Poets whom I love, and long to read their best out to you and share the beauty with you. You dear soul, you have swiftly come into my deepest life. So remain! *may envy never harm us*. If there is any innocence, it is love; and I cannot help loving you, *though far*

> *off is one whom I love. This, the common opinion would condemn, but I have spoken the truth.* What time may do, I don't know: but you will never pass from me.
>
> Your most affectionate Edmund.
>
> (31 August 1925; my italics)

Blunden ingeniously contrived a place for Aki to occupy in his work and life – she could not be his wife but could be his permanent secretary or copyist.

> The Proofs of my forthcoming book called 'English Poems' were on my table and I spent a great deal of the night in correcting them – they are to be published in November, so my list of Works is growing all the time. . . . I have had many letters of all kinds, and need a Secretary. Well, and I shall have one . . . yours unfailingly O sweet companion! Edmund
>
> (29 August 1925)

Apparently, he found two obstacles to this plan – one was that Aki was not with him in Tokyo but in Nagoya: 'It is miserable to think of days and days with you at Nagoya, me here' (31 August 1925). Nowadays it takes only two hours from Tokyo to Nagoya by bullet train, but sixty years ago, even by express, it took over eight hours. Aki, however, did not mind taking a night train from Nagoya so as to have more time to spend with Blunden in Tokyo. But Blunden was greatly concerned about her trying journeys. They meant that she had free time only on weekday evenings, using both Saturday afternoon and Sunday for travel.

One weekend Blunden planned to travel to Nagoya himself to meet Aki:

> It would be as well if you let me know what's best for my visit to Nagoya – date and trains – there is an express from Tokyo at 8.15 in the morning, getting in at 4.30 or so, but I am not quite certain. I hope I don't begin lecturing until the 15th. Curse lecturing – but that's what I'm paid for!
>
> (31 August 1925)

> Bless you, why aren't you here? must I go on counting past hours and living on retrospect? Tell me if I can bring anything from Tokyo which you need. But I suppose Nagoya is very

> modern. I can't picture it. But for your being there, I shouldn't want to: but now I am haunted by the name.
>
> (1 September 1925)

Though none of Aki's letters of this period have survived,[10] she must have written to Blunden asking about the possibility of their renting a house together. Blunden's answer was simple enough, stating that it would be more economical to stay in the Kikufuji Hotel – as Aki could easily book a separate room there whenever she came over – and above all they would be less open to malicious gossip.

> So far as I can see this hotel would be our best place until we begin the Secretaryship, and I take a house in this town. You can, I believe, get a room here for any short period, and we can see each other easily, without anxiety. Miss Collie is here, of course, but she doesn't supervise me after about 9 p.m. The staff leave me alone in a friendly fashion.
>
> (31 August 1925)

Another important question raised by their continuing relationship was whether Aki would remain on the staff of Anjo Girls' High School in Okazaki, near Nagoya, until March (which is the end of the academic year in Japan). The matter was still undecided in the letter of 31 August 1925, as well as the matter of plans for Christmas.

> At Christmas I'll go to Matsuyama and then we can meet at Kyoto or anywhere. We shall by then have our minds made up, you will know whether you will stop in Nagoya till March, and I shall have plans about a house &c. Meanwhile if I stay in this hotel I can save money, and that is very necessary.
>
> (31 August 1925)

Blunden's future also seemed to be uncertain, as Sassoon's suggestion that he should become a bookseller tends to imply. Meanwhile Blunden tried to share the beauty of poems with Aki, together with social activities like concerts and week-end trips. Thus, in a sense, he started to train her to be his literary assistant.

In September Aki returned to her work, and Blunden was left alone with happy memories of Karuizawa during the summer: 'All told, I am thankful for Karuizawa, & the scenery there is unsurpassed – honto ne? [isn't it?]' (1 September 1925). Particularly he was contented with the consummation of their love in the Green Hotel, Karuizawa. Aki thought herself rather 'reserved', but offered her heart, her body and everything to Blunden.

> I think with astonishment and delight of the love you give me, and the suddenness and completeness of it; I am happy in that love and only unhappy in my impatience to have you with me again. You write as though you had seemed rather reserved at the Green Hotel, but I never thought any such thing; the time there is beautiful to think about and your profound companionship gave me a new life and new poetry. 'I have offered my heart, my body and everything to you' – dear love, that I remind myself of all through the day, and my love seems to glow more and more. Your dear body has but a minor share in our mutual devotion – not to deny or despise physical love; but it is a part of love that could be excluded, and still love would prevail. We are in this world, creatures with bodies; and hence I think it's unnatural to act like hermits or icebergs; but still there's a deeper secret of love to worship most.
>
> (3 September 1925)

Blunden was delighted that Aki was sending him a *kimono*. His plan to go to Nagoya had been fixed: 'I intend being in Nagoya on the 11th, . . . and will look out for your letter about the hotel' (3 September 1925).

Apparently Aki's teaching job turned out be unsatisfactory.

> This is melancholy news about your new work and environment not at all answering your expectations. You must tell me all and ease your breast as much as you can.
>
> (3 September 1925)

She had moved school from Poole Girls' High School in Osaka – an Anglican mission school with a long and respected history – to Anjo Girls' High School near Nagoya. Advising Aki to come to Tokyo, Blunden also now referred to his secret but yet bold plan to take her to England; and that day was approaching.

> I hope England won't be another illusion scattered, [sic] when

you are wandering round some old estate, or a picture gallery, with joy, one day nearer. Your admiring and loving Edmund.

(3 September 1925)

Thus the first, and perhaps deepest part of Blunden's relationship with Aki was consolidated. With the arrival of early autumn another phase of their companionship was to unfold.

Aki was disappointed in her work, and Blunden's official work was also not what he might have expected. He found the classrooms dusty and noisy. The students were earnest in learning, and in befriending him on long walks and excursions. But neither comfort nor real contentment lay there. As for the buildings, Teidai was in quite a state, because most of the buildings had been destroyed in 1923 by the biggest earthquake Tokyo had ever experienced. (In 1929 Aki related her horrific experience of the earthquake to Blunden's youngest brother in Salcombe where his parents lived.) The Faculty of English itself was still a ramshackle temporary structure. One of Blunden's poems depicts the various stages of the rebuilding of the University:

Like men of fire, in painful night,
The Eastern builders thud
Their iron round; wild bubbles of light
From Babel's angles scud.[11]

The standard of English the students could manage was not high. Perhaps for most of them Blunden was the first foreign teacher they had had. Even such a prestigious University and English Faculty was allocated only one native speaker by the Ministry of Education. No wonder Blunden was looked on, and treated like, a very rare specimen, almost a museum piece!

The age-range of the students was mostly eighteen to twenty-two, and all were males, to whom Blunden lectured mainly on eighteenth-century English literature.[12] Blunden was encouraged to find that some of his young students were attentive and observant.

They soon found out that their new professor, whom they found very polite and kind, unlike his predecessor, was fond of such authors and poets as Dryden, Christopher Smart, John Clare and Hardy, whilst being rather hostile to Oscar Wilde and George Gissing. He seemed to prefer classic, observant, and yet suffering under-privileged poets, whose views illuminated their objective, meticulous, detailed and honest descriptions of their favourite theme, Nature. The students responded readily to Blunden's preferences because the traditional theme of Japanese poetry is the beauty and pathos of Nature; and its traditional method is the detailed and sensitive description of the changes Nature brings to human minds.

What were the students' impressions of Blunden? He was approachable because he was not too tall, and was thus easy to talk to. His nose was most impressive for its size – high and enormous. One student wrote that he was reminded of the nose of *tengu* – a Japanese demon noted for his outsize nose, and his love for drinking and outrageous behaviour!

As is shown in the fact that Blunden lived in a humble inn near the University, his life-style was never luxurious or extravagant. His modest upbringing (both of his parents were school-teachers) and the frugality of his education at Christ's Hospital were clearly lasting influences. For the students the proximity of his quarters was most advantageous. Whenever they wanted to ask questions (they would not have made comments) they could get hold of him by following him to his inn. They were reserved, partly naturally, but partly through awe of their former teacher, the English poet Robert Nichols, who had stayed in the most exclusive hotel in Tokyo, the Imperial Hotel. Indeed Nichols had opined that life in Japan was worse than the war, and never dreamed of modifying his Western life-style even in Tokyo. An extract from Siegfried Sassoon's diaries gives a good example of Nichols's attitude:

> April 18 [1922]
>
> But I'd ceased to believe in the importance of Smashaway this evening. An early copy of Blunden's new book of poems[13] was awaiting me here (sent by Mary B.) and, before I'd had time to do more than cut the pages, Bob Nichols arrived. He has been away fifteen months. Down he flopped in my armchair, and at once began telling me what hell he'd been through in Japan. 'It was worse than the War', he exclaimed. But he was only at the war for about three weeks, so I wasn't greatly disturbed, and merely asked him what he'd been doing since he arrived at Southampton in Mrs Asquith's liner from New York, which was a week ago . . .[14]

The students duly saw in Blunden a kind heart and a patient and careful listener, and took to him greatly. Yet some sharp minds also sensed a certain stubborn and proud Englishness in him. He disliked American wealth and materialism, even though this was contributing money to the reconstruction of Teidai. He loved cricket – a keen player himself – a true Englishman's sport, and highly curious to the Japanese students.

Blunden devoted some of his time to the Reading Society organised by the tutors and students. They read and discussed such works as Thomas Hardy's *Dynasts*. Sometimes they performed (by reading) Shakespeare's plays together. The students were much moved by Blunden's tears when he lectured on the undue hardships and miseries which such underprivileged poets as Christopher Smart and John Clare suffered. Blunden was probably reminded of his similar contributions and responsibilities as Secretary for the Grecians' Reading Society at Christ's Hospital, in which he took minutes and read a paper on John Masefield. He also read plays and was much acclaimed for his flair for drama – hitherto a hidden talent. The group took an excursion to Atami,[15] a famous hot spring and seaside resort, where Blunden enjoyed swimming with the students. He was young and ambitious – very proud that his book had been reviewed in the same newspaper as a volume of poems by Thomas Hardy.

On his way from University to his lodgings and in the streets, Blunden would encounter the unexpected and unwelcome attentions of street urchins jeering *Theio-jin* ('Westerners'). Initially much put out, he became more even-tempered under the influence of Aki.

> You have made a world of difference to Blunden, who otherwise can't help feeling like one in a dark prison, though I nowadays do not notice so keenly the points at which Japanese minds, manners and nerves entirely differ from ours. And I think I am a little closer in touch with the students at the University than when I came last year.
>
> (23 October 1925)

I enjoy the yellow flames of leaves which leap now from the chestnut trees – at Toranomon[16] they line the road.

I also enjoy the small children of this town, who hail my strange apparition with 'Theio-jin', and stop playing as though a giant was passing.

(7 November 1925)

However, it remained difficult for him to adjust to the Japanese climate. In Japan it could still be very hot even in September. In winter he would have had only a small gas heater, quite possibly prone to breaking down. These conditions were not ideal for an asthmatic.

I have not been able to write anything since you went, because of asthma and the sudden return to solitude.

(29 September 1925)

Dearest Autumn,[17]

I shall be at Tokyo Station on Sunday, unless your telegram cancels your plan, at 7.50 a.m., and shall wait if you don't arrive by that; . . . It's a delight to think of your coming, but the stress of such long night journeys gives me great anxiety for you. It's a pity I am not able to be the Dominant Male, and speak to you like a father! For my own part, I think now if I watch carefully what I do and don't hurry I may be free of asthma again for a period. It would have been the best remedies if you could have been here as you wished. I love you and your love.

(9 October 1925)

My throat is very sore, and I am a little anxious over it, in case asthma should follow.

(18 November 1925)

Apart from proof-reading *English Poems*, and writing articles regularly for the *Japan Advertizer* and newspapers like *Jiji*, Blunden's major project was to write about his memories of the war, which he later published as *Undertones of War*. As he himself mentions in a letter, he left his actual notebook in England, in which he had kept records during the war; accordingly he could not write in detail until he had checked the real facts in the notebook; but the memories haunted him obsessively.

There's a nip in the air now and the brown leaves begin to wander

> about. A great change from Kyoto[18] weather, only a month ago: I wish I was well for then it would be enjoyable. Ten years ago I was in the army & spent any spare time in long walks under the trees then serenely letting their leaves fall, while just over the Channel human leaves were falling in a wild bad storm. It is curious, but even then I often had asthma.
>
> (13 October 1925)
>
> . . . wrote a few more pages of my book on war experiences, which had been left uninspected since March.
>
> (10 November 1925)

Aki, for her part, helped Blunden to put his war poems in order, and they eventually formed the last part of the book.

The *Undertones of War* is indeed a classic and poetic account of a poet's war experiences. Compared with Wilfred Owen's memoirs, which were edited by Blunden, one of the striking differences is Blunden's sustaining detachment in the world of poetry and beauty – even amid the appalling reality of falling shells, blood-covered bodies, and bombardments. Blunden was never without a book of poetry, particularly always keeping with him Edward Young's *Night Thoughts on Life, Death and Immortality*. He was briefly infatuated with a country girl in a French village, praising the innocence of love:

> At Watten station something happened which you may laugh at, but I shall not. The train was not due to leave till the evening; after a visit to an estaminet, listening to a hero who was not ashamed of it, I sauntered by the canal, and then settled myself with my book in an empty cattle-truck. There came along a girl of fourteen or so, with a small brother, and looked in. We talked, and – we fell in love. That 'I' may be still in love with her, Marie-Louise of course, so black-eyed, and serious, and early-old with the inheritance of peasant experience – I have seen her alone since in many a moment of escape and fantasy.[19]

Blunden's war poems strangely retain an almost ethereal purity and serenity in the description of scenes which must in fact have been absurd, cruel and even horrific.

On the other hand, Owen seemed to be more directly engaged than Blunden, facing the real brutalities of the war, both outraged and terrified. For instance, Owen could not pay enough attention to a book of poetry given to him by his senior officer; his mind was occupied by sudden bombings and hosts of other practical difficulties and dangers, such as finding a chair.

> At the Base, as I said, it was not so bad. We were in the camp of Sir Percy Cunynghame, who had bagged for his Mess the Duke of Connaught's chef. After those two days, we were let down, gently, into the real thing, mud. It has penetrated now into that sanctuary, my sleeping bag, and that holy of holies, my pyjamas. For I sleep on a stone floor, and the servant squashed mud on all my belongings; I suppose by way of baptism.[20]

> 'Quite 10 years ago I made a study of this town and cathedral, in the Treasury. It is all familiar now!' He looked at the 'inoffensive sky' and his room, and reflected, 'I suppose I can endure cold and fatigue and the face-to-face death as well as another; but extra for me there is the universal pervasion of *Ugliness*. Hideous landscapes, vile noises, foul language, and nothing but foul, even from one's own mouth (for all are devil-ridden) – everything unnatural, broken, blasted; the distortion of the dead, whose unburiable bodies sit outside the dug-outs all day, all night, the most execrable sights on earth. In poetry we call them the most glorious. But to sit with them all day, all night – and a week later to come back and find them still sitting there in motionless groups, THAT is what saps the "soldierly spirit".'[21]

His poems convey harsher impressions of war in strong outbursts of human helplessness confronted by the savage mechanisms of war.

Aki was seriously worried by Blunden's asthma. She advised him not to come to Tokyo station to meet her when she came from Nagoya, and also to go out less frequently in the evenings in order to protect himself from sudden attacks. Blunden's weekend excursion to Nagoya was not repeated because Aki feared it would strain him, and thereafter they met only when Aki travelled to Tokyo.

Aki came up to Tokyo almost every weekend to meet Blunden, booking a separate room at the Kikufuji Hotel. They went out together to concerts or galleries; but they had one serious project particularly in mind. That was to save enough money to cover Aki's travel expenses to England. For that purpose they planned a small investment buying good yet comparatively cheap *Ukiyo-ye* paintings which were to be sold later in England at higher prices. Blunden tended to rely on Aki's taste and appreciation; for instance, praising her decision not to purchase a rather 'gaudy' painting. But Aki sometimes found it difficult to buy prints on her own, as the Japanese dealers were not used to selling such valuable paintings to a 'mere' woman. They were very suspicious of independent actions by women, an attitude which surprised and angered Blunden.

They eventually reached agreement concerning Aki's early resignation and she decided to join Blunden at Christmas. Her trunk (*kori* – a case made of knitted dried straw) arrived as a harbinger of Aki's own arrival.

> Your face cream, the same as before, is already bought: handkerchiefs and pastilles I will get. And I will have your Kori brought to my room, and glad to have such an assurance of yourself, quickly following.
>
> (20 December 1925)

Blunden wrote a letter to the hotel in Ikaho – a hot-water spa about two hours' train ride (nowadays) from Tokyo – reserving a room for Christmas. Following Aki's instructions, Blunden bought face cream for her which was probably only available in Tokyo, pastilles, and handkerchiefs. He himself had received a Christmas cake sent from his mother, and a woollen coat from his wife, who later reproached Blunden for giving it to Aki: 'I shall ask you to wear a little woollen coat, which I do not use; my wife has sent me a new one and altogether I have 4' (20 December 1925).

On the day of their departure for a brief get-together at Ikaho, which was on the 23 December, Blunden had to collect his salary at Teidai, then meet Aki so they could leave together. He asked her half-jokingly not to take a train going in the opposite direction and, in this symbolic manner, Aki became part of Blunden's life, sharing it with him for another thirty-seven years until her lonely death in London. Thus they embarked on a new adventure, perhaps fearing the judgment of Heaven, but definitely leaving for the same destination – which, at that moment in December 1925, was Tokyo, Ikaho, and eventually England!

Apparently, however, Aki was very anxious about the uncertain status of her relationship with Blunden. She persistently asked him to write a 'certificate' declaring his unending devotion and love. He responded to this request conscientiously, on 5 May 1926, though sometimes lamenting her naïvety in believing in a mere piece of paper!

> Aki asks me to write, –
> That I would sooner live with her,
> And be her love,
> Than with anyone,
> If I was not already married. E.B.
>
> Why question so often?
> Why rob me of my peace?
> Have I not shown you my spirit,
> made you the receiver of my intimate ideas,
> entrusted to you the desires of my heart?

but even giving a half-serious promise of marriage:

> Jan. 17 1927
> In case I should ever marry a second time I should in all likelihood marry Aki.
> Edmund Blunden.

Their Christmas break in Ikaho was rather like a honeymoon, though it was a secretive affair given its disregard for conventional behaviour. After the break Aki settled in the Kikufuji Hotel, and started sharing her life with Blunden, who was adamant that Aki should take no notice of malicious gossip in the hotel, which would soon dissipate. Blunden was uncharacteristically bold in this matter, partly because he knew that he was to leave Japan soon (within a year) and partly because in Japan a male initiative in adultery would not be as publicly stigmatised as in the West. However, Blunden was never open about his affair with Aki to his Japanese friends.

Before deciding on Ikaho, Blunden had several choices in mind – including such places as Kyoto or Nara. As a foreigner he might have chosen Kyoto for its history and its temple architecture, but for a Japanese this would be outweighed by the attractions of the hot spring – *onsen* – especially in winter, since it represented a source of natural warmth. For the Japanese a hot bath had a spiritual as well as physical significance, contributing to the cure of diseases, relaxation and the release of tension. In a resort one might take several baths per day – on arrival, after the luxurious meal, before going to bed, in the morning immediately after breakfast, etc. Hence, until recently, the favourite honeymoon choice for newlywed couples was a hot spring resort, though recent wealth induces people to travel abroad. Yet hot springs retain their medicinal and cultural mystique. Contemplative people remain alone, while the sociable mix with strangers. Thus a Japanese proverb says, people can wash their cares away in the stream of hot water. Usually hot spring resorts are located near beautiful scenery. Ikaho is among mountains and does not face the sea. As Blunden writes in his poems on Japan, such places can generate real peace of mind and comfort, the abundance of natural beauty delighting the aesthetic senses.

Later when Blunden was in a difficult mood and tired out by the stressful quarrels with his wife concerning her infidelity, he liked to stimulate Aki by mentioning their secret love in Ikaho, often in the half-finished sentence: 'Ikaho ni orimashita tokini . . . [When we were staying in Ikaho . . .]'.

In early 1927 Blunden asked the Mayor of Tokyo to grant Aki a passport. In those days women could not be registered in the census separately from their family, whose head always had to be the father, or if he were deceased, his eldest son. But in order to get a passport Aki had to demand to be registered separately from her family, in itself a courageous act.

On board with Blunden and Ralph Hodgson, Aki left Japan for good. It was April 1927, and Aki was full of expectations about England, knowing it only from maps, textbooks, and conversations with Blunden.

On 25 August, Blunden and Aki landed safely in Plymouth. He then had to arrange a visa for Aki, which was initially granted for only one month. In the document, previously submitted to the Japanese authorities, he declared that he would accept full responsibility for Aki, both financially and personally, during her stay in England.

> In respect of the application for a passport to England made by Miss: AKI HAYASHI, at present my secretary, I have the honour to inform you that I wish to retain her services in that situation in England; and accordingly I hereby guarantee to provide all her travelling expenses and all necessary expenses in England; and further I personally undertake all legal responsibility affecting her, and guarantee to fulfil exactly and completely all official

requirements concerning her. I beg therefore that Miss AKI HAYASHI's request for a passport to England may be granted.

(27 January 1927)

The most worrying matter for Blunden to face next must have been his wife's reaction to Aki's arrival. Mary seems to have been a rather jealous type of woman. Hearing about Mrs Hodgson visiting Blunden from Sendai, Mary sent him a note warning him that if ever he had an affair with Mrs Hodgson she would never forgive him.

With this temperament and after the long separation Mary must have been greatly upset by the arrival of Aki. Her children also had to suffer the shock. Consequently, Mary passed round the rumour that Blunden had brought a 'geisha' back with him.

Ironically, however, Blunden found himself still attracted to his wife, indeed more strongly and devotedly than to Aki.

I am *most anxious* that you should be happy and yet it is yourself alone who can make you so, for my home is intensely dear to me and I cannot help giving my life to it, with the hope that everything there will become as nearly perfect as a man can find, . . . but I can feel what loneliness and impatience you feel; they weigh on me among my other problems; I have you in my heart and feel that you are the only real gain I found in Japan. The chance of my renewing all that was beautiful in the love between me and my wife must dominate all my actions at present, and your devotion will not fail me in this, my overwhelming hope and great task . . .

If my feelings towards my wife had really died, I should not have to demand of you the sacrifice of being alone in London; but instead I find that I am inspired, by her excellent qualities and her own love surviving all the dreary discords of the past years, to love her as greatly as ever.

(Undated)

In her new unfamiliar environment Aki was no longer an essential mother-figure, and became more of a burden.

Blunden was very young, only twenty-one years old, when he married Mary, who was a country lass working as a waitress. They were both innocent and immature, believing in pastoral romance. Mary was not only a beauty but an intelligent woman who occasionally sent her poems to *The Nation* and other magazines. She was outgoing, lively, strong-minded, a bit selfish, and sarcastic. When a Japanese scholar was invited to stay with them in the village near Clare, Suffolk, they all went to the church together. Noticing a young girl with a red parasol standing near the church Mary teased him: 'Look, a pretty girl is waiting for you!'[22] Later, when he was in Japan, Blunden much resented that Mary was unkind to his parents, not having visited them as frequently as they had expected. It may be partly true that the relationship between Blunden and Mary suffered because of the death of their baby daughter Joy. Saddened much by her death, Blunden wrote the poem 'To Joy':

> Is not this enough for moan
> To see this babe all motherless –
> A babe beloved – thrust out alone
> Upon death's wilderness?
> Our tears fall, fall, fall – I would weep
> My blood away to make thee warm,
> Thou ne'er on earth hast gone one step,
> Nor heard the breath o' the storm.
> How shall you go, my little child
> Alone on that most wintry wild?[23]

However, Mary too had had an affair while her husband was away in Japan. During quarrels with Blunden concerning her adultery, she admitted her lover's inferiority. He was a mere manual labourer. Blunden received hints from his relations and the village vicar who had all known of his wife's love affair.

He confronted her, accusing her of using his money to live with this individual in his absence. Of course, Mary had just as much right to accuse Blunden of bringing Aki back with him from Japan – even if only as a 'secretary'. Mary accused him of giving the pullover sent for him to Aki. That 'allegation' Blunden laughed off as a mere trifle. The argument over Aki was only a curtain-raiser to the argument over Mary's behaviour. Aki was less and less the focus of dispute.

He found it impossible to live in the same house as Mary, who had continued meeting her lover while Blunden was out, even after his return from Japan. Finally he made up his mind to leave the house and move to London. During those trying and critical years Aki's support, dedication and self-sacrifice were his principal comfort and consolation. Moreover, she worked for him with much devotion, and made new discoveries of articles and passages important for his work.

Blunden found great relief in going out with Aki for a day in Cambridge, cycling from his troubled village home to spend a few hours with her.

The distress and misery caused by the estrangement from Mary were such that he often resorted to drink. This strain contributed to strange dreams and hallucinations. He imagined that Mary might be pleased to know that he was suffering so much. After some whisky, he had a dream referring to the tangled triangle of relationships: 'Last night I dreamed that you were riding in a bus with me, when someone touched my shoulder, & it was Mrs M. Blunden, who made a "scene"' (27 January 1930).

Siegfried Sassoon helped Blunden out by offering more than £50 as a financial base soon after his return to England. Blunden kept the offer secret from everyone except Aki, to whom he gave part of the money as an emergency fund.

> I have been thinking over the matter of dear Siegfried's promise, and how I might best use the gift, and during the night I decided when it comes to give you £50 of it so that you may feel no anxiety on the question of ready money during the next few months. I shall try to give you this sum in *cash*, in such a way that (except Siegfried) no one else knows of the transaction.
>
> (17 October 1927)

Now that Blunden faced the crisis of divorce, Sassoon was generous with his help. He suggested he could take all the responsibility for Blunden's two children, John and Clare. But Mary was determined not to sacrifice her children, and declined Sassoon's offer in a rude letter. 'There is no news about the other bothers. Except that a rude letter was sent to Mr Sassoon' (3 November 1929).

Blunden successfully obtained a position as a tutor of English at Merton College, Oxford, from October 1931. His private life, however, was still unsettled. His relationship with his first wife, Mary, was obviously hopeless, and the divorce was proceeding in the courts. Meanwhile, working for *The Nation*, Blunden met Sylva Norman (1901–71), a journalist whose work he encouraged and to whom he was attracted. She was of Armenian descent, strong-willed and career-minded. They agreed between themselves not to have any children.

Obviously Aki felt strongly about losing her last chance to marry Blunden, and her whole future seemed threatened. Until Blunden made known to Aki his love for Sylva, Aki identified with his feelings against Mary. Now her special place had been usurped, and she could no longer share things with Blunden in total confidence and trust. Blunden himself was very well aware of Aki's feelings, and inwardly much-feared her reactions to his new plans. She had been waiting for more than five years, and indeed possessed a number of Blunden's promises of possible marriage. He knew that very well too. Moreover, she might no longer be the docile Japanese woman who would follow her male partner's directions blindly. She had lived independently in London for five years, where the rights of women were much more widely acknowledged. Aki could have reacted more forcefully and self-assertively, as some of her English friends had advised. Hence Blunden's worries grew deeper, and his self-defensive reflexes became stronger. He had to be resolute in solving his crisis to his best advantage, by marrying Sylva Norman even at the cost of Aki's devotion and love for him. But he also knew that he wanted to keep Aki permanently in her special status of service to him.

> In short, should it become possible for me to marry Miss Norman, I ask you to show your gratitude to me, and your love for me, by treating that with the greatest reverence and good will. As you know, such a step on my part would not mean that your living in London and serving me is to be altered. You have my promise, and I mean it.
>
> (9 March 1932)

He even baldly stated that nobody mattered greatly to him apart from Sylva Norman, to whom he had been drawn not so much because of feminine qualities, but because of excellent literary talent.

> Woman or man makes little difference to me nowadays, apart from Sylva N. – and I am stirred by her not so much by feminine qualities as by general genius of which she has a share.
>
> (7 March 1932)

Indeed, she would be more useful in the social circles at Oxford.

Such thoughtless words must have been a great blow to Aki, who had to endure much humiliation and a series of distressing episodes during Blunden's continued courtship of Sylva. It is really pathetic to imagine Aki waiting at Paddington for Blunden to arrive from Oxford, while Blunden ignored her because he had an appointment with Sylva.

> I am sorry that you were so worried about my catching my train the other night, & that you ran such a risk by waiting on Paddington station for the Oxford train. Indeed I arrived by the 5.50, and was met by my Miss Norman, who took me up to Hampstead to dine with her father and mother; I had appointed that evening for her as you know, & so did not look out for you.
> (7 March 1932)

Indeed these letters frankly reveal Blunden's egocentricity; and no wonder Aki 'tried to make things difficult' for Blunden (9 March 1932). But her body had also suffered.

> Some things in your letter trouble me, above all your feeling so down-hearted about your illness. The need is for you to take action and to go to Dr Macduff as soon as you can.
> (7 March 1932)

At one stage he tried to plead with Aki to avoid adding any more black pages to his life. On another occasion he changed his tactics, trying to encourage her by reminding her of the valuable work she had been doing for him.

> I have the greatest wish to see you well and happy, and in steady good spirits, and continuing to work for me as you always have done; and although I may ask much of you in regard to letting me live my life as my new emotion & vision suggest it, yet you will know that I have a strong affection for you and that your place in my world is yours always . . . Your future is bright – you will be doing most valuable work, and honour and sympathy will be yours; whatever may be my lot, you will not be cut off from the essential fact that you will be helping me. – You would be surprised, perhaps, how often I bless you with words spoken to

myself, sometimes to others, because I think of you as a pattern of courage and goodness.

(7 March 1932)

These easy and superficial words may have appeased Aki because of the depth of her devotion, but his vain and childish attempt to placate her with such praises as 'you are a pattern of courage and goodness' only reveal his insensitivity.

But you are not really going to *gain money* from me, I know that well; you are trying to make things difficult for me, I am afraid. I have noticed that tendency in you, and forgiven it; but try not to hurt me!

(9 March 1932)

This episode soon ceased, though, because Aki retained her Japanese distaste for conflict and attempted a reconciliation with Blunden, even sending him a present. Indeed in ordinary Japanese life peace and unity are regarded as much more important even than 'justice', if obtaining that involves conflict. Thus Blunden managed to get his own way again. 'I am very glad that you liked Sylva, & she likes you. You need not think you gave a bad account of yourself at the meeting; far from it . . .' (24 October 1932).

Blunden obtained a second divorce in 1944, and married Claire Poynting in 1945, twenty-two years his junior, who was one of his pupils at Oxford. Blunden was forty-nine, and Aki Hayashi was in her middle fifties. Aki took to Claire, and much appreciated her kindness in sending small things from Japan while the Blundens were staying there during 1947–50.[24]

Aki wanted to become a naturalised British citizen, which Blunden supported, and this was eventually granted in 1949.

We have received your letter of the 8th with the excellent news that you are a British subject, after so long a period of trying to get this achieved; and I hope it means you can now find daily life a little easier in various ways.

(24 September 1949)

In fact, this is the only real rejoicing in the Blunden letters concerning Aki after 1925. Behind the scenes, there was the bitter experience she underwent during the Second World War as an 'enemy alien'. A letter from her old senior colleague, Miss Tristam, who was a former principal of Poole High School, suggests that Aki had planned to move to Durham in order to escape the escalating air raids. Blunden hoped that her new status would ease her difficulties in daily life, in which her milk bottles and eggs were constantly stolen. Unfortunately there was no evidence to show any improvement in her life.

Strangely, Aki asked Blunden to keep her status secret from her Japanese friends and relations. Her reason for this was:

> In case I forget, I have to ask you not to tell anybody including my relatives that I have been a British subject. . . . because it is entirely my affair – nothing to do with them.
>
> (17 April 1949)

She also sought to hide her address from Japanese visitors. Her strong tendency to secrecy about her life and status seems to imply a fear of Japanese gossip, and she was in any case ashamed of her one-room accommodation and single status. She tried to maintain her dignity and pride, hiding all her vulnerabilities. From 1956 her address was reported as 'care of the British Museum' in the alumni book of her College.

In 1953, three years after his return to England from Japan, Blunden embarked again, this time for Hong Kong and the Professorship in English at the University. When the news of Aki's death reached him there in December 1962, he was intensely shocked. She died alone in her small room in Worsley Road (now called Pilgrim's Lane), Hampstead, from a haemorrhage in the left cerebral hemisphere. But her loyalty and efficiency never failed her; she left all her property, including the considerable sum of her saved pension, to Blunden in her will, which had been registered in 1955.

> I devise and bequeath to Edmund Charles Blunden of the University of Hong Kong all my property whatsoever and wheresoever for his absolute use and benefit and I appoint the said Edmund Charles Blunden to be my Executor.

What Aki Hayashi attained in England, though with tremendous difficulty, was none the less a sort of dream for her contemporaries in Japan, whose freedom of action and life-style were severely restricted simply because they were women. The route to an independent career was extremely hard, and most of them withdrew into marriage. It was the age when women were expected to be modest and to stay in the home.

Notes

1. A district of Tokyo where Tokyo University is located.
2. One of the important industrial cities in central Honshu.
3. Inazo Nitobe (1862–1933), educator and cultural interpreter of the Western world.
4. Meiji Era (1868–1912), during which Japan began a rapid process of Westernisation, industrialisation and expansion in foreign affairs. Taisho Era (1912–26).
5. Tomomi Iwakura (1825–83) played an important role in the Meiji Restoration, and was a strong influence on the Emperor.
6. See Takako Yamazaki, *Tsuda Umeko*, Jimbutsusosho, no. 91 (Tokyo: Yoshikawa-Kobunkan, 1982; in Japanese).
7. Edmund Blunden, *An Elegy and Other Poems* (London: Cobden-Sanderson, 1937) p. 83.
8. Japanese genre paintings or wood-block prints, eighteenth and early nineteenth centuries.
9. An inn in Karuizawa.
10. The Humanities Research Center, Texas University, has about 200 letters from Aki Hayashi to Blunden, together with her diary and notes (see Bibliography).
11. Edmund Blunden, *Japanese Garland* (London: Beaumont Press, 1928) p. 34.
12. Most of the lectures were later published: Edmund Blunden, *Lectures in English Literature, given in the Imperial University, Tokyo*; first series (Tokyo: Kodokwan, 1927).
13. *The Shepherd and Other Poems of Peace and War* (London: Cobden-Sanderson, 1922).
14. Rupert Hart-Davis (ed.), *Siegfried Sassoon Diaries, 1920–22* (London: Faber and Faber, 1981) p. 142.
15. A hot spring resort, 90km west of Tokyo on the Pacific Ocean coast.
16. Avenue in downtown Tokyo near the Ministry of Education.
17. Aki's name is homonymous with the Japanese word meaning 'Autumn'.
18. The ancient capital of Japan and home of the Imperial Court from 794 to 1868.
19. Edmund Blunden, *Undertones of War* (London: Cobden-Sanderson, 1928) pp. 202–3.
20. Edmund Blunden (ed.), *The Poems of Wilfred Owen: A New Edition Including Many Pieces Now First Published, and Notices of his Life and Work* (London: Chatto and Windus, 1931) p. 12.
21. Ibid., pp. 19–20.

22. Tau Sigma, 'Mr Blunden Whom I Met in England', *The Study of English*, June 1927, p. 43 (in Japanese).
23. Edmund Blunden, *English Poems* (London: Cobden-Sanderson, 1925) p. 104.
24. Between themselves Blunden and Claire used to refer to Aki humorously as 'Old Hayashi'.

2

East and West

How English literature was taught in Japan
Blunden's relations with Japanese university and literary life
His poems in a Japanese context

Despite the significance of Blunden's influence upon the literary and educational circles in Japan since 1924 – which is at least as important as that of Lafcadio Hearn – there has been no substantial research on this topic, either in Japan or in England. This chapter intends to convey something of the cross-cultural milieu of Blunden and his Japanese friends from 1924 to 1962.

There seems no doubt that Blunden's relations with Japan and his Japanese students, and more particularly his emotional relationship with Aki, influenced his outlook and his poetry in a variety of subtle ways. No other English poet, and certainly no poet of the twentieth century, has been so surprisingly, and so sympathetically in touch with what might have seemed to someone as 'English' as Blunden a wholly alien oriental culture.

During his first stay in Japan as a Professor of English Literature at Teidai (Tokyo University), Edmund Blunden lectured mostly on eighteenth-century English literature, as well as Shakespeare and some Romantics, to classes of young men. He also tried to shed light on such minor and neglected poets as Christopher Smart and John Clare, emphasising the directness and purity of their work. One of his colleagues writes in Japanese:

> Professor Blunden gave lectures on 18th-century literature and 19th-century essayists in the first year, and in the following year Shakespeare, Survey of Literary History, and in the final year Literary Criticism, together with Masters and Masterpieces of English Literature. He also gave short lectures on various subjects from Chaucer to the Modern Period surveying the general trend of English Literature. . . . It was specially significant that through him for the first time systematic methods of studying English Literary History had been taught to Japanese students.[1]

Blunden's inaugural lecture greatly impressed the Japanese audience with its fresh insights into literature and humanity. The Japanese students who were so used to the impersonal formality of their lectures were amazed by it. One of them recalls how they were struck by his stress on individualistic approaches and the free appreciation of literature. Blunden mentions:

> But let us keep an ideal before us, – the enquiring spirit, the finer kind of curiosity. I, now coming before you as a Professor of English Literature, have spent many days happily in chosen areas of research. I have found, if I am not mistaken, that recognition of beautiful writing is not inevitable; that even the best editions and biographies sometimes err; that what struck Dr Johnson as being a splendid sermon has no striking power for me; that the eighteenth century was not swept into the dustbin by the Romantics; that the Romantics, in turn, do not pale in the improved lighting system introduced by Tennyson, Morris and the rest; with many other things of the kind. . . . For practical purpose, I am your guide, endeavouring to note the main interests, producing a sort of chart or diagram. But books are living things, are characters and men, and *our affinities are our own*. I love an enquiring spirit, and one who dares to find beauty for himself.[2] [my italics]

Equally, the students took to his unpretentious character, and his lectures must have contrasted sharply with the authoritarian style of other Japanese professors at that time. Mr Ogura writes: 'One of Professor Blunden's favourite words is said to be "humanity", and I think that it well conveys the truth of his personality.'[3] His approach to literature was welcomed by the Japanese students because it upheld the priority of humanity and individuality, and it stood to liberate the old style of education (modelled on German tradition), which seemed to aim at cultivating minds useful only for the prosperity of the country.

> And there is an accumulated force and movement in this approach of young Japan. There are cross-currents, it is true, of a jealous nationalism, and a kind of lethargy sometimes creeps in, necessitated, it may be, by the great burden of education forced on boys who must acquaint themselves first with Chinese characters and presently with our widely variegated language and one or two of the others. But the air of that country,

> traditionally kind to mental and spiritual careers, is still cultural. Conscious that there are worlds to conquer, the Japanese student sets about the campaign with a seriousness that sometimes hardens into mechanical dryness, but usually is like a blossoming.[4]

Thus the students who had suffered unwittingly under the old system were provided with a fresh source of inspiration in Blunden, whose liberal mind supplied what that particular era – Taisho democracy – needed. One student bears witness to the prevailing atmosphere of indifference at the university: 'Some students simply graduated from the University without remembering their professors' names.'[5] In contrast to this, Blunden offered warmth and sensitivity:

> We are truly indebted to Prof. Blunden for inspiring us with fresh facts of literary history. We have had great contentment in finding ourselves understand the outline of what English literature means. Truly, his mission for teaching the Japanese students about how to appreciate the facts of literature was finely accomplished.[6]

Whether he knew it or not, Blunden successfully changed the quality of English literary studies in Japan, since almost all of his pupils subsequently became influential teachers in the field.

Besides lecturing, Blunden was willing to help his students in their extra-curricular activities. Though extremely busy with his own work, he regularly attended the monthly meetings of the English Reading Society, and the students responded to his genuine interest with admiration and gratitude. Professor Y. Sakai, one of Blunden's pupils, and former professor of Tokyo University, recalls the foundation of the Society:

> While Mr R. Nichols (Blunden's predecessor) was teaching, our hopes for organising a group for reading drama and discussing literature were in vain. But the plan became feasible, when Professor Blunden came to the University. With earnest support being accorded with Professor Ichikawa's encouragement, we successfully launched the first meeting of 'The English Reading Society' in October 1924. We have had twenty meetings to date, and are most grateful to Prof. Blunden for having given us both

> his encouragement and his academic knowledge. . . . Mostly, we have read such Shakespearean dramas as *Hamlet, King Lear, The Tempest, A Midsummer Night's Dream; The School for Scandal* by Sheridan; *The Good-Natured Man* by Goldsmith and Hardy's *Dynasts* and *Strife* by Galsworthy.
>
> Thanks to Prof. Blunden's earnest guidance, we have enjoyed a much friendlier atmosphere than in the lecture rooms.[7]

This private seminar not only fired the students' interest and enthusiasm for English literature but it cemented the relationship between Blunden and his students. It was very rare, and hence valuable, for students to be on an equal standing with their professor; usually there was a feudal style of apprenticeship between the Japanese teachers and students. Indeed, one of the students thanked Blunden for his friendliness; he reminded him of a 'senior student' rather than a 'professor'.[8] This may have been partly due to the proximity of age between them, but was mostly due to Blunden's unaffected and open-minded attitude to the students. Interestingly, Blunden found the students' polite attentions rather awkward, and he hints at his dissatisfaction in the following:

> Here, a simple story may speak clearest. 'What is this, *sensei* [professor]?' 'That's a shoe-horn – a little ancient.' 'Is this the ordinary English shoe-horn?' 'It is. . . . Would you like it?' Smiles, and 'We don't see these in Japan. . . . I am very much obliged to you for your kindness.' (1930)[9]

Blunden's uneasiness with the Japanese way of relating to people may be easily understood when we bear it in mind that he was so used to the English way of treating other people on equal 'Christian name' terms. However, his understanding of the students gradually increased as he came to know them better, as he writes in a letter to Aki:

> Even here the general attitude is passive and lazy, but there are stirrings of intellect, and several of my students please me well with their keenness and their genuine, unborrowed ideas.
>
> (7 October 1925)

The personal approach which Blunden had cultivated in Japan is revealed in another feature of his teaching at the University – his private 'tutorials'. Students would eagerly visit this sympathetic teacher in his room in the Kikufuji Hotel in order to ask questions. He is remembered for having responded kindly, trying to provide some sort of answer, even when the queries fell outside his special fields.

> In his room we were chattering, with some chocolates. Then Prof. Blunden showed me some references to Joseph Conrad about whom I had asked, and he lent me some of Tomlinson's works.[10]

Blunden himself writes about such an occasion:

> That drowsy, heavy youth who comes up at the end of the morning with some query (precisely what, it is hard to hear) on the biography of Mr Galsworthy, or the length of a Yule-log, will be grateful for a careful answer, which he goes off meditating. In a year he will be a cheerful, not unconventional visitor, unwrapping from his silk handkerchief[11] – by that time his teacher has begun to use one instead of a portfolio – a copy of some newly acquired book, or a Japanese clay figure for the *sensei*'s table.[12]

Blunden, on another occasion, greatly impressed the Japanese students by his readiness to express emotions openly. Professor Sakai writes that he was much moved by Blunden's tears when he was talking about John Clare to the English Reading Society. Naturally, the young Mr Sakai was not accustomed to seeing the more humane side of his teachers, and would never forget the scene. He also recollects Blunden's defence of John Clare, in which he said that Clare's greatness lay in the fact that he never claimed worldly recognition for himself but firmly stood by his own beliefs as expressed in his pastoral poems.[13] This unauthoritarian approach to poetry and literature in general had a considerable impact on the Japanese students who saw in it a means of liberation from the old 'feudalistic' system and thought-structures of the Meiji Era, whose ghost, they believed, was still haunting them.

Blunden (who later became an associate editor of *The Times Literary Supplement*) engaged in literary journalism in Japan, and influenced pupils in this field.

> Since he came to Japan, Professor Blunden has contributed a number of articles to *English Studies, Japan Advertizer, Rising Generation* (*Eigo Seinen*) and *Eigo Kenkyu*. He edited *The Oriental Literary Times* which unfortunately ceased to be published after the publication of its sixth volume.[14]

Yoshio Nakano, a controversial critic and journalist, was a pupil of Blunden's at Teidai, and was encouraged by his teacher's interest in his career. Blunden, realising that most of his students were to be English teachers after graduating, warned them that they should be much more honest with themselves about their individual vocations, and should think carefully before following the set pattern of becoming a teacher. In fact, his advice came too late, or perhaps it just sounded too unrealistic, given the actual system in Japan: most of his pupils in fact became successful teachers. None the less, Nakano, though he became a teacher and advocate of peace causes, still followed Blunden's advice to some extent and made a name as a Shakespearean critic, writing for a wider audience.

> Shortly before graduation, Prof. Blunden recommended I make journalism my career, yet I feel ashamed of myself for not yet having reached the standard he set. I often remember the interest he showed in Japanese journalism, as I do his kindness in holding an umbrella over me quite unexpectedly, one rainy day.[15]

Not only as a teacher and critic-cum-journalist but also as a poet, Blunden impressed his Japanese pupils, and the accounts of his second stay during 1947–50 and subsequent short visits in 1955, 1959, 1960, 1962 and 1964 are clearly reflected in his poetry. Indeed, much wider and more varied subject matters are treated in *Poems on Japan: Hitherto Uncollected and Mostly Unprinted* – from a thought of Prince Chichibu[16] to a newly opened English-style pub in Kobe.[17] Dr Takeshi Saito, who had invited Blunden to the Teidai in 1924, and had compiled and edited the book, tells of his endeavours:

> After his lectures, even on such visits, he was always surrounded by a crowd of people and not infrequently asked for his autograph on a *Shikishi*[18] so that his pen was busy writing extempore poems. But he was so free with these poems that, so far as I know, he kept no copy of them.

> Therefore I tried to trace all of them if possible, and thanks to the kind response of those having such poems in their possession, I am delighted to have received seventy, most of which have not been previously published. . . . I am afraid, however, that there may be some unknown Blunden manuscripts treasured here and there and which thus have yet to see the light, and so this small book cannot claim to contain all of Blunden's poems on Japan and her people.[19]

What struck the students most with regard to his poetry seems to have been his sympathy as an English poet with nature, that intuitive intimacy and sympathy which appears in poems like Edward Thomas's 'Adlestrop' (much admired, incidentally, by Blunden), a poem whose impact and subtlety would not be lost upon a Japanese poet, who would see in it something of the Japanese attitude to nature. Blunden's poems such as 'The March Bee' and 'The Veteran' display the same lyrical and sensuous glimpse into the world of natural objects. In 'The March Bee' the poet hears a bee buzzing among the still leafless branches of a little wood on a sunny day in March. The contrast is between the summer associations of the sound and the wintry bareness of the season, symbolised by the plain black and white bird, the magpie, who is seen 'steering round from wood to wood'. (Note the delicate accuracy of perception expressed in the word 'steering', which conveys the motion of the bird as he slowly flies, seemingly steered by his long tail.)

'The Veteran' is a celebration of the tranquil rural life, among fruits and flowers, beehives and apple-trees, of an old soldier long retired from the army. Blunden rejoices in the sights and sounds which now surround him, contrasting them with the former barren discipline of his military life. Now the cobwebs over the mantelpiece 'trace the outline of his rusty gun'; and if he wakes in the night it is not to the sound of the bugle or a night alarm but to hear 'his bellman cockerel crying its first round'. Blunden's poems frequently turn on contrasts of this kind, between the seasons and sights of nature and the response to them of human beings, set free from their own worldly or mechanical concerns. A very early poem, 'The Midnight Skaters', describes a frozen pond near the home of Blunden's parents at Yalding in Kent. Here it is nature itself which is cold and inhuman, the black water locked up in ice over which the skaters in the moonlight joyfully wheel and turn like happy birds in the sunshine. A telling detail which gives the poem its central image is the stack of hop-poles which stand beside the pond.

> But not the tallest there, 'tis said,
> Could fathom to this pond's black bed.[20]

These poems, like Blunden's interest in cricket and other English sports, are purely English in feeling and subject-matter, and yet an audience accustomed to Japanese poetry would find many shared resonances. The Japanese have traditionally been close to nature; it frequently occupies scenes both in poetry and paintings. One of Blunden's friends, who later became a famous poet, Taketomo Sófú (1891–1954), writes in his tributes to Blunden's three years' teaching in Japan:

> Professor Blunden's power to catch the subtlety of nature is not to be compared with other earlier English poets. I admire his 'First Snow' most, and the last stanza is especially impressive: . . . reading the line of 'How silent comes the snow' I can spontaneously visualize the scene in which the first snow is falling over the fields with its faint yet clear-cut sound.[21]

T. Yokoi, another pupil, similarly observes:

> Professor Blunden loves nature, and firmly believes in 'the truth of nature'. All of his poetry and criticism is born out of this strong affection for nature.[22]

One of the other factors which might have enabled the Japanese to feel close to Blunden was his remarkable ability to describe things in detail; for description has been one of the prime concerns of Japanese poetry – further common ground in this celebrated Anglo-Japanese friendship.

> In his poems Blunden also shows remarkable intimacy with birds and flowers – for example, 'their steepling hollyhocks' – [note the use of the same accurate but unexpected image as in 'The Midnight Skaters'] – as well as almost everything else in rural life. He is a great painter of nature, expressing his impressions in words with absolute certainty. If the use of epithets is any criterion for evaluating poetical works, there is no question about his superiority.[23]

Perhaps Blunden's poems reminded his pupils of the descriptive and picturesque poetry of China – *Kanshi*, with which they were already familiar.

By comparison with his gentle personality – as Dr Saito said, 'gentleness is power'[24] – Blunden's poems have not been sufficiently discussed in Japan. His kindliness and humanity, and his generous concern for the students have become almost legendary in Japanese literary and educational circles, but his influence as a poet has been left unresearched. There appears to be a considerable number of 'buried' poems which await discovery.

Blunden started with mere descriptions of things, but gradually acquired the skill of combining his own unique thoughts and ideas with them, thus maturing his poetry. We shall examine his poetic development in those of his poems which represent his interest in Japanese scenes and people.

Japanese Garland is a collection of poems published in 1927 which records Blunden's experiences and impressions of Japan. Only 390 copies were published, and one was presented to Aki. The inscription inside reads:

To the best flower
in any Japanese Garland,
Aki Hayashi,
with E.'s love. July 5, 1928.

Most of the poems contained in this volume are descriptive, as, for example, his account of carpenters at work on the frames of the Library of Tokyo University.

Like men of fire, in painful night,
The Eastern builders thud
An iron round, wild bubbles of light
From Babel's angels scud.

The hammer's fierce brain-battering shout
In bursts of power rebels,
Puts unheard melodies to rout,
Drowns heaven's songs and bells.

In vain, it serves their quiet will,
It builds them one more home

Where nooks shall be most kind and still
  For the great Muse to come.[25]

As a poem, this is not one of his best. Blunden is said to have 'striven for utterance'[26] in order to find the right words, which in the end only tended to render his poetry difficult to read and slightly remote, especially for the Japanese students. But Blunden's feelings were always genuine, and well conveyed, when his emotions were stirred by human misery or the suffering of animals. One poem written on this theme tells of a small dog thrown out on the street, almost dead. Blunden was deeply hurt by the maltreatment of dogs and cats in Japan. He observes a similar sad incident in his prose, too:

> I mention a few details at random out of the many in which a Japanese city makes itself felt. The worst side is perhaps the meeting with dogs and cats evilly diseased and apathetically driven on to their release. Bewick's *Waiting for Death* is nothing to it.[27]

On a Small Dog, Thrust Out in a Tokyo Street
Soon After His Birth, and Rescued in Vain

ANIMULA *vagula blandula*, foundling dear,
So deep a hold have you already won
On my tired heart? so great a joy have you to give?
So sharp a fear?
Can your tininess unseal so hot a tear
And prayer, that you should live?

Like these cherry flowers here
Whose life thin-spun
Seems by its own ghost haunted – but no more words!
Save, all heaven's luck befriend you,
Blind eyes and feeling hands,
That take me for all-surety and all-love,
And so to sleep.[28]

Somehow the sympathy expressed here echoes Blunden's lament for his dead daughter, Joy. The short-lived beauty of cherry blossom is often regarded as a symbol of the transitoriness of life, *ukiyo* in

Japanese, which literally means 'floating world', where nothing is secure. A strong spring wind could easily scatter the blossom, leaving the pink-white petals dead upon the ground. This sadly fated beauty would appeal to the aesthetic sensibility of the Japanese, and in turn seems to have influenced Blunden's sense of beauty and happiness; he shows great interest throughout his poetry in the transitory contentment of life, with its undercurrent of anxiety.

> I particularly appreciate in Blunden the niceness of the observation – sometimes it is finical – and the subtle way human unease is hinted at in much verse which at first sight would appear to be purely descriptive.[29]

Another impressionistic poem, 'The Daimyo's Pond' conveys his youthful wish to draw as much attention and admiration as possible to his talent and charm, vanity in this case as it was partly in the previous one. He wishes it would work, as an old man beating a bucket like a drum near the pond lures a number of colourful fish out of the unseen depths of water and tangled weed. This is one of the best poems written in his early years; it successfully combines the minute descriptions with his complex psyche.

Look, how that old man, face like parchment tanned,
Wrinkled, mouth-shrivelled, silently is come
To the high bank, a bucket in his hand –
He beats upon it as it were a drum:
He beats a solemn summoning monotone,
And through the secrecies that under shroud,
The water-shapes steal towards his gonging drone,
The lonelinesses gather in a crowd.

Moon-pallid some come gliding through the green,
Great fishes, yet for phantoms passing well;
Others like opals rosy-rayed convene,
Jewels of June waters, to that simple bell;
Dark as barbaric dreams, there others swim,
And now to that old labourer's wish a host
Of splendours circle mingling, to the brim
Fanning and fawning, flame and dream and ghost.

Would that I might by means as plain as this
Bring many a mystery from life's shadowy pool,
Enchant the live gems from the unknown abyss,
And make them seen, the strangely beautiful.

He concludes the poem with Blakean questions on the mystery of life:

What measured syllables must I resound,
Oh what most simple and most secret spell
For hidden fancies waits there to be found?
Who knows that incantation, and will tell?[30]

'The Daimyo's Pond' is in the compound of Tokyo University and is famous for the cherry blossoms around it in spring. *Daimyo* means 'a feudal lord', and this pond belonged to the estate of Lord Maeda.

His Japanese students and colleagues owe Blunden a debt of gratitude for the introduction of varied Japanese scenes in fine poetry to the British reader. Whatever 'measured syllables he resounded', his wishes seem to have been fulfilled, because he achieved remarkable success as a teacher certainly 'enchanting the live gems from the unknown abyss' – the minds and hearts of the Japanese – if not in the Coleridgean way as described in this poem. In 1927, shortly before leaving Japan, Blunden was still humble about his success and apologetic for his 'incompetence'.

Forgive what I, adventuring highest themes,
  Have spoiled and darkened, and the awkward hand
That longed to point the moral of man's dreams
  But shut the wicket-gates of fairyland:
    So by too harsh intrusion
    Left colourless confusion.

. . .

Forgive that eyeless lethargy which chilled
  Your ardours and I fear dimmed much fine gold –
What your bright passion, leaping ages, thrilled
  To find and claim, and I yet dared withhold;
    These and all chance offences
    Against your finer senses.

The Japanese students, responding to this kind of humility which was so similar to their own, much regretted Blunden's departure from Japan. Blunden affectionately thanked them for their devotion and friendship.

> And I will even pray for your souls' health,
> Remembering how, deep-tasked yet eager-eyed,
> You loved imagination's commonwealth,
> Following with smiling wonder that frail guide
> Who hears beyond the ocean
> The voice of your devotion.[31]

Indeed, he generously offered his continued guidance to the English Reading Society from England – or to the Shepherd's Society, as it became known. Thus the ties of admiration and devotion between the two countries were to continue.

Throughout his long career as a poet, Blunden wrote a number of fine poems which pay tribute to the friendship he had with the Japanese people. One of these is about his enjoyable stay in a friend's villa in Chigasaki, a famous seaside resort near Yokohama. Blunden wrote to Aki:

> And I have written some verses about Chigasaki scenes, as yet only rough and unshaped. You will think me vain to tell you such things. I feel content to have you to tell them to.
>
> (1 October 1925)

In 'The Cottage at Chigasaki' Blunden's interest focuses on the Japanese poetess, Kaga-no-Chiyo, who graciously withdrew when she found the ancient well-bucket already taken over by the twine of the morning glories. This sort of *okuyukashisa* (reticent gracefulness) much appealed to Blunden, whose modesty is somehow of a similar kind.

> That well you draw from is the coldest drink
> In all the country Fuji looks upon;
> And me, I never come to it but I think
> The poet lived here once who one hot noon
> Came dry and eager, and with wonder saw
> The morning-glory about the bucket twined,
> Then with a holy heart went out to draw

His gallon where he might; the poem's signed
By him and Nature . . .

He then develops a lively scene commonly seen on Japanese beaches where the people 'wash away the salt and sand carried from the sea's blue fire'; then discuss water-melons, probably having some slices; and finally:

Though comfort is not poetry's best friend,
We'll write a poem too, and sleep at the end.[32]

Here the leisurely and contented pace of a summer's day is depicted. Oddly, Blunden's friend seems to have forgotten to tell him that the poet was a woman! Nonetheless, Blunden adds this note:

> Perhaps the most familiar Japanese poem is that which says, approximately, 'The morning-glory has taken hold of the well-bucket; I'll borrow some water elsewhere.'

In *Poems on Japan*, published in commemoration of Blunden's seventieth birthday, friendship is the main theme celebrated, and is epitomised by yew trees and their 'rubies' in the following poem:

To Koichi Nakane

By my old house a yew-tree stood,
A huge dark tree, and like a hood
Obscured our roof; its berries red
Were underfoot and overhead.

Outside this eastern house, once more,
The yew-tree wears the jewels it wore,
Its rubies; but the quiet age
Has suffered from a desperate rage.

Sad years, strange difference! But be sure
In this kind house all's as before;
And as the dark red-berried yew
Unites the vanished with the new.

So our good Host's warm welcome mends
All defects, and makes perfect friends.[33]
(18 September 1948)

Not only on his second visit from 1947 until 1950 when he worked for the British Embassy as a lecturer and cultural adviser, but also during his subsequent short stays, Blunden met a wide range of people, exerting great influence on them through his amazingly numerous lectures – no less than six hundred – delivered throughout Japan from northern Hokkaido to southern Kyushu. Dr Saito comments about Blunden's lecture on English literature on one such occasion, remarking at how patient the audience was, especially those who had to stand for the whole three hours because of a shortage of seats. Even a Buddhist temple was temporarily used as an auditorium due to its spaciousness.

> Wherever he spoke, he attracted huge audiences, not only of students of English literature, but of the reading public in general. On two occasions I had the honour of being another lecturer with him. One afternoon at Osaka, in April 1948, about two thousand people came to the City Hall (formerly a theatre) to hear his lecture on 'The Growth of English Literature'. They occupied even the small extra chairs that had been packed into the gangways and passages for the occasion; and many others had to stand or lean against the walls. One of his former students and well-known novelist, Tomoji Abe, acted as interpreter for his lecture. The whole meeting, including the translation and my own speech, lasted three hours; but the audience did not move till we had left the hall. Another time, at Asahikawa in Hokkaido, in July 1949, we were taken to a Buddhist temple because in those days it was the largest building in the city. Blunden spoke on *Hamlet* to an overflowing audience. It was, I think, his first and last experience of lecturing from a place like an altar, almost surrounded by Buddhist sculptures.[34]

Blunden describes his busy yet rewarding tour up and down the country in 'The Summer Journey':

Even as we travelled, travel seemed
Not so much actual as dreamed,
And long delightful days at last
Were merging with the distant past.

We paused indeed, from place to place,
Enjoying grandeur, pastoral grace,
Kindness and welcome, a still hour,
Antiquity and modern power;
And castles, temples, waterfalls,
Statues and lost memorials,
This grove of cedars, that immense
Avenue and bright byways thence
With endless cottage roofs and flowers
And yellowing ricefields, all seemed ours.
Long we might stand, or sit, and stare,
And fall in love with what lived there,
Or we might hasten to and fro
From shop to shrine, while all aglow
The hope of winning something true
And beautiful lit up anew.
But soon that sullen verb 'forget'
Obscured the vision. Forth we set,
And as we travelled on and on
Again a thousand signals shone:
'HERE is the best. Here, please to stay;
This crowns the whole; O, but one day!'
And speed, denying, whirled us away.[35]
(1963)

Obviously, Blunden enjoyed the work, and had sufficient energy left over for writing short verses for his admirers. One of these occasional poems was given to a newly opened English-style public house in Kobe:

The King's Arms, Kobe

Elizabethan England, rise
To bless this happy enterprise,
Look up: the favourite Sign!
And enter where all weather's fine.
Upon this ground in old Japan
Our cordial host bids every man
Take his best ease, in such an inn
As Shakespeare's feet would speed to win;

The welcome warm, the feast at hand,
All set for kindness to expand,
For wine to sparkle and for wit,
And the brave Arms bright over it.[36]
(1951)

At the other end of the scale, Blunden could draw poetic inspiration from meeting royalty. Indeed, the recipients of his poems included a wide variety of people such as mayors, scholars, editors, poets, painters, sculptors, women's colleges and groups. One poem is dedicated to Princess Chichibu and concerns her husband, the Prince, who studied at Oxford in his youth and who continued a close association with England until his untimely death.

On a Picture of
H. I. H. Prince Chichibu

So we once saw him, and no more
May see upon time's changing shore;
So kindly he, as this records,
Accepted what old time affords,
The great occasion or the small,
The rise of nations or the fall,
The public or the private sphere –
How pleasantly he greets us here,
With quiet friends and dear Princess,
Looking across all pain and stress
With courage good, a Prince in truth
Who signified perennial youth.
(17 June 1956)

To Princess Chichibu
with the affectionate respects of
Claire and Edmund Blunden.[37]

The poem contains no literary merit, but clearly marks the meeting of the poet with the royal couple, hence portraying the important ties between England and Japan.

Among these impromptu poems, there are some pieces which display a distinct affinity not only with things Japanese but with the style in which Japanese poets describe them. 'The Tea House' must be counted as one of them, with its subtle descriptions of the serene Japanese countryside and an inn, and the individual quality of Blunden's love for them.

> When on the mountain side we saw the tea-house
> Overlooking so many tilled green lowlands,
> We wrote no poems; all were written for us,
> And in the night there was no need of writing.
> The picture in the bedroom held the secret
> Of all our journey, springs insisted nightlong
> On telling us the magic of the mountains.[38]

'Flowers of the Rock' belongs to the same category. This poem was later slightly revised or, rather, edited, in *A Hong Kong House*. The original bears the following inscription by Blunden:

> To my friend Torao Uyeda who is by no means 'averse from general good'.

The Flowers of the Rock

UPON that cliff, that rock upright
  A thousand weeds
  In life delight:
Even saplings dance their boughs; how bright
That perilous lily-bloom!
                    The seeds
Of thought, of flower of fancy too,
  Of whims, designs and deeds
Whether by good or bad winds blown,
Have found in many a breast of stone,
  Averse from general good,
  Their laughing livelihood.[39]
                    (16 January 1950)

This poem suggests one of Blunden's characteristic traits – his tendency to side with the less conspicuous and fortunate. He preferred and cherished thoughts, fancies, and plans which were averse from 'easier' general good, and found their place in a much harder breast of stone. Perhaps the flowers of the rock were favoured by Blunden for the sake of their plainness, in contrast to the grandeur of roses or chrysanthemums? Blunden's preoccupation with John Clare, Christopher Smart and Robert Lloyd, and his troubled love for Aki Hayashi seem related to this kind of preference. One of his early students recalls:

> Professor Blunden's clear-cut character and his distinct taste for favourite and unfavourable things are in every way noticeable. . . . His favourite literary figures are Charles Lamb, Coleridge, Leigh Hunt, Keats, Shelley, John Clare, Gilbert White, Fielding, Sterne, Trollope, Marryat and Emily Brontë; among some present authors Hardy, Bridges, Sassoon, Hodgson and H. M. Tomlinson might be counted as his favourites. On the other hand, he has never praised Galsworthy, Drinkwater or Wells during his three years' lectures. He dislikes Gissing and Wilde, and especially Wilde for whom he seems to have a strong distaste.[40]

However much he valued his friendship with the Japanese people, and his delight in their countryside, he remained a firm patriot. His love for cricket – 'our most beautiful and subtle game'[41] – which was said to be difficult for the Japanese to understand, testifies to this.

Cricket, I Confess

'Sir, I cannot profess to understand
One thing in England' – and Sakabe scanned
My face to be sure there was no offence astir, –
'It is cricket, I confess. In the English character
That's the chief Puzzle I have.' '"My horn is dry."
If you don't understand it, no more do I.'[42]

Again his loyalty to England and dislike of America are clearly remembered by Y. Nakano.

> It was when the Rockefeller Foundation donated a considerable sum of money to build the University Library. Professor Blunden used to walk around the classroom among the students during their breaks, but one day stopped at my desk and spoke to me. He asked me when the Library would be finished or something like that. 'Within several years, I suppose,' I replied in shaky English, adding very vaguely, 'Some donations have been made by

> America to cover the construction charges.' Then to my great surprise, Professor Blunden's face changed and he spoke with a rather authoritative tone, stiffening slightly. 'Make no mention of America, but Britain has made some fine contributions.' I was stunned to hear this . . . replying with some unmeaningful words: 'Yes, yes . . .'.[43]

The strength of Blunden's patriotism clearly surprised the Japanese students.

Regarding Blunden's influence upon the Japanese poets, Torao Taketomo, alias Sófú, probably received considerable benefit from him. Blunden himself dedicated a small poem to him duly paying tribute to this poetic talent.

> To him whose own poetic power might yield
> Far finer harvest than my stony field,
> I write this word, and thank him that he cares
> To set my 'Waggoner' where gladly fares
> His 'Scholar Gipsy', and where Tristram shines,
> And the sky glitters with poetic signs.[44]
>
> (12 December 1924)

A comparative study of both poets, which has not yet been attempted, would certainly be rewarding. Shiratori Seigo is another poet whom Blunden mentions in two short verses commemorating the honours he shared with Shiratori on a famous island, Matsushima (see p. 172). Here again, comparative study would almost certainly reveal shared outlooks and would provide a substantial topic for future research. Further, Blunden wrote a preface for Ishii Hakuson's poetical work.

One of Blunden's most attractive poems about post-war Japan features three young women students whom he glimpsed in the garden of Tokyo Women's Christian College. The original version was written on 13 August 1963, but it was later published with minor changes in *Eleven Poems* in 1966.

Written in the Women's Christian College, Tokyo

I SAW three graces under dark green boughs,
  Young girls of new Japan, together talking
Earnestly, it might be of marriage vows,
  Of books and plays, or plans for highland walking.

Grouped on cool grass, beneath old time's own trees
  Early one morning in idle summer weather,
These all deserved, it seemed, some new degrees,
  Achieving such calm threefold grace together . . . .

When I had found my books, pen, ink and paper,
  And tried to add to last night's pondered lines,
My window drew me, vainly an escaper, –
  No such kind picture now below the pines;
Which still with luck will, generations hence,
  Shade shrine-like other friends in 'mercy, soul and sense'.[45]
(Reischauer House, 15 August 1963)

Blunden's sincere tributes to Japan are also expressed in the poems, 'Japan Beautiful' and 'Nearing Yokohama: 15 August 1960'. Blunden is scarcely ever sentimental in his poems, but here he seems to be exceptionally overwhelmed by his longstanding affection for Japan. Perhaps it was particularly because he was travelling with his own family.

Nearing Yokohama
15 August 1960

Over these evening waters, snowy-crested,
Beneath a light blue sky and clouds cool-breasted,
  The French ship takes her way, a noble way.
And among all who young and old await
Tomorrow's landing, surely fortunate,
  I come again, the greyest of the grey.

And more than half a long life-span ago,
This was a future I could not foreknow,
  With wife and children thus surrounding me, –
Since then it has been known, and change has brought
With lessening powers of action as of thought
  New sense of blessing while I pass this sea.

This last stanza sums up Blunden's by now strong emotions for Japan and her people:

This is a land, my children, worth your learning
Whither like me in after years returning
  You shall have visions as your ship draws near, –
Not only loveliest lakes and woods and highlands,
Old roads high-avenued and templed islands,
  But personal genius and the soul sincere.[46]

Japan Beautiful

What most we love we do not well express,
Or do not oftenest try to put in words;
We are content with well-known happiness,
With memories echoing rather than clear chords.

And so it will not be my luck to write
One poem in Japan that will not die;
Let those who know me tell my heart's delight
In new Japan and in Japan gone by.

Gone by? and can The Mountain's wonder fade
Seen westward on a cold sad sunset, can
The peasant homes anigh – the bamboo shade,
With thatch and bloom and sprout, not say 'Japan'?

While I was thinking thus, a vision rose
From other than great Fuji's lordship. Hail,
Strange northern lakes, ancients, – I think of those,
And savage harmless life, and down the vale

Of usual travelling I scatter time
Among the tea plantations and the rice,
Time all too brief, – and temples too sublime
For sketches, and sweet nets stretched out to entice

On the seashore folks like me, when fishes rest,
And so we walk, and beauty reigns once more,
Beauty not quarrelling over East and West,
Beloved; the woods above, the pine-loved shore.[47]

Using the traditional images familiar to Japan – majestic Mount Fuji, tea and rice plantations, sublime temples, and 'pine-loved' shores – Blunden expresses his considered passion for the country, the land for which he had a lifelong affection. Here he is content, full of happiness and satisfaction; and 'Japan Beautiful' must have implied 'Japan Always and Forever'.

Notes

1. Haruji Ogura, 'Our Gratitude to Mr Blunden', in *Edmund Blunden: His Professorship and His Writings – Appreciations by Some of his Students and Friends* (Tokyo: Kenkyusha, 1927); special issue of *The Study of English* (June, 1927) p. 46. All articles are written in Japanese. Subsequently referred to as *Edmund Blunden: His Professorship and His Writings.*
2. As cited by Yasuaki Okamoto, 'Professor Blunden', ibid., pp. 59 and 60.
3. Ogura, 'Our Gratitude to Mr Blunden', ibid., p. 47.
4. Edmund Blunden, *The Mind's Eye* (London: Jonathan Cape, 1934) pp. 93–4.
5. Yoshitaka Sakai, 'Professor Blunden and the English Reading Society', in *Edmund Blunden: His Professorship and His Writings*, p. 66.
6. Okamoto, 'Professor Blunden', ibid., p. 59.
7. Sakai, 'Professor Blunden and the English Reading Society', ibid., p. 66.
8. Tokuji Yokoi, 'Remembrances', ibid., p. 70.
9. Blunden, *The Mind's Eye*, p. 96.
10. Yokoi, 'Remembrances', ibid., p. 70.
11. A common Japanese way of carrying books or other objects is to knot them inside the four corners of a silk square.
12. Blunden, *The Mind's Eye*, p. 93.
13. Sakai, 'Professor Blunden and the English Reading Society', pp. 66–7.
14. Yoshitaka Sakai, 'Favourite Reviewer', in *Edmund Blunden: His Professorship and His Writings*, p. 64.
15. Yoshio Nakano, 'Professor Blunden', ibid., p. 72.
16. Prince Chichibu (1902–53) was a brother of Emperor Hirohito.
17. Capital of Hyogo Prefecture, western Honshu, and one of Japan's leading ports. The city is known for its cosmopolitan atmosphere.
18. A hard, square Japanese paper often beautifully decorated and painted for writing poems on or for calligraphy, being used for presentation or ornamentation purposes.
19. Takeshi Saito, 'Edmund Blunden', in *Edmund Blunden: Poems on Japan – Hitherto Uncollected and Mostly Unprinted*, compiled and edited in honour of his seventieth birthday by Takeshi Saito (Tokyo: Kenkyusha Press, 1967) pp. 72–3. Subsequently referred to as *Poems on Japan*.
20. Edmund Blunden, *Masks of Time: A New Collection of Poems Principally Meditative* (London: Beaumont Press, 1925) p. 23.
21. Sófú Taketomo, 'Impressions Personal and Critical', in *Edmund Blunden: His Professorship and His Writings*, p. 31.
22. Akira Tomita, 'Professor Blunden', ibid., p. 68.

23. Takeshi Saito, 'Edmund Blunden' in *Edmund Blunden: A Tribute from Japan*, ed. Masao Hirai and Peter Milward (Tokyo: Kenkyusha, 1974) p. 7.
24. *Poems on Japan*, p. 71.
25. Edmund Blunden, *Japanese Garland* (London: Beaumont Press, 1928) p. 34.
26. Shunzo Kashiwagura, 'On *The Shepherd*', in *Edmund Blunden: His Professorship and His Writings*, p. 20.
27. Blunden, *The Mind's Eye*, p. 90.
28. Blunden, *Japanese Garland*, p. 37.
29. *The Penguin Book of Contemporary Verse*, ed. Kenneth Allott (Harmondsworth, Middx: Penguin, 1962) p. 136.
30. Blunden, *Japanese Garland*, pp. 14–15.
31. Ibid., pp. 38–9.
32. Edmund Blunden, *A Selection from the Poems of Edmund Blunden* (Long Melford: Lavenham Press, 1969) p. 16.
33. *Poems on Japan*, p. 16.
34. Takeshi Saito, 'Edmund Blunden', in *Edmund Blunden: A Tribute from Japan* (Tokyo: Kenkyusha, 1974) pp. 13–14.
35. *Poems on Japan*, pp. 66–7.
36. Ibid., p. 34.
37. Ibid., p. 40.
38. Edmund Blunden, *A Hong Kong House: Poems 1951–1961* (London: Collins, 1962) p. 27.
39. *Poems on Japan*, p. 25.
40. Nakano, 'Professor Blunden', p. 73.
41. Blunden, *A Selection from the Poems of Edmund Blunden*, p. 17.
42. Ibid.
43. Nakano, 'Professor Blunden', p. 71.
44. *Poems on Japan*, p. 2.
45. Ibid., p. 61.
46. Blunden, *A Hong Kong House*, p. 36.
47. Ibid., p. 35.

3

Poetry in Love

The nature of Blunden's relations with Aki Hayashi, and the influence of their intimacy on his outlook and poetry

---

Aki Hayashi undoubtedly had a considerable effect, directly and indirectly, on Blunden's writings and particularly on his poetry. The poetry he wrote in Japan, and on Japanese subjects after his return to England, is suffused with the particular sense of, and feeling for, Japan, which he had acquired from his relations with her. He could, and did, also confide to her his feelings about the First World War; and his letters to her often refer to it, sometimes associating Japanese landscapes with what he had seen in Flanders.

The scenery of Tohoku District which Blunden had passed on board the train to see Ralph Hodgson reminded him of Flanders.

> The journey was stuffy and uncomfortable but I enjoyed the snowstorm outside, and the appearance of the lonely places with groups of farm buildings, flat roads, ditches and short avenues of trees suited my war-book, resembling Flanders. I missed my glimpses of the sea, but no doubt they would have been very dull & imperfect ones.
>
> (21 March 1926)

In the summer of 1932 he visited 'the old country of the war', and sent a postcard to Aki describing the then peaceful sight of 'countless wild flowers' and 'clear sparkling streams'.

Postcard Paris

> This is a half-way house for us, my dear A., on our wanderings; we first passed through the old country of the war, from Cassel to Béthune and to Amiens, and have been almost 2 days here. As the skies have been cloudy (not very different from London) the bright colours that this picture shows have not been obvious. . . . Have been very slack in writing letters &c., but not otherwise – we took some very long walks, two of them in the old battlefields of

the La Bassée and the Beaumont Hamel one. Hardly any trace of war would meet your eye there now if you were not told what to watch for; and by Hamel the river valley is fresh and beautiful, with countless wild flowers and clear sparkling streams. . . . will write again in a few days, I expect from Perigueux in south-west France. We found my friends the Bonnerots at Amiens, saw them again here, and shall catch them up on the sea shore not too far from Perigueux.

(4 August 1932)

Blunden tried to 'transfer' these scenes into a novel on which he was collaborating with Sylva Norman.

Cleave's Yalding

There is something dear A which you can usefully do at once for me at the Museum. I want to have by me while writing my new book with Sylva Norman such passages from *Froissart's Chronicles* as may serve. It is a famous old book but I have no copy. The passages I shall need are those relating to the English in Périgord, and especially their wars and so on in these places: Domme, Brive, Sarlat, Périgueux, Rocamadour – all which we lately visited.

(8 September 1932)

War memories were brought back to him by small incidents, such as an article in a Sunday paper (28 May 1936), in which the Prince of Wales was reported to have recollected his narrow escape from arrest as a spy, and his encounter with Lieutenant Blunden. Yet Blunden himself could not recollect that incident and found the article strange, 'though Canal Bank in 1917 was enough to make one forget anything!'

Today a friend of Sylva's sent her a cutting from a *Sunday Pictorial*, in which the Prince of Wales is stated to have been nearly arrested as a spy on the Canal Bank, Ypres in 1917, and to have been brought to our Battalion H.Q. where Lieut. Edmund Blunden all alone received him! This is passing strange. I don't think I should have forgotten the episode, though Canal Bank in 1917 was enough to make one forget anything! Mr Mottram has published a new book on the Western Front in which he several times mentions me very handsomely.

(28 May 1936)

The volunteer service of Blunden's son John during the Second World War also evoked the memory of his own volunteering during the First World War. As a father he was concerned about his son's action.

> Merton College, Oxford
>
> My son writes that he has volunteered for the Air (as a pilot), though still under the age of conscription. It is all rather unhappy to me. I was a month or two older when I joined in 1915.
>
> (1 February 1941)

The cloudy summer weather again brings another memory of the War – a fierce battle in the Passchendaele region.

> Merton College, Oxford
>
> We have cloudy weather and the summer seems to be breaking up – but so it was in 1917 at this date when like so many others I was about to attack the Germans in the Passchendaele region!
>
> (29 July 1941)

About 16 years before this letter, in Japan, Blunden related the result of some battle:

> Kikufuji Hotel, Hongo, Tokyo
>
> Today, 9 years ago, my battalion attacked and captured a German trench; in which proceeding I played some, alas! too insignificant part, and experienced more in 48 hours than some old gentlemen in all their lives.
>
> (21 October 1925)

Blunden seems to have desired that Aki too should share and understand his unforgettable memories.

No wonder Claire Poynting told a reporter that 'their lives were dominated by it (war), and that up until he died in 1974 no day passed in which he did not refer to that war'. In particular changes of weather used to fill him with memories.[1]

Blunden was not only obsessed by vivid memories of the war and driven to re-visit the old scenes of action, but was actually involved with service for the War Graves Commission.

9 Woodstock Close, Oxford

Perhaps you saw in Monday's newspaper that I have been called on to serve (no salary attached!) on the War Graves Commission. A sudden series of messages on Friday and Saturday, then a visit by Major-General Sir Fabian Ware – and the deed was done.

(4 March 1936)

Friendships developed during the war, which resulted in continued reunions of the old soldiers for a long period of time afterwards.

Went to Brighton on Saturday for our annual dinner of Old Soldiers, lots of beer was drunk and many stories were told once more.

(7 March 1939)

67 Pembury Road, Tonbridge

. . . On Saturday afternoon I go to Worthing, for the annual dinner of our old Royal Sussex battalions; will be back at Tonbridge on Sunday evening, & here as usual on Monday.

(12 March 1953)

Even in Hong Kong Blunden seems to have been unable to escape such ties. He had to send a message to the annual Dinner of his old Royal Sussex battalions, or was concerned about his old friends' state of health and 'youthfulness'.

The University, Hong Kong

. . . General Harrison writes quite often, as he has done since 1918, and tells me that my old companion Sergeant Worley of Worthing has had a troublesome operation. Alas, the years do make these changes in us. I can only be thankful that G. H. H. has kept so young, and some more of the old Royal Sussex. They had their annual Dinner at Worthing and I had sent a message which G. H. H. read out.

(6 April 1954)

He was requested to write something for the fortieth anniversary of his battalions.

The University, Hong Kong

> The Royal Sussex (South-down Battalions) are to celebrate their 40th anniversary at Bexhill &c. in September, and I am desired to write something for the 'souvenir programme.' I wish one of them would arrange a quiet seaside week for you by way of rewarding me.

(15 June 1954)

Blunden was given 'a present, a 4-page letter from Dickens to Forster' from an old war friend:

The University, Hong Kong

> . . . Lately a gentleman who was in the same Division as me in War I and read my book about it sent me as a present a 4-page letter from Dickens to Forster. I have not many such things here and this is accordingly a special Benefit.

(26 April 1955)

His truest and most serious feeling, however, towards his fellow soldiers killed in the War is conveyed in the following passage, in which he says neither himself nor Sassoon would be pleased with the grand ceremony for the fallen – which he regards as a mere 'show-piece'.

The University, Hong Kong

> On Sunday we must attend a show-piece – the unveiling of a War Graves Memorial; shall be happy when this is all over, the captains & the kings depart, and we can go peacefully home. It will no doubt be a stately ceremony, led by a famous General from England. My spirit like S. Sassoon's hardly rejoices in any such public performances concerning the fallen.

(15 February 1955)

Meanwhile, his books on the First World War seemed to find increasing favour. A new edition of *Undertones of War* was to be published in the World's Classics Series and his pamphlet on the War Poets of 1914–18 in the British Council Series was published.

The University, Hong Kong

What else? There is to be a new edition of 'Undertones of War' in the World's Classics series (Oxford Univ. Press.) I owe this to my friend D. Hudson of Merton College who is now I think in charge of that series. So I must before long get together a new Introduction & in it I shall have a chance of speaking about Philip Tomlinson. A great shame that he has not lived to see the new edition, and perhaps the introduction would have come from *his* pen.

(7 July 1955)

UNIVERSITY OF HONG KONG
DEPARTMENT OF ENGLISH

. . . When you are near B. M., call at 59 New Oxford Street, – Albion House – on Mr Brander, and he will give you a copy of my pamphlet in his British Council Series, on the War Poets of 1914–18. It will have been published when this reaches you. It is chiefly about Rupert Brooke, W. Owen and S. S. who is given an unusual photograph, from 1916, . . .

(18 July 1958)

More than anything else, his mind always wandered back to his 'old Somme villages', which he would visit whenever he had the opportunity.

Sylva leaves for Italy tonight and we may meet her in Rome early in June – as yet we have no address in Rome & we shall be a bit of a party – C., E., 4 girls 1 amah, 2 young ladies from the English Department. I was intending to visit Shelley's last home in Lerici, but have had to put the thought from me; alas. – One day perhaps. In July we may be in Paris awhile, & once more my desire is to return briefly to our old Somme villages, but it can hardly be fulfilled. In 1963, I tell myself, but nobody can be sure that way – . . .

(25 April 1961)

When he returned to Oxford again after the First World War, Blunden seemed to be always looking for a sense of surety and certainty. His poem 'April Byeway', published in *A Queen's College*

Miscellany in 1921, conveys some of the despair and suffering he felt as a result of his fierce War experiences. Here he was looking for certainty and stability in a changing world – an 'unseen friend' who alone seems to represent such reality.

But the old forge and mill are shut and done,
The tower is crumbling down, stone by stone falls;
An ague doubt comes creeping in the sun.
The sun himself is shaken, the day appals,
The concourse of a thousand tempests sprawls
Over the blue-lipped lakes and maddening groves,
Like agonies of gods the clouds are whirled,
The stormwind like the demon huntsman roves –
Still stands my friend, though all's to chaos hurled.
The unseen friend, the one sure friend in all the world.[2]

This last stanza echoes Yeats's poems which are similar in tone and written in the same period.

The Second Coming

Turning and turning in the widening gyre
The falcon cannot hear the falconer;
Things fall apart; the centre cannot hold;
Mere anarchy is loosed upon the world,
The blood-dimmed tide is loosed, and everywhere
The ceremony of innocence is drowned;
The best lack all conviction, while the worst
Are full of passionate intensity.

Surely some revelation is at hand;
Surely the Second Coming is at hand.[3]

A Prayer for My Daughter

. . .

Considering that, all hatred driven hence,
The soul recovers radical innocence
And learns at last that it is self-delighting,
Self-appeasing, self-affrighting,

And will that its own sweet will is Heaven's will;
She can, though every face should scowl
And every windy quarter howl
Or every bellows burst, be happy still.[4]

Yeats treats the theme of 'despair and anarchy' in a larger historical context, associating it with the image of the Second Coming; and again in 'A Prayer for My Daughter', he hopes to see salvation and a new security coming from the sweet will of Heaven, with which his daughter's soul, recovering radical innocence, should be united. Blunden's hope lies in his friend, 'The unseen friend, the one sure friend in all the world', which is a much more personal response to the trauma than Yeats's universalism. Perhaps, this is one of the reasons why Blunden's poems have largely failed to appeal to the twentieth-century reader.

It was not long after this that Blunden was to find altogether new kinds of security – and insecurity – in Japan.

Turning to the poetry which Blunden wrote directly under the influence of Japan and his relations with Aki Hayashi, let us begin with two very moving examples: 'Lonely Love' and 'Ainu Child'.

Lonely Love

I love to see those loving and beloved
Whom Nature seems to have spited; unattractive,
Unnoticeable people, whose dry track
No honey-drop of praise, or understanding,
Or bare acknowledgement that they existed,
Perhaps yet moistened. Still, they make their world.

She with her arm in his – O Fate, be kind,
Though late, be kind; let her have never cause
To live outside her dream, nor unadore
This underling in body, mind and type,
Nor part from him what makes her dwarfish form
Take grace and fortune, envy's antitone.

I saw where through the plain a river and road
Ran quietly, and asked no more event
Than sun and rain and wind, and night and day,
Two walking – from what cruel show escaped?

Deformity, defect of mind their portion.
But I forget the rest of that free day of mine,
And in what flowerful coils, what airy music
It led me there and on; those two I see
Who, loving, walking slowly, saw not me,
But shared with me the strangest happiness.[5]

Ainu Child

On the straggling scanty hedge out there
We are shown the remnants of an unlucky bear,
And the hunter is proud.
Then the little crowd
Drifts back to the street; and the children share
A handful of sweets, and stare and stare.

In the sunshine, the grass is bright green; time half sleeps;
But the thought of dead bears like a cold shade creeps
On our minds, and the gloom
Of a race in a tomb,
Where old age itself no more harvest reaps
Than the bones of bears torn from their woodland deeps.

Among these small children one larger child waits,
Her eyes on the strange woman; contemplates;
And she has good eyes,
We begin to surmise
She implores that strange woman to challenge her fates,
And take her and break for her all the locked gates.[6]

'Lonely Love' is very 'un-Japanese' – it illustrates the great difference between Blunden's response to life and the Japanese one. He doesn't care about the *absence* of grace and beauty in the people and in the poem. He *loves* it! This would seem strange to a Japanese.

To love pathos and deprivation is characteristic of Blunden as it also is of Hardy and Larkin as poets.

As Larkin has himself wryly remarked: 'Deprivation for me is what daffodils were for Wordsworth.' What is perfect as a poem is what is imperfect in life.[7]

In this respect the three poets are very similar. There seems no doubt that his feeling for Aki is reflected in 'Lonely Love'. He also had affection for sad, deprived and unloved writers, as is shown by his interest in such poets as Lamb, Clare and Smart, and also in the First World War poet Ivor Gurney. On the other hand, some of Blunden's poems are very close to the Japanese. The 'meticulous' nature poems show not only his poet's eye for the country, but the influence of Aki's knowledge of Japanese poetry, which she imparted to him.

Another feature of his poetry is the seasonal description of nature, which is also evident in his letters. Blunden's descriptions result from his detailed observations and sharp senses, in both his poetry and his letters to Aki. Indeed he is opposed to the Modernist way of transforming things into symbols of the poet's psyche – represented by such a poet as T. S. Eliot – which, he declares, is not the sort of poetry he enjoys (19 October 1954). Blunden prefers to preserve nature in poetry in its purest and most natural form, as can be seen in his descriptions of the vivacity of nature – the living, growing, changing life of flowers, birds, light, wind and animals.

> At last the world of birds, flowers, bees, even worms thinks the spring is coming, and I expect you hear the early morning music much as here.
>
> (17 March 1942)

Blunden can be sharp enough to discern changes in the quality of birdsong:

> Easter Monday, but it does not feel much like a holiday, though some of the birds are holding a concert (rather sharp voices until the spring really brings forth the sweetest singers.)
>
> (6 April 1942)

> You must hear all the birds sing that you can the next week or two, for when the summer gets drowsy so do they; they are almost without music then until the autumn.
>
> (18 June 1931)

The dramatic power of transformation by light is described with a romantic touch:

MERTON COLLEGE, OXFORD

> . . . Here it's a fine spring day, which I hope makes some sunshine for you also in London; a glorious rainbow here yesterday appeared to spring from the back of a sheep feeding in the meadow below my window, & in its light all the flock had a dark dusky gold fleece.
>
> (22 April 1932)

'Lonely Love' certainly shows Blunden's appreciation of Aki's solitude and his realisation of her position, as well as his tenderness for her. Undoubtedly Blunden came to feel, through her, emotions in his poetry he would not otherwise have had. In a similar vein Blunden's poems on Japan published in *Near and Far* record his first impressions of Japan, the shock he experienced in assimilating the different culture and sensibility, and above all, his clandestine love for Aki Hayashi. Many of them correspond well with his comments on Japan and its people written in his letters to Aki during this period. Indeed, the combination of the poems and the letters reveal much about his reactions to the different culture and to 'forbidden' love.

Near and Far, which was published in 1929, contains principally *Japanese Garland* and *Moods, Conjectures and Fancies*. As the flyleaf of the book explains, the poems here were written during his stay in Japan, and the two years immediately following his return to England in 1927; and would ideally reveal his emotions during this period.

> Several of the pieces in this new volume are on Japanese subjects. The rest are the work of the last two years. They offer some fresh melodies to those who still desire the music of verse. Inevitably, the note of English country life is expected from Mr Blunden's poetry, and will be heard here; but the spirit of man is his wider field.

Without dedicating *Japanese Garland* to Aki, Blunden presented her with a copy whose flyleaf bears in his own hand the tribute: 'To the best flower in any Japanese Garland, Aki Hayashi'. One of the reasons for his avoiding the form of a dedication may have been that his love for her had to be kept secret because he was still married to his wife Mary. He asks Aki in his letter to keep the matter secret.

I hold you so fast in my love and honour, you must be my refuge if ever my friends forsake me. But it will help us, if we can keep a secret.

(31 August 1925)

Perhaps in response to this effort to hide true emotions, the tone of most of the poems in *Near and Far* acquires a *haiku*-like quality, impressionistic and 'detached' – because of the frequent lack of specific cases. Often, the person(s) involved, or even the time and place, are only abstractly sketched, in the manner of the paintings of Turner or Japanese ink-paintings.

Indeed, Blunden himself seems to be well aware of this 'trick'. In his Prefatory Notes he indicates that he has made an effort to hide his true emotions – trying to disguise the Japanese scenes with allusions to England and vice versa. He apologises for this 'transformation', and tries to explain it away by saying that there is not much difference between cherry blossom and rose, rice and bread, and so on. In fact, though, his poems do not greatly disguise his 'true' feelings and reactions.

Prefatory Note

These poems are chiefly the product of the last two years. The Japanese pieces, however, are mainly reprinted from a volume issued by Mr C. W. Beaumont in 1927 in a limited and decorated edition. . . .

It is not my habit to reply to my critics, who have been generous to me as a versifier for years. But, in respect of the Japanese pieces which I have written – and I hope to write more – I may be allowed a word. They were blamed here and there for their English tone, and their author was described as an incorrigible 'Briton'. Those, however, who go from England to Japan without succumbing first to Japanesery will find that there is no great gulf between the old experiences and the new. Substitute cherry-blossom for rose, and rice for bread, and Alps for Chilterns – you do not thereby produce a mystical incomprehensibility. That is better (and worse) provided by avoiding Japan and the Japanese and just being 'Oriental'.

He also writes to Aki:

> I await news of my 'English Poems', which should have been issued last month in London; lately I wrote two pieces, one short & one long. The short one I will copy for Aki now. It is an English scene but it may resemble something here. My unalterable blessings and love, Eddie.
>
> (3 December 1925)

In a sense, it is also true that his 'difficulties' and sense of 'strangeness' were greatly mitigated by his gradual absorption into Japanese society, much assisted by Aki.

> I nowadays do not notice so keenly the points at which Japanese minds, manners and nerves entirely differ from ours.
>
> (23 October 1925)

But the effects of that absorption do not seem to penetrate far below the surface. In reality his poems implicitly disclose how deeply he *was* puzzled by the 'mystical incomprehensibility' and inscrutability of the Japanese culture and by his complex attraction to a Japanese woman.

His suppressed and secret love for Aki and its uneasy emotion and probable guilt are disclosed in his use of dark and passionate words in the poems – 'steals away' and 'witch-like' in 'Far East'; 'Defines the daemon's murderous work' in 'Eastern Tempest'; 'luring sails', 'deflection dark', 'waiting vultures of the night', 'Each pirate blackness skulks', 'a murderous mark', 'apprehension's baffling destiny' in 'Inland Sea'; 'sabred shades', 'black voice' of the bell, and 'dead man's eye' of Buddha in 'The Quick and the Dead'; such lines as 'The murmur runs along their rugged lines, "What black ship waits the crash of our typhoon?" ', 'jealous gods', 'Their mysteries luring that young seraph-cloud' in 'The Inviolate'; 'nooks' in 'Building the Library, Tokyo University'; 'ghost' of cherry-flowers, 'Blind eyes' of a small dog in 'On a small Dog, thrust out in a Tokyo Street soon after his birth, and rescued in vain'; 'So by too harsh instrusion / Left colourless confusion', 'my gloomed perspective in strange mood', 'eyeless lethargy', 'My hobbling commonplaces', 'a frail guide' in 'The Author's Last Words to his Students'. On the other hand, some of his phrases suggest a quest for the safety of a secure home – 'binds' in 'Far East' or 'And build them one more home . . . For the great Muse to come!' in 'Building the Library, Tokyo University – Night Scene'.

Fine fields, wide-lapped, whose loveliest-born
  Day's first bright cohort finds,
And steals away; where lustier corn
And red-faced churl invades at morn
  And proud as Caesar binds –[8]

O swiftly serve thy quiet will,
  And build them one more home
Where nooks shall be most kind and still
  For the great Muse to come![9]

He also writes to Aki of his wish for a home.

> It is like your strong and active love to go to your Canadian friend's house & see how some things are done abroad. I shall not cause you a lot of trouble and difficulty, for I know you will do everything well. It will seem like liberty itself & delight with it to me, after almost two years of no-home –.
>
> (14 November 1925)

Under the spell of love, Blunden seemed to feel things around him more intensely than usual as if the 'dark' and 'mystical' undercurrents were moving and skulking like the 'waiting vultures of the night' whose 'murmur runs along'. In his calmer period, perhaps before meeting Aki in the summer of 1925, Blunden must have been a sober, rather lonely, and yet youthfully ambitious teacher who aspired to be a successful poet like Thomas Hardy. He longed to 'Enchant the live gems from the unknown abyss, / And make them seen, the strangely beautiful'.[10]

> I had a letter from Mrs Thomas Hardy, but nothing very definite in it except that Mr Hardy is publishing a volume of poems this autumn. So am I!! and curiously enough when T. H. published last, I did too, and the editor of the *London Mercury* honoured me by reviewing my pieces in the same column with Mr Hardy's.
>
> (23 October 1925)

The incantation of 'love' came to him swiftly and unexpectedly.

> But still how gentle and beautiful a love has awakened between

you and me! I shall rely on it and live on it in many solitary hours. It is a charm to keep me going. I am most distressed that I cannot fulfil all that I ought to Autumn, as things stand now – but you have unselfish patience and a splendid courage. When I was with you, the cares of this hurried and bilious world ceased to touch me. I loved whatever gave me the chance to do some slight thing for you: and, as it has been, so it will continue to be.

(29 August 1925)

The second poem of *Japanese Garland*, 'Ornamentations', records the acute and powerful shock reactions of Blunden's western sensibility to its first encounter with the strange art of curving cranes, red-eyed war-gods and demi-lions. The poem begins in similar vein to Yeats's depiction of his slouching monster in 'The Second Coming'.

The curving cranes with serpent necks
  Knotted on these enamelled streams,
The gloating mouths thrust out to vex
  The red-eyed war-gods' frenzy dreams,
The inscrutable and dog-like grin
Of demi-lions lock me in!

With countless crafty manacles,
  Dead men's dexterity strives to bind,
Like some machine that all but feels,
  The amazed and apathizing mind.
Cornices, crannies, shape in shape,
Bud glittering eyes, defy escape.[11]

Again there is depicted a similar world to Yeats's 'Byzantium' – the craftsman's realm of art. Yeats writes:

A mouth that has no moisture and no breath
Breathless mouths may summon;

. . .

Miracle, bird, or golden handiwork,
More miracles than bird or handiwork,
Planted on the star-lit golden bough.

. . .

. . . The smithies break the flood,
The golden smithies of the Emperor!
Marbles of the dancing floor
Break bitter furies of complexity,
Those images that yet
Fresh images beget,
That dolphin-torn, that gong-tormented sea.

The difference lies in that Blunden's cranes do not scream or crow whereas Yeats's golden bird does and even 'scorns aloud'.

Can like the cocks of Hades crow,
Or, by the moon embittered, scorn aloud
In glory of changeless metal
Common bird or petal
And all complexities of mire or blood.

In other words, Yeats 'regards' or treats lifeless artifice as a living object, which is clearly indicated in his open declaration:

I hail the superhuman;
I call it death-in-life and life-in-death.[12]

Though they did not know each other, both Yeats and Blunden had a great interest in Japan and its art; but Blunden preferred a plainer and more straightforward expression of his feelings. Did Yeats borrow from Blunden? The similarity of 'images (ornamentations) and gongs (drum, knell, etc.)' is striking. Blunden's poem was published in 1928, two years before Yeats's 'Byzantium'.

Though tormented by the gloating mouths of the ornamental cranes and dog-like grin of demi-lions, he praised the craftsmen's dexterity in binding pieces together, and the glittering eyes of artifice. Yet, he feels the mind present in these ornamentations rather uncongenial and disagreeable – 'The amazed and apathizing'. Blunden's sensibility had been so shaped by the aesthetic of gentleness and smoothness that he was taken aback by the oriental aesthetic of terror and 'monstrosity'. He much preferred to escape into the gentler and more peaceful world of 'roses and daffodils'.

Heavily hangs this haughty air,
   Drum, knell and drone commingling slow;
Claw-tendrils reach, man-monsters glare;
   The victim heart prepares to know
Art's terror, dragon genius – till
Thought spies one rose or daffodil.[13]

Thus Blunden conveys his culture-shock on a much less grand scale than Yeats would do – 'till Thought *spies* one rose or daffodil'.

Here is the contrast between the 'feminine' sensibility of western art and culture and 'masculine' culture represented by Japanese art's 'terror'. Western culture reveres not only women's beauty but the gentle and peaceful gracefulness of Nature much more than its eastern counterpart, which can sometimes reflect an aesthetic of cruelty disguised as manly vigour and sustained by a male-dominated society. Blunden's poem 'The Match' conveys that aspect of cruelty: he observes an 'ordinary scene' for any Japanese who loves baked eels – cooking eels alive in front of the shopper in order to capture the meat at its tastiest.

The Match

In a round cavern glass, in steely water
(None yet so comfortless appalled the day)
A man-eel poised, his lacquer-skin disparted
In desert reds and wharfy green; his eyes too
Burned like beads of venom.
Beyond the glass the torturer stood, with thrustings,
Passes, grimaces, toothy grins, warped oeillades.
To this black magic mania's eel retorted
With fierce yet futile muzzle, and lancing darted
In an electric rapine, against the wall
Of glass, or life: those disputants of nothing,
So acidly attracting, lovingly loathing,
Driven by cold radii, goblin lovers, seemed yet
The difficult dumb-show of my generation.[14]

Yet Blunden's western pacifist eyes reacted to the scene as nothing but a sign of barbarism. The trained cook of eels stood for a torturer. In a similar vein, what aggravated Blunden most in Japan was the prevailing social *apathy*, associated with his observation of the absence of a charitable mentality in Japan as I mentioned in the previous chapter in connection with the 'small dog' poem.

The apparently expressionless faces of the Japanese, sustained by their effort to hide emotions and feelings, have always been an enigma to western observers. Those traits helped to create the famous image of inscrutable orientalism, and Blunden might at first have fallen victim to the cliché; also the initial language barrier probably contributed to his impression of Japanese 'apathy' – which was probably in fact the impact of Japanese stoicism.

Blunden recognised another apathy prevailing in the atmosphere of Tokyo University. He writes to Aki:

> Some letters are just in from England, with urgent command that I return; and indeed, for all the University deserves of me, I should not be wrong to do so, but there is more in question than the apathy and discourtesy of that 'Academic Body'.
>
> (18 December 1925)

One of the benefits for Blunden of his direct contact with the opposite cultural sensibility to his own was to bring to his poems a 'masculine' touch – some strength and dynamism. He uses more pointed verbs like 'invade' or 'climb' (in 'Far East') together with emphatically masculine images, which are rarely perceivable traits in Blunden's early poems about English scenes such as 'The Waggoner' or 'Almswoman'.

For instance, 'Eastern Tempest' conveys a vivid description of the blind rage of a storm which attacked the whole country in early September – the time of tempests. Blunden depicts the violence of the storm in the first part of the poem; but it passes quickly, and is replaced by a very fine blue sky and sun – the Japanese phrase 'after the typhoon' refers to the natural passing away of tumultuous disturbances:

> That flying angel's torrent cry
>
> . . .
>
> In Chance's eye what desperate deed?

The sudden transformation of the storm into a peaceful blue sky seems to the western eyes of Blunden like a merciful deed of a beneficent god.

A kinder god discerns, replies,
And stills the land's storm-shouts to sighs;
The clouds in massy folds apart
Disclose the day's bright bleeding heart,

. .

From flame to flame the vision glows,
Till all the pools of heaven unclose
The lotus-light, the hue, the balm
Of wisdom infinitely calm.[15]

Blunden again takes refuge in a 'kinder god (who) stills the land's storm-shouts to sighs' from the eastern 'daemon's murderous work', as he once had sheltered himself in the world of 'rose or daffodil' in response to the monstrous ornamentations.

Another 'charity-minded' poem, 'Sir William Treloar's Dinner for Crippled Children' describes 'an ancient England in the new' where 'greatness and good-nature, still thrive', and where we hear Blunden's great sigh of relief after his traumatically hurtful experiences in Japan.

This is an ancient England in the new;
Hear how those thousand children leap and sing.
Their dreams, their wonder and their pleasure ring
Through England; young expectancy comes true,
While Mayor and Alderman and Usher bright
With robes and jewels out of a fairy story,
And brighter hearts, wish them their heart's delight,
And music shows them sudden streets of glory.

Here walks the shade of Whittington in bliss;
O greatness and good-nature, still you thrive.
I thank my God, Charles Lamb is still alive
In these new Londoners; they shall not miss
The crown of life; here's Coram, Dickens, Hood,
Christmas and Christ profoundly understood.[16]

To the same category of commonplace poems belong 'On a Biographical Dictionary' which contains Blunden's celebration of the exclusive entry of 'men and women of great soul/Replying, singing to their genius' in the prestigious book.

Proud is assembly, and the anthem proud
That populous nave and aisle and gallery raise
In conscious strength, till God in his bright cloud
Seems hovering to that multitude of praise.
Yet from this mild prosaic book, as loud,
As strong, as various, from as many throats,
I hear the Gloria of a golden crowd,
And there the heavenly wing still brighter floats.

I hear the trumpet and alarm of time
Appeal, and men and women of great soul
Replying, singing to their genius climb;
Deep wisdoms hearten, organ-yearnings roll;
Tried faith transfigures every imperfection
Into one chant, one radiance and election.[17]

In 'The Quick and the Dead', Blunden finds much happiness in walking with friends in Nara – the most ancient city of Japan where the dead, including the huge Buddha, appeared to be more powerful than the living.

Once we three in Nara walked
Where pomp and fame look through the leaves;
With sabred shades we walked and talked
By lacquered gates and bow-like eaves,
By pools where carp doze through their green
Eternities, to lonelier shrines
Where mossy courtyards lie serene
Beneath some peasant-planted pines.

Less of that giant, surly bell
Whose black voice warned us at all hours
My late remembrance likes to tell,
Less of the Buddha as he lours
With thick curled skull and dead man's eye,
Of old wives' faithful groan of prayer,
Of fire-robed ritual trooping by,
Than the plain joy, three friends walked there.[18]

Blunden cares less for the giant bell and historic Buddha than for the company of his friends. Yet, if we replace the number three by two, the poem turns into a love poem, depicting Blunden enjoying Nara in the company of Aki – 'the plain joy' of walking together. Indeed, one of his letters to Aki suggests he was very fond of that city.

> I wonder if another time we might not rather go to such a place as the Nara hotel or the Kyoto places; though it might be difficult for you to get away. This point too we must try to think over. In expense the Nara hotel w^{d} be considerably less, & it's very finely furnished & managed. (5 September 1925)

Despite Blunden's efforts to hide his love affair with Aki, this poem fails somehow to disguise the aura of secret joy. Another interesting point is Blunden's fondness for the images of 'walking' and 'passing'. 'The Lonely Love' depicts such a scene – two deformed people in love pass Blunden without noticing him; yet the strange sensation created by seeing them inspired him to write the poem. Blunden *loved* feeling such unusual sensations, especially if private to himself – only a wasp could compare!

> . . . Here came my flitting thought,
> The only visitor of a sunny day,
> Except the half-mad wasp that fights with all, . . .[19]

The enchantment of the combination of 'unwanted' and the 'kind touch' of God or Nature is another recurrent image. 'The Kiln' is a very good representative:

> Beside the creek where seldom oar or sail
> Adventures, and the gulls whistling like men
> Patrol the pasture of the falling tide,
> Like Timon's mansion stands the silent kiln.
> Half citadel, half temple, strong it stands
> With layered stones built into cavernous curves,
> The fire-vault now as cool as leaves and stones
> And dews can be. Here came my flitting thought,
> The only visitor of a sunny day,
> Except the half-mad wasp that fights with all,
> The leaping cricket in his apple-green,
> And emerald beetle with his golden helmet;

While the south wind woke all the colony
Of sorrels and sparse daisies, berried ivies
And thorns bowed down with sloes, and brambles red
Offering a feast that no child came to take.

In these unwanted derelicts of man
Nature has touched the picture with a smile
Of more than usual mystery; the far heights
With thunderous forest marshalled are her toil,
But this her toy, her petty larceny,
That pleased her, lurking like a gipsy girl,
My thought came here with artfulness like hers
To spy on her, and, though she fled, pursued
To where on eastern islands, in the cells
Of once grave seers, her iris woos the wind.[20]

Blunden was often thrilled by the movements of walking, passing and running (of streams and rivers); and 'Epitaph' conveys the symbolism he wanted to embody in those images. There 'running stream' suggests the pathos of passing years and the never-static phases of human life; as a Japanese proverb says, 'Man can never stand in the same stream again': exactly the same thought as that expressed by the ancient Greek philosopher Heracleitus 'you cannot bathe twice in the same river'. The classic Greek and the classic Japanese have the same sadness and also, sometimes, the same cruelty. But Blunden's poetry is never cruel.

Happily through my years this small stream ran;
It charmed the boy, and purified the man;
Its hollowed banks were my romantic caves,
Its winter tumults made my ocean waves.[21]

Ironically, though ceaselessly moving, the stream is always in the same place, whereas a man might go abroad and change his abode. In fact, Blunden loved long walks and he wrote to Aki:

Thank you so much for praising my poems, but I repeat you will like them more when you have spent some little time in the country which gave them life. It gave me life too, but a little too much asthma with it. Love, my love to you Edmund.

(13 October 1925)

> . . . and I wish I could go for a walk with you even there or anywhere. . . . Every day & hour I think of you my very deeply loved Aki. It's wretched to find how slowly some days go by.
> (6 October 1925)

The second stanza envisages an Aki-like face mirrored in the stream among foxgloves. He brought her to England 'who was gone' (to London?), while Blunden sat and meditated on his life, talking to and counselling the running stream of Yalding; he was surrounded by the wealth and consolation of Nature, now in its 'English' colours.

With all my years this pretty stream sang on.
I brought one here to praise it; who is gone,
Yet in that crystal soul her mirrored face
With foxgloves looking in still finds a place.
Even the Muse's 'melody unheard'
For me is woven with this water's word,
Since here I sat to read immortal song;
The ripple played to that, nor answered wrong.
All that deep-sighing elegy might mourn,
Glad lyric hail, and sonnet-thought adorn,
The changeful rivulet from stone to stone
Enchanted into anthems of its own.

My travel then! my wealth, my dream, my love,
True Golden Treasury and Golden Grove!
Accept one weakness, let one pale shade cling
Where with so strong a life you run and sing.[22]

His adoration of 'running' seems to be related to his concern with the idea of passing Time. He mentions it in 'Summer Rainstorm':

Joy's masque and fashion of Time's Samson-passion
Deceives no lark that springs from weed and clod.
    Through their frank sight
    I feel the bright
Angel-event of sunset's fresh creation
And fields made lovely with the living God.[23]

In fact, Blunden dedicated to Aki a small fragment of a

Shakespearean sonnet, using the image of Love's faith in his love letter.

A. H. E. B.
28.8.1925

Love's not Time's fool, though rosy lips & cheeks
In compass of his bending sickle come;
Love changes not with his brief hours and weeks,
But bears it out e'en to the edge of Doom.

Comparing the English 'Summer Rainstorm' with the 'Eastern Tempest' reveals the much smaller scale of Nature's disturbance, seen as joyous and even merry – in the western isle.

Sweet conversations, woodland incantations
Are thrilling through the tides of gale and shower,
  Which now conceal,
  Now blue-reveal,
Across the fallow's russet undulations
A broken windmill and a silent tower.

And sometimes glancing through the top sprigs dancing
Elf-wings set out on visit and patrol.
  Though the full cloud
  Frowns monster-browed,
Those merry wild-folk chirruping and chancing
Know the kind truth; would I had such a soul!

Joy's masque and fashion of Time's Samson-passion
Deceives . . .[24]

Similarly, if we compare 'The Quick and the Dead' with 'Epitaph' as poems both suggesting Blunden's clandestine love, we can see how strongly the poem on Nara is imbued with *haiku*-like quantities.

A *haiku* is a 17-syllable verse form consisting of three metrical units of 5, 7 and 5 syllables respectively, and the focal point which the author wants to stress usually falls on the last metrical unit. Now the second stanza of 'The Quick and the Dead' has a similar effect:

Less of that giant, surly bell
Whose black voice warned us at all hours
My late remembrance likes to tell,
Less of the Buddha as he lours
With thick curled skull and dead man's eye,
Of old wives' faithful groan of prayer,
Of fire-robed ritual trooping by,
Than the plain joy, three friends walked there.[25]

Not only does the main message of the poem come at the end – 'the plain joy' – but we may see as equivalent to the first metrical unit of a *haiku*, the image of the bell, up to 'My late remembrance likes to tell', and as the second metrical unit ('Less of the Buddha . . . trooping by'), which concerns the fearsome godhead and the measured gestures of the devout.

On the whole, the poem written in England, 'Epitaph', carries much freer, richer, diversified and more direct emotions unrestricted by the influence of a confined use of syllables, the neat 'nothingness' of *haiku* poems.

A much deeper influence of the *haiku* may be traced in 'Inland Sea' and 'The Inviolate' – in both poems the surface messages are simple: 'in the moonlit sea, The fishers wind their ancient ways'; or 'on the white Pacific shore the pines still serve their jealous gods, . . . God-gates and temples glow with changeless noon'. All the remaining phrases are 'ornamentations' supporting the main message.

Inland Sea

Here in the moonlit sea,
While swift we fly, while tranced we gaze,
The fishers wind their ancient ways:
Now like sea-lilies loom their luring sails,
Or heaven's envoys walking fountained vales;
And now by one deflection dark,
Like waiting vultures of the night
Each pirate blackness skulks, a murderous mark
Begotten by a thing of light,
Like apprehension's baffling destiny.[26]

The Inviolate

There on the white Pacific shore the pines
  Still serve their jealous gods, and late and soon
The murmur runs along their rugged lines,
  'What black ship[27] waits the crash of our typhoon?'

And in this vigil circled, calm and proud,
  God-gates and temples glow with changeless noon,
Their mysteries luring that young seraph-cloud
  Swan-like between the mountain and the moon.[28]

The *haiku* shares some features with Japanese forms of 'politeness'. Both tend to avoid self-imposing assertions; hence a poem's message is likely to be indirect, blurred and ambiguous leaving the final interpretation to the reader. Blunden seems to have followed this fashion in writing 'Inland Sea' in which he tried to convey 'apprehension's baffling destiny' in association with the picturesque scene of 'the fishers wind[ing] their ancient ways in the moonlit sea'. Equally in 'The Inviolate' there lies no explicit message. Blunden was impressed by the inviolate god-gates and temples seemingly formed by the trees on the shore which stood calm and proud despite the 'malicious' murmurs concerning the omen of the black ship; and their mysterious stance lured the swan-like cloud.

The expression not only of thought and emotion, but also of colour tends to be restricted in the *haiku*. The influence of this is especially marked in the above poems. Only 'darkness and light' are depicted in 'Inland Sea'; in 'The Inviolate', the green of the pines and the 'red' of god-gates and temples are intentionally unmentioned, reflecting the poet's fear of disturbing the balance of black-and-white like in an ink-painting.

'The Deeper Friendship' confirms in a more open manner Blunden's reliance on 'one final hold' – *probably* suggesting Aki's love and support for him, though Blunden uses religious imagery: 'I know one hearth, one love that shine beyond fear'.

Were all eyes changed, were even poetry cold,
Were those long systems of hope that I tried to deploy
Skeletons, still I should keep one final hold,
Since clearer and clearer returns my first-found joy.

I would go, once more, through the sunless autumn
in trouble;
Thin and cold rain dripping down through branches black,
Streams hoarse-hurrying and pools spreading over the
stubble,
And the waggoner leaving the hovel under his sack

Would guide me along by the gate and deserted siding,
The inn with the tattered arbour, the choking weir;
And yet, security there would need small guiding.
I know one hearth, one love that shine beyond fear.

There, though the sharpest storm and flood were abroad,
And the last husk and leaf were stripped from the tree,
I would sue for peace where the rats and mice have gnawed,
And well content that Nature should bury me.[29]

After his return from Japan to Cowlinge in Suffolk and to Yalding – where his parents lived – in August 1927, Blunden had to endure the humiliation of his wife Mary's infidelity during his absence. Even his pent-up expectations concerning home-coming were despoiled by the rift with her – the way he felt she had deceived his trust and love. A number of poems truthfully convey his sadness and disappointment.

I knew Seraphina; Nature gave her hue,
Glance, sympathy, note, like one from Eden.
I saw her smile warp, heard her lyric deaden;
She turned to harlotry; – this I took to be new.

Say what you will, our God sees how they run.
These disillusions are His curious proving
That He loves humanity and will go on loving;
Over there are faith, life, virtue in the sun.[30]

In his plight nothing more seemed to console Blunden than Aki's devotion to him and assistance with his work; but he desperately tried to believe in the love of God – 'These disillusions are His curious proving / That He loves humanity and will go on loving'.

The measureless houses of dreams,
And the magic of hours within hours;

And those who pass by like clear streams,
Pass by us, on a journey not ours!
The eyes that we know and we fear,
As waters of Castaly clear,
That gaze that should once have been sweet,
Now a terror to meet!
– Yet, both in one corridor narrowly led,
Those steps in another intensity tread;
There is space that convenes us, but holds us apart;
Sunlight and sunlight, distinctly combined,
As a wish with the wind
And all heaven with one heart.[31]

This poem could be associated with Blunden's remark in a letter to Aki about a curious dream, in which he was on board a bus together with Aki and Mary:

> – Last night I dreamed that you were riding in a bus with me, when someone touched my shoulder, & it was Mrs M. Blunden, who made a 'scene'.
>
> (27 January 1930)

He seems to be struggling with the problem of whether reconciliation was possible; he seems to have been torn, too: 'There is space that convenes us, but holds us apart'.

In these great difficulties Blunden took comfort in the support of his family.

. . . Come,
And see how kindly all's at home.
No sweeter things than these I rhyme,
And this by much their sweetest time.[32]

The shadow of his loneliness became deeper, and his happy and optimistic familiarity with the Nature of the village sounds vain:

Familiarity

Dance not your spectral dance at me;
I know you well!
Along this lane there lives no tree
But I can tell.

I know each fall and rise and twist;
You – why, a wildflower in the mist,
  The moon, the mist.

Sound not that long alarm, gray tower,
  I know you well;
This is your habit at this hour,
  You and your bell!
If once, I heard a hundred times
Through evening's ambuscade your chimes –
  Dark tower, your chimes.

Enforce not that no-meaning so,
  Familiar stream;
Whether you tune it high or low,
  I know your theme;
A proud-fed but a puny rill,
A meadow brook, poured quick and shrill –
  Alone and shrill.

Sprawl not so monster-like, blind mist;
  I know not "seems";
I am too old a realist
  To take sea-dreams
From you, or think a great white Whale
Floats through our hawthorn-scented vale –
  This foam-cold vale.[33]

War's People

Through the tender amaranthine domes
Of angel-evenings echoing summer song,
  Through the black rock-tombs
Of winter, and where autumn floods prolong
  The midnight roar and tumbling thunder,
  Through spring's daisy-peeping wonder,
  Round and beyond and over and under,
    I see our homes.

. . .

From low-gorged lairs, which outshine Zion's towers,
Weak rags of walls, the forts of godlike powers.
  We went, returned,
But came with that far country learned;
Strange stars, and dream-like sounds, changed speech
    and law are ours.[34]

Confused and saddened, Blunden was disturbed by his awareness of other people's eyes upon him:

In animation beautiful
Returns your chance; now wander with
The sparkle on the living seas,
Nor fear that in these green estates
  Ambushed may lie
The hooded serpent with the human eye . . .[35]

His troubled mind continued to suffer:

Would understanding win herself my vote,
Now, having known this crisis thirty years,
She should decide me why it overwhelms
My chart of time and history; should declare
What in the spirit of a man long schooled
To human concept and devotion dear,
Upraised by sure example, undefiled
By misery and defeat, still in the sun –
What stirs in him, and finds its brother-self,
From that late sky. Again that sky, that tower,
These effigies and wizardries of chance,
Those soundless vollies of pale and distant birds
Have taken him, and from his whirring toils
Made him as far away, as unconcerned,
As consonant with the Power as its bare trees.[36]

Clearly he had to reassure himself many times that he would keep his own spirit intact – 'undefiled / By misery and defeat' during his personal crisis. The carefree innocence of 'Inland Sea' in Japan now turned into the sea of sighs – like Matthew Arnold's famous poem 'Dover Beach'.

Hear on the shore too the sighed monotones
Of waves that in weakness slip past the purled stones;
The seethe of blown sand round the dry fractured hull,
Salt-reeds and tusked fence; hear the struck gull
With death in his bones.

Slow comes the net in, that's filled with frustration;
Night ends the day of thwart discreation;
I would be your miracle-worker, sad friend,
Bid a music for you and a new star ascend, –
But I know isolation.[37]

Again, 'Return' suggests there was no real relief for Blunden to enjoy at home, all the sadness of broken loves awaiting him:

And Love, even Love, has dropped her lilies
On the hot highroad; once she knew
How columbines and daffadillies
Created her own sun and dew.

Return; how stands that man enchanted
Who, after seas and mountains crossed,
Finds his old threshold, so long scanted,
With not a rose or robin lost!

The wise, from passion now retreating
To the hamlets of the mind,
In every glance have claimed the greeting
Of spirits infinitely kind.[38]

During this difficult period Blunden often met Aki who was living and working for him in London; and one such outing took place in Cambridge.

Once again I have to tell you that I have been in a melancholy state and unable to attend to anything. I hope you got your train and reached home safely; it was a most happy afternoon in the air and in the church too, though as you know so well England is not at her best in the present mood. I cycled from Cambridge through the dark, & was somewhat troubled by the speed and glaring lamps of the motor-buses and cars, but got home in a little more than 2 hours. The next day we went to Felixstowe; it was a failure. M. said she would send you a present, & that was almost the only kind thing she said all day.

(9 July 1928)

Blunden's poem 'A Quartet' ('The Mikado' at Cambridge) tells of the production which he saw on a different occasion.

> Deep-moved I mark their choral master-piece,
> Their union in each swell and dying fall.[39]

He also wrote in his letter to Aki:

> No need to copy mere scraps and commonplace, but anything with real information or vivid interest. So much, my dear Aki, for work: I have no news, except that Plomer wrote & sent you his good wishes. . . . (Went to Cambridge last night saw 'The Mikado' which was very melodious and amusing, w.d have made you laugh at the 'Japanese' girls & costumes.)
>
> (5 May 1928)

A connotative poem, 'Values' concludes the book *Near and Far*, implying Blunden's high evaluation of English culture in which a kinder God and truth dominate. This was the precious rediscovery and re-appropriation of the ethos of his *own* country after his traumatic encounters with Eastern demi-gods, Buddha's dead eyes and ghoulish ornamentations in Japan – all appearing to him excessively implacable and intimidating. He also argues that Japanese value-judgements, which rigorously demand social standards of perfection, are wrong – and so also any other form of absolutism. In this context, the last poem of *Japanese Garland*, 'The Author's Last Words to his Students', well represents an aspect of Japanese sensibility – formalised modesty – which influenced Blunden.

Values

> Till darkness lays a hand on these gray eyes
> And out of man my ghost is sent alone,
> It is my chance to know that force and size
> Are nothing but by answered undertone.

No beauty even of absolute perfection
Dominates here – the glance, the pause, the guess
Must be my amulets of resurrection;
Raindrops may murder, lightnings may caress.

There I was tortured, but I cannot grieve;
There crowned and palaced – visibles deceive.
That storm of belfried cities in my mind
Leaves me my vespers cool and eglantined.
From love's wide-flowering mountain-side I chose
This sprig of green, in which an angel shows.[40]

In the sonnet 'Values' Blunden embodies several of his conclusions concerning the differences in values and 'sensibilities' between England and Japan. The first is: 'It is my chance to know that force and size / Are nothing but by answered undertone'. 'Force and size' could imply an army or even the Buddha, and may refer to both his major historical experiences – the War, and Japan.

In the latter half of the octet ('No beauty . . .') he tries to make it clear that he values undertones much more than force and size; that he much prefers England where 'the glance, the pause, the guess' are appreciated more deeply than absolute beauty or perfection. In the poem: 'Raindrops may murder, lightnings may caress'.

The relevance of this message is two-fold; firstly to the sensibilities of his Japanese students and secondly to his relationship with Aki.

The Author's Last Words to his Students[41]

Forgive what I, adventuring highest themes,
Have spoiled and darkened, and the awkward
hand
That longed to point the moral of man's dreams
And shut the wicket-gates of fairyland:
So by too harsh intrusion
Left colourless confusion.

For even the glories that I most revered,
Seen through my gloomed perspective in
strange mood,
Were not what to our British seers appeared;

I spoke of peace, I made a solitude,
Herding with deathless graces
My hobbling commonplaces.

Forgive that eyeless lethargy which chilled
Your ardours and I fear dimmed much fine
gold –
What your bright passion, leaping ages, thrilled
To find and claim, and I yet dared withhold;
These and all chance offences
Against your finer senses.

And I will ever pray for your souls' health,
Remembering how, deep-tasked yet eager-
eyed,
You loved imagination's commonwealth,
Following with smiling wonder a frail guide
Who hears beyond the ocean
The voice of your devotion.[42]

From the beginning he sounds very apologetic, 'Forgive what I . . .' – which is a sure sign of Japanese influence in which absolute value dominates the rest; hence as perfection will be the *ultimate* goal, one has to be always apologetic for one's failure to attain it.

In the context of his relationship with Aki, Blunden mentions in a letter how much he misses her in his room adding 'even an imagination can hurt'. Such kinder, tender, sympathetic, lyrical concepts of life and Nature were in the background when he wrote that 'Raindrops (not even the army or eastern tempest) may murder, lightnings may caress'.

My Autumn
. . . I can see you too, but imagination is not the life itself, and hurts as much as it pleases.

(31 August 1925)

These were the mixed feelings of his reaction to the prevailing Japanese reality he had experienced, in which the people had to suppress those aspects of their sensibilities which would enable them to understand the undertones of things – politeness, substituted for sympathy; they narrowly concerned themselves with the values of visible things – shape, force and size; in this sense one might compare the poem with Yeats's 'The Statues'.[43]

Lacking real encounters with Greek culture, Yeats's poem could be said to remain too general and abstract. The feminine sensibility at the base of western culture, which Blunden favoured, clashes interestingly in his poem with more masculine eastern sensitivity that could be fierce, brutal and less caring.

In the sestet, Blunden's message is simple, 'visibles deceive'. Thus he returns with relief to the womb-like protection of 'vespers cool and eglantined'. The couplet of the poem summarises:

> From love's wide-flowering mountain-side I chose
> This sprig of green, in which an angel shows.[44]

Thus he ultimately chose the 'sprig of green (Nature), in which an angel shows'. By thus closely associating Nature with the supernatural – like an angel or love – Blunden follows western mental patterns which place special value on the supernatural as a higher and more enlightened form than the natural world; whereas the Japanese value-judgement tends to terminate in the perfection of natural, hardly aspiring to supernatural existence in its true sense. This might be attributable to the different cultural concepts of God. Hence, he seems to have risen into love, not only his own personal love but a wider Christian love (cf. 'Deeper Friendship'). The association of love and the angel, bearing in mind also the images of bells and drums in other poems, could direct us to the famous passage on love in I Corinthians: 13 in the Bible:

> I may speak in tongues of men or of angels, but if I am without love, I am a sounding gong or a clanging cymbal. I may have the gift of prophecy, and know every hidden truth; I may have faith strong enough to move mountains; but if I have not love I am nothing. . . . Love is patient, love is kind and envies no one.

Finally then, in his deferential way, Blunden seems to be hailing the triumph of Christian love over the unsympathetic gaze of Buddha's dead eye. This is perhaps his basic judgement on the Japanese culture which he had encountered; and if so, is a measure of the shock of that encounter.

Notes

1. Caroline Moorehead, 'The Poets We Nearly Forgot', in 'Women at War', *The Times*, 9 November 1981, p. 9. (The newspaper erroneously gives 1976 as the date of Blunden's death.)
2. *A Queen's College Miscellany* (1921) p. 20.
3. W. B. Yeats, *The Collected Poems of W. B. Yeats* (London: Macmillan, 1965) pp. 210–11.
4. Ibid., pp. 213–14.
5. Edmund Blunden, *An Elegy and Other Poems* (London: Cobden-Sanderson, 1937) p. 82.
6. Edmund Blunden, *A Wanderer in Japan: Sketches and Reflections in Prose and Verse* (Tokyo: Asahi Shimbunsha, 1950) p. 61.
7. John Bayley, *Selected Essays* (Cambridge: Cambridge University Press, 1984) p. 93.
8. Edmund Blunden, 'Far East' in *Near and Far: New Poems* (London: Cobden-Sanderson, 1929) p. 22. Subsequently referred to as *Near and Far*.
9. 'Building the Library, Tokyo University', ibid., p. 30.
10. Edmund Blunden, *Japanese Garland* (London: Beaumont Press, 1928) p. 14.
11. Blunden, *Near and Far*, p. 21.
12. *The Collected Poems of W. B. Yeats* (London: Macmillan, 1965) pp. 280–1.
13. Blunden, *Near and Far*, p. 21.
14. Edmund Blunden, *Retreat* (London: Cobden-Sanderson, 1928) p. 66.
15. Blunden, *Near and Far*, pp. 25–6.
16. 'Sir William Treloar's Dinner for Crippled Children', ibid., p. 65.
17. 'On a Biographical Dictionary', ibid., p. 61.
18. 'The Quick and the Dead', ibid., p. 28.
19. 'The Kiln', ibid., p. 50.
20. Ibid.
21. 'Epitaph', ibid., p. 59.
22. Ibid., pp. 59–60.
23. 'Summer Rainstorm', ibid., p. 49.
24. Ibid.
25. 'The Quick and the Dead', ibid., p. 28.
26. 'Inland Sea', ibid., p. 27.
27. A 'black ship' was a foreign warship such as those introduced by Commodore Matthew Calbraith Perry (1794–1858), a US naval officer who reopened Japan to the Western world after more than 200 years.
28. 'The Inviolate', in Blunden, *Near and Far*, p. 29.
29. 'The Deeper Friendship', ibid., pp. 55–6.
30. 'Report on Experience', ibid., p. 58.
31. 'Dream Encounters', ibid., p. 43.
32. 'Autumn in the Weald', ibid., p. 52.
33. 'Familiarity', ibid., pp. 37–8.
34. 'War's People', ibid., pp. 41–2.
35. 'Fragment', ibid., p. 47.
36. 'The Correlation', ibid., p. 51.

37. 'The Blind Lead the Blind', ibid., p. 57.
38. 'Return', ibid., pp. 53–4.
39. 'A Quartet', ibid., p. 62.
40. 'Values', ibid., p. 67.
41. In the School of English Literature, Tokyo Imperial University, 1924–7.
42. Blunden, *Near and Far*, pp. 32–3.
43. The significance of shape and appearance is represented by such art forms as flower arrangements, the tea-ceremony, or Noh plays, or even the films of Kurosawa in which all movements and emotions tend to be stylised, and concentration put on intensity and aesthetic perfection.
44. Blunden, *Near and Far*, p. 67.

4

Letters

A selection of Blunden's letters, with annotations

NOTE: Japanese place names and personal names have only been annotated where they are relevant to Blunden's immediate activities or to his relations with Aki Hayashi. The dates in parentheses signify those of Blunden's letters which record the events explained in my text. The exact dates on which particular events took place cannot be inferred from them.

References to 'Kirkpatrick' are to B. J. Kirkpatrick, *A Bibliography of Edmund Blunden* (Oxford: Clarendon Press, 1979).

Karuizawa Hotel[1]

1 August 1925

Dear Miss Hayashi

I came back here today, and think of remaining 10 days or a fortnight. Do you care to look in? I shall be delighted. I hope this time to be fairly free & at ease; my last few days were not so; but there are many earnest acquaintances of mine in the town! Tomorrow evening (2nd) I am invited out to dinner; can you dine here the evening after? please come & tell me you can.

Yours sincerely
Edmund Blunden

Note

1. Located in the north-west Central Mountain District, Karuizawa is two hours by train from Tokyo. The district is marked by lofty mountain peaks of the Japan Alps, averaging well over 3000 metres in altitude, ensuring cool, fresh air and low humidity during the summer. One of the most popular resorts in Japan with its volcanic mountain, Asama.

218 Karuizawa

17 August 1925

My dear

I hope this will reach you with the medicine. It's another wretched day & our excursion w.^{d} have been impossible; perhaps you will come but I rather think you must stay in the dry & rest. How beautiful it was to see you last evening & be at peace; I am still happy because of those happy hours. I woke up looking the way you are & sending you my blessings. If you can come tomorrow, I shall be here & free I believe: or perhaps you will send me word where & when to meet you. What of the concert this evening? Well, I wait and see.

With my love
E.

218 Karuizawa

Monday 7 p.m.
[undated]

Dear one

Just had your dear note. I'll say quickly, as the messenger was waiting some time before I returned: – If you're better, be at the Post Office at 10.30 tomorrow morning like a darling: if not better, be at the station at *11*, where I should go on to meet you. It's not the fear of catching your cold which keeps me here this evening, but – respectability! that curse.

O, much love to you
Edmund

We seem to be going to the concert, wish you were.

A.H. E.B.
28.8.1925

Love's not Time's fool, though rosy lips & cheeks
In compass of his bending sickle come;
Love changes not with his brief hours and weeks,
But bears it out e'en to the edge of Doom.[1]

Note

1. Shakespeare's Sonnet no. 116. Blunden seems to have avoided quoting the first eight lines of this sonnet to Aki, as they praise the bliss of fidelity in love.

c/o E. Hori Esq
Higashi-Kaigan
Chigasaki

29 August 1925

My very dear Autumn[1]

But still how gentle and beautiful a love has awakened between you and me! I shall rely on it and live on it in many solitary hours. It is a charm to keep me going. I am most distressed that I cannot fulfil all that I ought to Autumn, as things stand now – but you have unselfish patience and a splendid courage. When I was with you, the cares of this hurried and bilious world ceased to touch me. I loved whatever gave me the chance to do some slight thing for you: and, as it has been, so it will continue to be. This train is going in your direction – a pleasing thought, but only partly so. The colours of circumstances are always rather ironically mixed. I ought to forget to stop at Chigasaki![2] and would if life had no complex calls upon us.

There is a 'John Clare'[3] at Kikufuji H.[4] ready but I didn't have time to send it – when I come, will that do? and I hope to have a copy of my Poems[5] in a small sixpenny edition for you. This cheap edition is intended to sell very widely but it may be a dream. The Proofs of my forthcoming book called 'English Poems'[6] were on my table and I spent a good deal of the night in correcting them – they are to be published in November, so my list of Works is growing all the time . . . I have had many letters of all kinds, and need a Secretary. Well, and I shall have one. I do trust you're ever so much better in health, and no bad news or troubles. This must end, I think I am nearly at Ch. With true love and all my blessings, Dear

yours unfailingly O sweet companion!
Edmund

Notes

1. 'Autumn': 'Aki' means 'autumn' in Japanese, though at the town office the registered name of Aki (Hayashi) is spelt in *katakana*, which allows various readings of 'Aki', and not in *kanji*, where the *only* possible translation is 'autumn'. However, as Aki herself gave 'autumn' as the meaning of her name to Blunden, he thus addresses her 'Dearest Autumn'.
2. Chigasaki is located in the area of Shonan Seaside, about an hour's ride from Tokyo. Blunden's friend Professor Eishiro Hori, who later became Professor of English at Keio University, invited him to stay at his cottage, and there Blunden wrote 'The Cottage at Chigasaki'. In his letter of 1 October 1925, Blunden writes: 'I have written some verses about Chigasaki scenes, as yet only rough and unshaped. You will think me vain to tell you such things. I feel content to have you to tell them to.'
3. *John Clare, Poems Chiefly from Manuscripts*, note by Edmund Blunden and Alan Porter; biographical signed by E. Blunden, 2000 copies (London: Cobden-Sanderson, 1920). (Kirkpatrick B3.)
4. Kikufuji Hotel is located in Hongo, near Tokyo (Imperial) University. It was founded in 1897 by Konosuke Haneda and his wife, Kikue, and in 1914 became 'Kikufuji Hotel'. On 10 March 1945 its fifty years of history ended in a bombing raid. The site where it stood is now marked by a memorial stone. Among those who stayed there for considerable periods of time were many eminent literary figures and scholars – novelists Tanizaki Jyunichiro, Naoki Sanjugo, and Masamune Hakucho to name but a few. See Plate 7.
5. *Poems 1913 and 1914* (Horsham: Christ's Hospital, Price and Co., 1914). (Pamphlet, 100 copies.) (Kirkpatrick A1, 3.)
6. *English Poems* (London: Cobden-Sanderson, 1926). (Kirkpatrick A20.) This book was first published in 1925 and dedicated to Mary Blunden.

[Kikufuji Hotel
Hongo
Tokyo]

31 August 1925

My Autumn

. . . I have just had a letter from my friend Siegfried Sassoon,[1] the greatest of poets in England now. He closes with the suggestion that I sh.[d] become a Bookseller when I go back, and he will provide the capital at the beginning. Alas, my dear, I am afraid he would utterly change his mind if he knew about us; and yet, shall I grieve for that? Even that I could endure, if the worst came to the worst – I hold you so fast in my love and honour, you must be my refuge if ever my friends forsake me. But it will help us, if we can keep a secret.

I don't feel like sleep; so restless and so alone. My room is untidy, I'll spend some hours in straightening things. I have here some Poets whom I love, and long to read their best out to you and share the beauty with you. You dear soul, you have swiftly come into my deepest life. So remain! may envy never harm us. If there is any innocence, it is love; and I cannot help loving you, though far off is one whom I love. This, the common opinion would condemn, but I have spoken the truth. What time may do, I don't know: but you will never pass from me.

Your most affectionate
Edmund

Note

1. Siegfried Sassoon (1886–1967); noted as a First World War poet. His works include three autobiographical novels: *Memoirs of a Fox-Hunting Man*, *Memoirs of an Infantry Officer* and *Sherston's Progress*, collected together as *The Complete Memoirs of George Sherston* (London: Faber and Faber, 1937); and *Collected Poems* (London: Faber and Faber, 1947), and *Collected Poems, 1908–1956* (London: Faber and Faber, 1961). He was a great friend of Blunden and one of the first to realise Blunden's poetic talent. They first met in 1919 and shared a keen interest in poetry and cricket. Sassoon helped Blunden with both financial and family matters. Aki undertook a burdensome copying task for him (15 October 1931).

Kikufuji Hotel
Hongo
Tokyo

1 September 1925

Greatly dear,

I must speak to you a little, and send you my greetings and kindness. You have begun your work, now, I suppose – take it easy! imitate Blunden. I feel it is wasted time, alone here, without enthusiasm for anything even among my books and papers; it is as though I should never be able to resume my former way of thinking and doing. Even Mr Hardy's Poems[1] remain on the shelf – This is a mood and must be shaken off, or I shall be a failure. To work and achieve used to be my principle and no doubt is so still, though just now the solitariness to which I have returned makes me so uninterested. My dear Autumn, I shall soon see you again, that's a good and delightful thought. Each departing day repeats that. I have been expecting a telephone message from Mr Hori,[2] but none has come, so he may not be returning to Chigasaki until the 3rd. I shall not stay longer than the 8th in any case. I am inclined to take a private student or two if any apply to me, so as to put aside a little money – this day, going to the bank to send home what I could, I was much aggrieved to find that the *yen* had dropped considerably. It was already very low, and my appointment is not worth what it appeared to be in London – if I had been a man of business ability, I should have refused a contract that didn't allow for fluctuating currency. But I am always grumbling about something; particularly this! The remedy is for me to become really active . . .

Your deeply longing
Edmund

Notes

1. Thomas Hardy (1840–1928), *Collected Poems* (London: Macmillan, 1919).
2. See note 2 to the letter of 29 August 1925.

c/o Eishiro Hori
Higashi Kaigan
Chigasaki

3 September 1925

My dear soul

When we got here in the rain this afternoon I was not disappointed, for your first letter from Nagoya was here. It brightens a dark day, and is really *you*. I think with astonishment and delight of the love you give me, and the suddenness and completeness of it; I am happy in that love and only unhappy in my impatience to have you with me again. You write as though you had seemed rather reserved at the Green Hotel, but I never thought any such thing; the time there is beautiful to think about and your profound companionship gave me new life and new poetry. 'I have offered my heart, my body and everything to you' – dear love, that I remind myself of all through the day, and my love seems to glow more and more. Your dear body has but a minor share in our mutual devotion – not to deny or despise physical love; but it is a part of love that could be excluded, and still love would prevail. We are in this world, creatures with bodies; and hence I think it's unnatural to act like hermits or icebergs; but still there's a deeper secret of love to worship most. . . .

Your admiring and loving
Edmund

c/o Eishiro Hori
Higashi Kaigan
Chigasaki

5 September 1925

Most sweet & dear

Today the usual course of things here was vastly improved by my getting at the same post your letters of the 3rd and 4th. I daresay Hori[1] felt a little curious about the writing which must already be familiar to his eye. Well, that does no harm. I take the greatest delight in all the beautiful things you say to me, and feel as you do that this living at distance is a severity and pain all the time. We will discuss the future when I come to N.[2] next week, and I am thinking that I shall be appointing a Secretary about Christmas! Actually I can find her plenty to do for I have undertaken to produce 2 School books at least – (1) Odes &c. by Keats,[3] for an English publisher (2) British Poets, selections for Japanese readers, to be included in a series edited by Vines[4] & Hori – and the sooner I get those under hatches, the better. There is much more exacting work and of finer texture to be done. And the articles on Japan Within should be finished while I am in the mood. So you see the urgency. It may suit, if you are unhappy in Nagoya; but possibly your work will turn out more agreeably in course of time.

I am writing in bed, & feel very 'salty', having bathed twice today in a somewhat violent sea. Did you wake up with the small earthquake this morning? I did & wondered how it affected you.

The thought of seeing you, & happy you, before long, has been growing stronger in me as the hours went by. Though the hotel is absurdly dear yet I can manage, and on Friday 11th I'll be on the 8.45 express from Tokyo. Meet me if you can at 4.32 I shall love that. On the Monday (I intend beginning my lectures on the 15th whether the University like it or not) I hope you will do as you say & come part way on the returning train – it should be, *all the way*. But duty no doubt rules. You are good to tell me about the trains & above all to make inquiries at the hotel. I wonder if another time we might not rather go to such a place as the Nara hotel or the Kyoto places; though it might be difficult for you to get away. This point too we must try to think over. In expense the Nara hotel w.[d] be considerably less, & it's very finely furnished & managed.
Goodnight, my blessings to you whom I love and lack so much.

Notes

1. See note 2 to the letter of 29 August 1925.
2. Nagoya: now two hours by the Shinkansen (bullet train) from Tokyo, and one of the important industrial cities in central Japan.
3. *Shelley and Keats as They Struck their Contemporaries: Notes Partly from Manuscript Sources*, edited by E. Blunden (London: C. W. Beaumont, 1925). (Kirkpatrick B16.)
4. Sherard Vines, Visiting Professor of English at Keio University: author of *Yofuku, or Japan in Trousers* (London: Wishart, 1931), and *Movements in Modern English Poetry and Prose* (Tokyo: Humphrey Milford, Ohkayama, 1927).

Kikufuji Hotel
Hongo
Tokyo

18 Sept. 1925

Deeply loved,

Your letter of yesterday cannot hide the fact that you are ill, which is depressing. I wish I could help, but perhaps by writing I can do you some little good. I continue to feel your absence and naturally when I go out (as I did this morning to the 2nd hand bookshops) I want to be talking to you & hearing your words just as so many happy times. And you are reading the Bonadventure![1] now quite an ancient history. I felt sure you would easily take the voyage with me, and am delighted now that you send me your appreciation and prove my confidence was sound. Just so I believe you will be able to share in the experiences set down in my War Book,[2] not yet published and only half done; I intend to bring it to a completeness, but before arranging its publication I must go over it with the aid of my old notes and letters from the trenches and similar papers now lying in my study in England. It has all been written in the light of memory, which is not nowadays so radiant as I should like.

You ask what 'Georgian' means. It means, of the present period in England.

Q. Victoria 1837–1901 (or so)	– 'Victorian'
K. Edward VII 1901–1910	– 'Edwardian'
K. George V 1910 –	– 'Georgian'

There is a little confusion, as we had a succession of King Georges in the 18th century, but as used lately 'Georgian' means 'contemporary'.

I see that the Diet has been burned down, so our visit will not take place! We'll go to the Pictures instead. This is a wonderful town for Fires – it passeth all understanding: and I never feel absolutely easy in my mind when I'm away, for I should hate to lose my private papers here & some of the books are irreplaceable if they should happen to join in some little blaze. – Yes, sometimes I feel easy about that, even that: in Kyoto I didn't trouble at all, for my heart and my mind were occupied only with the present and that meant You. And I am still wholly moved by you and for you, save that far off there is a profound and gentle love as you know. That is too much a part of my life to be changed, tho' something may seem to change it abruptly;

but else you have my heart. Do not allow yourself to sit in doubts and shadows, but trust and be at rest, for that is how my love for you should persuade you, you dear woman. You must be happy in my happiness, or it is more like another of this life's disenchantments.

It's late and I must be about early in the morning to get my lecture ready. So I'll close this little letter and go on thinking of you and speaking to you though unheard. How nobly you offer me money; but, Autumn, that's my privilege and I make you the same offer by way of reply! The inexhaustible sums which the Japanese Government pay foreign professors enable us to buy Prints, the Japan Advertiser, Whiskey and indeed Pipe Tobacco. Why then –

With my faith and my love
yours, my Autumn,
Edmund

Notes

1. *The Bonadventure: A Random Journal of an Atlantic Holiday* (London: Cobden-Sanderson, 1922). (Kirkpatrick A12.)
2. *Undertones of War* (London: Cobden-Sanderson, 1928). (Kirkpatrick A28.)

Kikufuji Hotel
Hongo
Tokyo

Sept. 20, 1925

Ever my dear,

I send you my blessings and greatly wish to hear that you are better – perhaps the morning will bring me word from you. In spite of what I said about writing twice a week I feel a painful dissatisfaction on any day when there is no letter from you; and also I feel each day impelled to write to dear you. Dully and feebly do I go about my work – I take hours to begin, pick up a book to refer to some passage, lay it down again without finding what I meant to find; I can't go ahead. I want in my deepest being *to go back,* and be with you at Kutsukake[1] watching you come into the room, or at Kyoto (but it was too hot) with you kneeling at my chair. The present is a fruitless time.

This day a young woman . . . came to see me. She has come occasionally and is very kind; she had lunch with me and we walked in Ginza.[2] I tell you this because I think it's fair to do so. I longed that it might be you and I was thinking of you all the time she was in my company. O, had it been you I should be now in the best mood in the world, but I feel instead heavy and all alone.

We shall soon meet again! that's glorious. The days go by and bring us nearer. Do tell me if for any reason your letter to this Hotel brings no answer or an unsatisfactory answer. We could no doubt fix up elsewhere if necessary but here is best perhaps. I am threatened with asthma lately – the well-known and hated symptoms in my chest and nose have several times given warning. But care and tranquillity may get me past this stage. I will be as fresh as May when you come. We'll make good use of the time, which is the sole duty of man. I hope it gets a little cooler here. At present it is quite airless and oppressive, so that one feels drowsy.

The public holiday on Wednesday doesn't save me anything, as that's my blank day always: but I hope you will gain a leisure hour or two by it. The next public holiday, I hope, we'll spend together at Atami[3] or some such place.

To my natural regret an Income Tax demand has reached me! Well, these things must be, and in England the Government is much more exorbitant. Taxes there are certainly the greatest fault we have to find with our country. I don't think they'll tax Aki-san. She'll be Free and without any duty. I believe we shall be going together – something tells me that. Well, the voyage alone will be a joy, not to mention the sequel. I'm now going to bed, as I am rather asthmatic and having to burn my powder: in the morning I'll add a little to this. Love to you, goodnight my darling – and shall I be contented? O heavens, no.

Notes

1. A village near Karuizawa.
2. The main shopping street in Tokyo.
3. See p. 16.

Kikufuji Hotel
Hongo
Tokyo
24 September 1925

My great Love,

Having your letters of the 21st & 23rd I was about to answer this evening when two French friends came and got me to go out with them, I failed to have this ready in time for the post. Perhaps it will reach you at home nevertheless, before you start on your journey this way. It is now only two days before I see Aki – less, for it's now just on midnight. The rain is coming down in floods, so quite likely it will have stopped by the time you come. I shall be at the station studying the crowd that pours out of the train at 9.30 for one sweet face. You will be very tired I fear and this wretched cold & headache will oppress you. I shall try to make you take things easy during your few hours – few! – with me, but I am not very good at that myself.

You send me most loving and thoughtful letters. I always open them with a hurried hand and read them with a heart refreshed. It is a different Japan nowadays, although the pain of absence sometimes makes a day go slower than ever; but ordinarily the sense of your deep love and the words of comfort and intimacy which you send carry me through much dreariness better than all. A photograph of you is sadly missing here. I should be delighted with one, so don't dodge the question! But I see you and am with you in a surprising way, until some trifling idea breaks the spell and absence resumes its power again.

The English people are so optimistic about Japan that the truth would be valuable there. I shall try to get you a good hearing, my dear. But will Japan ever hear? I as an outsider feel that the national failing is still that 'children of heaven' complex.[1] But I am only a hasty observer.

My old 'Bonadventure'[2] was quite well received – so I have taken you with me, have I, through weeks of sea-water, sea-arguments and sea-mealtimes? I get a new pleasure from having written the book, and hope we may one day share a somewhat similar experience, though a passenger-ship and a 'tramp' are as far apart as a duchess and a ploughman. Still, we can go ashore and 'blithely spend the day'.

Your noble, generous, most womanly thought of 'self-sacrifice' is in itself a great thing done for me. I want you, and I shall try not to give you any opportunity for that self-sacrifice: you always will be putting me to shame with your active love.

I write with *your* kimono on, but the air is chilly and finding its way in, so I must soon finish. Yesterday with much mental protest I ground out two more articles for the Japan Advertiser,[3] and I shall perhaps get back some of my English fluency in prose if I don't get disturbed too frequently. Students occasionally come & some of 'em leave me to do *all* the talking, in the elementary English which may be easy to them but is vilely difficult to me. However, they are entitled to a closer view of the English type (if I can be so called!). . . .

Your ever affectionate
Edmund

Notes

1. This idea was peculiar to, and prevailed among, the Japanese people until after the Second World War, and especially during the Shinto revival of the eighteenth and nineteenth centuries. It was based on the traditional myth that the Emperor was the incarnation of the great sun god and that the Japanese belonged to a prestigious 'divine' race. An example of this belief occurs in the ancient story of the warships of the Mongol invasion which were saved from destruction by a sudden gale from heaven.
2. See note 1 to the letter of 18 September 1925.
3. The English-language paper. See note 5 to the letter of 30 May 1941.

Kikufuji Hotel
Hongo
Tokyo

29 September 1925

Most sweet and dear

I have just had your letter as a consolation for the gloomy day, and was sorry to read you did not get to sleep in the train because you were worrying over my asthma. It is as if I was myself in want of sleep: however, I daresay in a few days you will feel as well as usual. My asthma has not gone yet, but I gave my lecture yesterday: &

luckily today is a holiday. I must try & reach Yokohama[1] as I promised Mr Rose-Innes,[2] so after writing this I'll set off.

Though you were here such a little while you brought me great joy and peace of mind and I still feel the glow and gentleness of our hours together. The Autumn equanimity of things shares my mind with ideas of your enjoying this season presently in England. I don't argue that English autumn is more beautiful than any others – no, but there is a fine spaciousness of air and earth, a selectness or crystal clearness about the distant trees, farms, mills, spires and cities. One of the best pieces in Tennyson describes this space and visibility well: it is in 'In Memoriam' and begins, 'Calm is the morn without a sound.'[3] I tried in 'The Waggoner' – the poem is called 'Leisure'[4] – to show how the country lies serene and clear-cut at this time. And one day I shall try again.

You ought to make an anthology of poems on Autumn. Or perhaps you will do that in England, when you will come across many pleasant books for a few pence each, with a real touch of truth & enjoyment from page to page. (I have just found an old cutting which is typical of the affectionate rural literature of the English – I think you'll catch the spirit of it. Perhaps we shall one day visit the very place).

I have not been able to write anything since you went, because of asthma and the sudden return to solitude. It would please me highly if I found myself entering upon a poem of large design and something like satisfactory newness of metre and words. But there is no use in trying and wishing to write a poem. If the sky falls we shall catch larks.[5]

Don't fret but take all the chances of life as always. I ought to have remembered that 'wine' – excuse the inverted commas, – but next time we'll not omit. All my kindness, all I am capable of, sets like a spring breeze towards you, and I am conscious of you and your love all day long. The new year will be a blessing.[6]

Your deeply loving
Edmund

Notes

1. Yokohama is a sea-port town near Tokyo and the capital of Kanagawa Prefecture. Many Westerners have settled down there and the town has a cosmopolitan atmosphere.
2. Arthur Rose-Innes; a good friend of Blunden who lived in Yokohama and who often invited Blunden to dinner while he was staying in Japan.

He was a linguist and author of *Beginners' Dictionary of Chinese–Japanese Characters with Common Abbreviations, Variants and Numerous Compounds* (7th edn, enlarged, Yokohama: Yoshikawa Shoten, 1932; American edn, Cambridge, Mass.: Harvard University Press, 1942).

3. XI

Calm is the morn without a sound,
   Calm as to suit a calmer grief,
   And only thro' the faded leaf
The chestnut pattering to the ground:
. . .

4. And calm and marvellous the wide lands lie
Dim with awakening notes of little birds;
And the delighted Spirit in the dells
      Woos the sun's opening eye
With his droll night-whims, puffballs' pepper-gourds,
Startling white mushrooms and bronze chantarelles.

5. Blunden here recalls an English rural proverb.
6. This sentence suggests that Blunden's plan to live together with Aki from the new year had been firmly agreed between the two by then.

2 Oct. 1925

Dear heart

I have not yet sealed up my letter of last night and now can add a hasty word; delighted just now to read your message of the 30th and to have for myself the little picture of you which gives me something of your presence. It's my day for foreign mail so I am hard at it scribbling: my asthma is not cleared away altogether but less burdensome that it was. Do not on any account alter your intentions: I shall suffer if you do so: but you'll see what I wrote last night & be guided by that. I don't know the Lakes, my dear, but they seem to live up to their reputation, and we shall find them as fair as their pictures. Many and many a book exists on them, and some are finely illustrated – there too you will gather in a little collection. You Anglophile! lover of England – she needs lovers nowadays, for her enemies are sufficiently numerous. We'll talk over the cushions next time you are here: there's no hurry for my room is not noticeably aesthetic. Don't learn *Leisure*, I beg you: it's too imperfect. . . .

Many and loving blessings for
Autumn herself
Edmund

Kikufuji Hotel
Hongo
Tokyo
7 October 1925

Kindest Love,

. . . I am sorry your day's work is so dreary. Your acute and enquiring mind must be isolated completely. Even here the general attitude is passive and lazy, but there are stirrings of intellect, and several of my students please me well with their keenness and their genuine, unborrowed ideas. Then there are bookshops, music, pictures and the cinematograph, even if my standard in those matters is rather in the way of my enjoyment. And, in point of price, they are too dear here. The common cinema at 1*y*.20 or 1*y*.50[1] is not half as good value as the shilling seat at home – as Aki will not unwillingly see presently . . .

My dearest love to Autumn
Ever your Edmund

Note

1. Blunden was earning approximately 150 yen per month, about the equivalent of £50. A cinema seat costing 1*y*.20 was thus correspondingly much more expensive than in England.

Kikufuji Hotel
Hongo
Tokyo
9 October 1923 [?1925]

Dearest Autumn

No more than a note. I shall be at Tokyo station on Sunday, unless your telegram cancels your plan, at 7.50 a.m., and shall wait if you don't arrive by that; but perhaps before Sunday I shall hear from you exactly what train you will take. It's a delight to think of your coming, but the stress of such long night journeys gives me great anxiety for you. It's a pity I am not able to be the Dominant Male and speak to you like a father![1] For my own part, I think now if I watch carefully what I do and don't hurry I may be free of asthma again for a period. It would have been the best of remedies if you c[d] have been here as you wished. I love you & your love. Last night I attended a Reading Society[2] and this afternoon I am to address a little class of Saito's.[3] It is raining in true Tokyo fashion now, so probably I shall have to get a boat over to the University.[4] I have heard that there is a holiday on Oct. 30 as well as Oct. 31; does this help Aki at all, or is she tied to duty or marriage feasts?[5] Enter Miss Collie[6] with my lunch. She really is a kind soul. And makes excellent soup.

It is a long way to England. I wanted you to have the sixpenny poetry book before now. And I must write to my publisher soon & get copies of The Shepherd,[7] John Clare[8] & 'English Poems'[9] (due to appear in November) for you. Lazy Blunden – that's putting it mildly too, for wherever I turn my mind's eye I am aware of things postponed and neglected. As you say, this is a foreign climate for me, but at home it is much the same story. When you come here, or wherever we shall be, do you think you can reform such a confirmed idler?

Well then, I shall be seeing you on Sunday and we'll rejoice and be exceeding glad. Many blessings and my love

Your affectionate
Edmund

Notes

1. Blunden may be referring to the general attitude of Japanese men toward women at that time.
2. An extra-curricular activity to enhance students' knowledge of English literature. It was guided by Blunden. See Chapter 2 for more details.
3. Takeshi Saito (1887–1982), Emeritus Professor of English in the University of Tokyo, honorary KBE. He wrote many studies of English literature, and his *History of English Literature* (in Japanese; Tokyo: Kenkyusha, 1938) has been for many years a standard textbook for students of that subject. His book *Keats' View of Poetry* (London: Cobden-Sanderson, 1929), was published in England with Blunden's help. He was Blunden's closest Japanese friend and arranged for Blunden to be offered the professorship at Tokyo University in 1924. He himself was an austere man and a stoic Christian. Coming from humble origins he attained the prestigious post of a professorship in Teidai. The personal and literary friendship between Blunden and Saito is recorded in Blunden's letters to Aki which number about 64 in all dating from 1925 to 1962. The most interesting accounts are as follows. 'Saito had a lot of fine photographs of England' (13 October 1925). 'Saito wanted a long article for a new English Literature Quarterly' (8 December 1925).

Blunden sent a long literary letter to Saito (14 February 1928). Saito's book came out, had a notice and was reviewed (17 November, 29 November and 8 December 1929). Blunden sent cuttings of the reviews to Saito (13 December, 19 December 1929, and 20 January 1930). Saito sent a letter to Blunden who showed it to Aki (14 January 1930). Saito hoped Blunden was coming to Japan (6 February 1930).

Blunden sent Saito an article on Keats for *Saito's Studies* (15 May 1931); in return Saito sent Blunden a cheque for books accompanied by an admiring letter (18 June 1931). Saito sent a book dedicated to Blunden together with a photograph and Keats's *Endymion* (23 August 1931). Aki found a Keats poem for Saito (18 November 1931). Saito sent a book on Japanese art to Blunden (17 January 1932). A letter from Saito arrived in Karuizawa (a summer resort) (23 August 1933). Saito sent another letter regarding the possibility of a post for Blunden in Japan (9 September; also relevant are the letters of 19 August, 4 September, 20 September 1934).

Saito sent a Japanese translation of *Undertones of War* to Blunden (13 November 1935), but said nothing about Blunden's introduction to it (28 May 1936) which surprised Blunden. T. Sato and Saito quarrelled about Blunden's appointment in Japan (12 May 1937) because T. Sato invited Blunden to Keijo, Korea.

Saito's daughter and a friend came to England to pay Blunden a short visit and sent photographs (17 January 1940). Blunden commended Saito's edition of *A Song to David* (see *A Song to David, with Other Poems by Christopher Smart*, chosen with biographical and critical preface and notes by Edmund Blunden [London: Cobden-Sanderson, 1924]). Saito's edition was published in Japanese in *Fukuin to Gendai* (February 1958). Blunden planned to meet Saito in Tokyo (28 November 1947). In Japan Saito translated Blunden's speech (13 January 1948), and presided over the founding of ICU – International Christian University (20 February 1948). Blunden noticed that Saito's personality was changing for the better (26 October 1948). He attended the wedding of Saito's son Makoto (5 December 1949), whose son was tragically to kill Saito on 4 July 1982. Saito was due to retire in Spring 1954 (4 December 1953).

Saito was going to America for funds (19 February 1954) and was to visit Blunden in May (30 April 1954). Saito came to Hong Kong and was disappointed that Blunden could not come to Japan (15 June 1954). Blunden mentioned Saito's dictionary on World Literature (19 October 1954) and praised Saito's editing of *King Lear* (15 February 1956).

Saito always welcomed Blunden's friends at his home in Ushigome (29 March 1959). He wrote a contribution for Blunden in an issue of *Today's Japan* (8 February 1960); Blunden wrote that he thought old friends stayed alive a long time! (17 April 1960). In 1961 letters from Saito informed Blunden that he had been very busy (17 September and 31 October) even after seven years of retirement. Blunden was impressed with Saito's humorous and humane lecturing (14 September 1962); Saito wrote on Hodgson (6 November 1962). There exists unpublished typed correspondence between Dr Saito and Blunden: see Chapter 5, section (c).

4. It was established as the first Japanese university in 1877 by the unification of Kaisei Gakko and Tokyo Igakko, which had been founded in the Edo Period (1600–1868) as the Shogunate-sponsored centres of Western learning Kaiseijo and Igakujo. Renamed Tokyo Imperial University in 1886, it was the only such university until the establishment of Kyoto Imperial University in 1897. In 1947 its name was changed back to Tokyo University and in 1949 it was reorganised to incorporate the First Higher School and Tokyo Higher School.
5. The autumn is the most popular season for Japanese wedding ceremonies.
6. A co-lodger at Kikufuji Hotel, and very kind to Blunden in a motherly way.
7. *The Shepherd and Other Poems of Peace and War* (London: Cobden-Sanderson, 1922). (Kirkpatrick A10.)
8. *John Clare Poems, Chiefly from Manuscripts,* edited by Blunden and A. Porter (London: Cobden-Sanderson, 1920). (Kirkpatrick B3.)
9. *English Poems* (London: Cobden-Sanderson, 1925). (Kirkpatrick A20.)

Kikufuji Hotel
Hongo
Tokyo

13 Oct. 1925

My delightful Aki

You have treated me very nobly in writing on the 11th. and again on the 12th. This second one greeted my return just now from the usual dusty and noisy class-room – it is hard to lecture there at any time, but when my throat and chest are bad it's really unpleasant. I have had a fresh attack of asthma, due as usual to catching a violent cold, and as I write I can't make up my mind whether to try & keep my engagement with Mr Rose-Innes in Yokohama this evening or not. If I don't go I think I can shake off my enemy. Surely I shall be all clear when you come. I may call on a friend on Friday evening, but shall be at the station at 8.30 or 9.30, whichever you tell me. The future is quite bright for once with the expectation of you.

You need not bother about the typewriting; there is much to do, but we can arrange later. Instead of copying some things for my intended schoolbooks, there will be a means of finding suitable books on second-hand stalls & cutting out the wanted passages. That alone will be quite a business. – It is just like your modesty to say you are 'ignorant and stupid' in the middle of a letter written with such expressive freedom in a foreign language.

There's a nip in the air now and the brown leaves begin to wander about. A great change from Kyoto weather, only a month ago: I wish I was well for then it would be enjoyable. Ten years ago I was in the army & spent any spare time in long walks under the trees then serenely letting their leaves fall, while just over the Channel human leaves were falling in a wild bad storm. It is curious, but even then I often had asthma. At Mr Saito's last night I saw many fine photographs of English towns, abbeys, and river scenery; he did well to buy such things, which at home I always leave to their fate on the second-hand bookstall.

This hotel is not changed since you were here – just as casual, I think, but it doesn't make much difference. I need but little – I wish I had my British Museum Library, that's all! . . .

Too much literature in my head today, dear; I can't help getting headaches. Your school seems to expect rather unusual duties of you. In any event it could not have been your 'spiritual home'. Thank you so much for praising my poems, but I repeat you will like them more when you have spent some little time in the country which gave them life. It gave me life too, but a little too much asthma with it.

Love, my love to you
Edmund.

Kikufuji Hotel
Hongo
Tokyo

15 Oct. 1925

My Autumn

It's a splendid day and if the week-end is like it we ought to be thankful; I at present am not clear of my asthma though I have tried hard to be – I gave my lecture as usual this morning but had a struggle to do it; hurried back for my remedy, and found your letter of yesterday which helped me much. Should I be *perfectly* well tomorrow evening, my conscience would take me to the Station to meet you; but as you tell me so strongly not to go there, and as indeed it is essential for me not to be having attacks of asthma while you're here, I shall most probably obey and await you here. Send me a message by the maid as soon as you're in, or come yourself to my room: I am not sure where they'll put you, as the room you had last appears to be occupied now. Well, *you're coming*: the rest will be easy.

It is passed round that Monday also will be an unofficial holiday at this University, but I fear that won't be any help to you my dear. I shall also have a day off on the 26th, after an expedition by the Literature Course (24th, 25th) which I suppose it's right for me to join.

Not much to report. I am a little anxious at not hearing from my home for some weeks. A friend tells me that S. Sassoon is still very anxious to start me as a bookseller when I get there again. *If* all goes smooth, you see what this might mean for you.

In the *Times Lit. Suppt* just received here is an unexpected and generous notice of a small book on Shelley & Keats[1] which I had left with the publisher on leaving & forgotten since. I should like to see it! another imperfect but at least amiable book, Mine!

With love to you, dear child
Edmund

Note

1. See note 3 to the letter of 5 September 1925.

Kikufuji Hotel
Hongo
Tokyo

21 October 1925

My dearest Autumn

. . . I hope your parcel arrived. My wish is to send you something every day but looking round my dreary den I see nothing – except *your* Bananas and Grapes which are now much thinned out. They solace my sleepless intervals, after burning my magic powder.[1] – Today, 9 years ago, my battalion attacked and captured a German trench; in which proceeding I played some, alas! too insignificant part, and experienced more in 48 hours than some old gentlemen in all their lives. Every blessing and my longing love

Autumn
your
Edmund

Note

1. Medicine for asthma.

[Kikufuji Hotel &c]

23 October 1925

Dearest & kindest

I got up so late this morning that I am obliged to write to you in the train on the way to Yokohama, where I am going to have lunch with my friend Mr Rose-Innes.[1] He used to invite me to dinner but at present the risk of going out in the evening obliges me to ask myself for lunch. There's no news to tell you, I fancy. I had a letter from Mrs Thomas Hardy,[2] but nothing very definite in it except that Mr Hardy is publishing a volume of poems this autumn.[3] So am I!! and curiously enough when T. H. published last, I did too, and the editor of the *London Mercury*[4] honoured me by reviewing my pieces in the same column with Mr Hardy's. Time is moving fairly fast – already it is a week since you came to see me, and only a week until you come again. I have been unusually busy over Mr Hardy's 'Dynasts'[5] which presents great problems to anyone wanting to arrange it for a meeting of a small Reading Society. And Miss Collie has been at war with the hotel over our oil stoves, which have been tampered with, and useless parts substituted for good ones. As a result we can only get warm by filling the room with foul-smelling fumes, not much help to my chest as you can imagine. I hope you are as well as you ever are, and not finding your life at the school even more uncomfortable since you have announced your resignation.[6]

Well, soon I shall be writing to my mother about a young Japanese lady who wants to see the land of her dreams and would be a great delight to have as a guest. I wonder though whether you would not find a small town in the West of England[7] rather monotonous. But as a first resting place in England it might do well, and you would find them all so natural and familiar that it would be the best way of beginning. Afterwards your experience of London and other places would be easily arranged – or more easily.[8]

I received a deep impression of contentment & love when I woke up last Sunday morning and saw in the early light your eyes studying me. I shall never forget that look, among many others which I clearly recollect and dearly value.[9] You have made a world of difference to Blunden, who otherwise can't help feeling like one in a dark prison, though I nowadays do not notice so keenly the points at which Japanese minds, manners and nerves entirely differ from ours. And I think I am a little closer in touch with the students at the University that when I came last year. . . .

With my abundant love, and
continual wishes for your presence with me
Edmund

Notes

1. See note 1 to the letter of 29 September 1925.
2. His second wife Florence, whom he married in 1912.
3. *Human Shows* (London: Macmillan, 1925).
4. Founded and edited by J. C. Squire. From its beginning in 1919 it was for a decade or more the leading English literary and art monthly but lost its hold as new, experimental types of writing became common. It ceased separate publication in 1939 and was merged with *Life and Letters* (which ran from 1928 to 1950).
5. *The Dynasts: A Drama of the Napoleonic Wars* (3 parts, 1903–8; 1 volume, 1914).
6. Thus Aki has decided to join Blunden for good.
7. Salcombe, Devon, where Blunden's parents lived. Tennyson's poem 'Crossing the Bar' is traditionally associated with his visit to Salcombe in May 1889.
8. In fact Aki lodged in a single room in London throughout her stay in England, right up to her death.
9. Thus it is clear that Aki was a protective mother-figure for Blunden.

Kikufuji Hotel
Hongo
Tokyo
23 Oct. 1924 [1925]

Poor dear

I am sad that you did not get a letter from me in good time. On Wednesday evening I gave one to a student (who called on me) to post, and I told him it was important; I hope he didn't forget it. And this evening, as I got back from Yokohama, I posted another from Tokyo station. You should not apprehend there is something wrong when you do not hear very quickly from me – I often am interrupted and forced to miss a day. It is painful to think how many letters I owe friends in England, but laziness is partly to blame for that; & climate to some extent. Your card shall be kept & may prove useful another day. After my journey, though such a short one, I feel pretty tired; yet better than usual lately. In my earlier letter I mentioned a rumour that I could get a rough bedstead for 10 yen; but this seems to be quite wrong, prices having advanced. So I am wondering if I can fix up something for myself on the lines of our improvised 'beds' behind the trenches in France – canvas stretched across two strong poles , the poles supported at the ends on boxes or upright timbers. It is drawing towards winter, so the question begins to press. When you come we must talk over this & similar things again. Tell me soon if you will be coming on Friday night – I shall be at Mr Rose-Innes' to lunch again and could perhaps meet you at Yokohama station? but you'll see – Poetry stands still just now. The asthma drives it silly. –

Love always
your most affectionate
Edmund

1 Aki Hayashi (on the far right) with her mother and family in Japan (*c.* 1905).

2 Aki Hayashi (far right, front row) at her graduation from Tsuda College in 1909 with the Principal, Umeko Tsuda.

3 Aki Hayashi (farthest left, front row) with her alumni classmates in Tsuda College.

4 The modern gate of Poole Gakuin where Aki Hayashi taught.

5 The Chapel of Poole Gakuin.

6 Aki Hayashi (third from left, second row) as a teacher at Poole Gakuin High School in 1912.

7 The memorial stone of Kikufuji Hotel.

8 Edmund Blunden during the First World War.

9 Portrait of Edmund Blunden by Ralph Hodgson, 1921.

10 Edmund Blunden aboard the *Hakone Maru* in Royal Albert Docks, London, on 28 March 1924. Photograph shows Downing, Blunden, Nagasawa, P. Tomlinson and Hodgson.

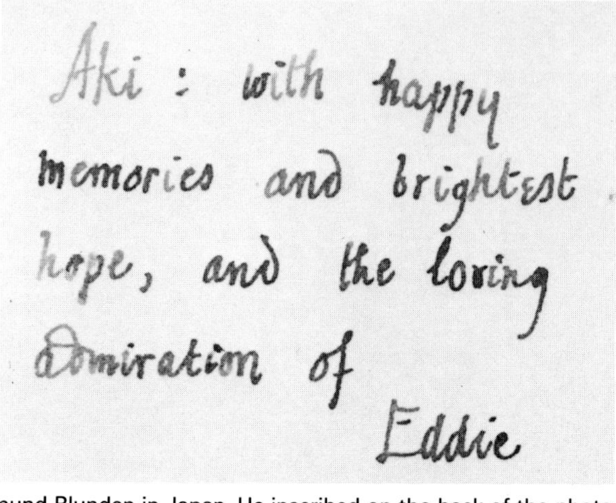

Aki: with happy
memories and brightest
hope, and the loving
admiration of
Eddie

11 Edmund Blunden in Japan. He inscribed on the back of the photograph: 'Aki: with happy memories and brightest hope, and the loving admiration of Eddie'.

12 Aki Hayashi with her friends in England (Easter 1933). On the back is inscribed in her own handwriting: 'at Miss Stevenson's, Easter 1933'.

13 Aki Hayashi in March 1933 in England. On the back Blunden wrote, after her death: 'Miss Aki Hayashi was for many years my worker at the British Museum reading room. She underwent the War years with great patience. Died in December 1962. She had become a British subject. E. Blunden' (postmarked 8 March 1933).

14 Aki Hayashi and Edmund Blunden in Kobe, *c.* 1925, when they spent their happiest days together.

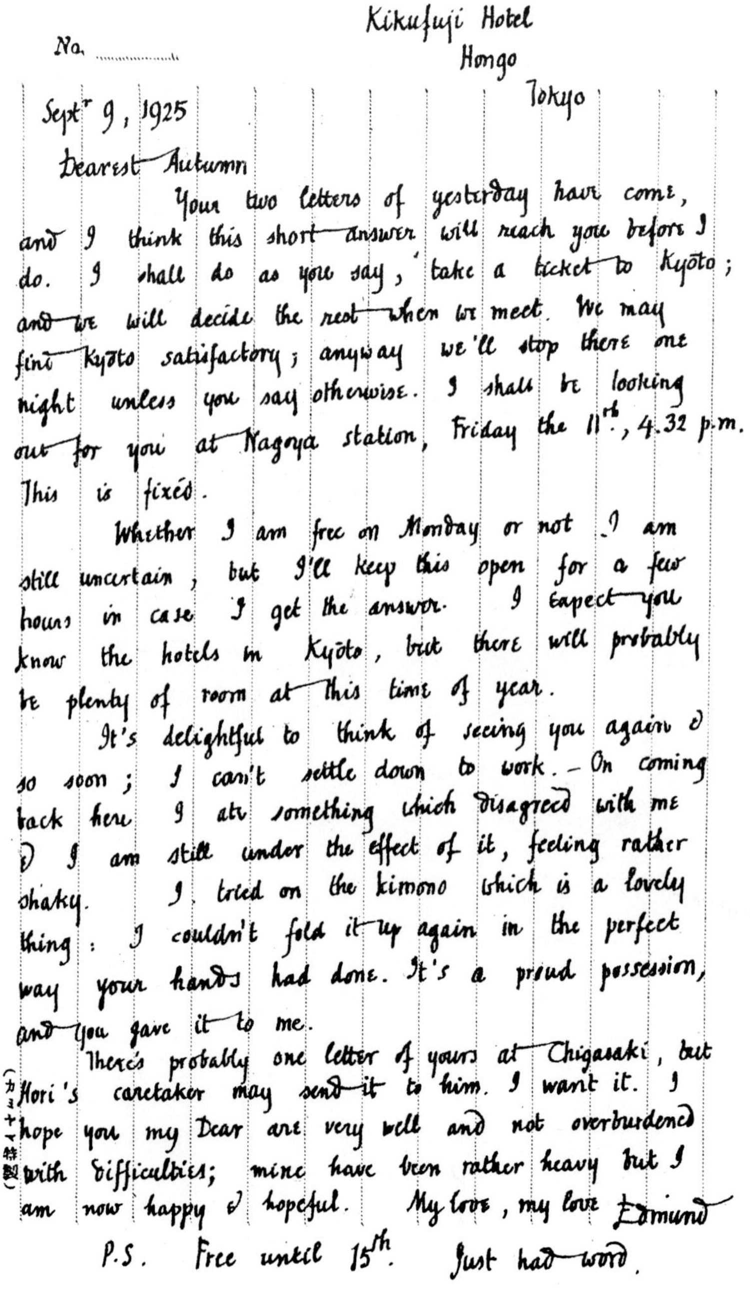

No. ....

Kikufuji Hotel
Hongo
Tokyo

Septr 9, 1925

Dearest Autumn

Your two letters of yesterday have come, and I think this short answer will reach you before I do. I shall do as you say, take a ticket to Kyōto; and we will decide the rest when we meet. We may find Kyōto satisfactory; anyway we'll stop there one night unless you say otherwise. I shall be looking out for you at Nagoya station, Friday the 11th, 4.32 p.m. This is fixed.

Whether I am free on Monday or not I am still uncertain, but I'll keep this open for a few hours in case I get the answer. I expect you know the hotels in Kyōto, but there will probably be plenty of room at this time of year.

It's delightful to think of seeing you again & so soon; I can't settle down to work. – On coming back here I ate something which disagreed with me & I am still under the effect of it, feeling rather shaky. I tried on the kimono which is a lovely thing: I couldn't fold it up again in the perfect way your hands had done. It's a proud possession, and you gave it to me.

There's probably one letter of yours at Chigasaki, but Hori's caretaker may send it to him. I want it. I hope you my Dear are very well and not overburdened with difficulties; mine have been rather heavy but I am now happy & hopeful. My love, my love Edmund

P.S. Free until 15th. Just had word.

15 A letter to Aki Hayashi from Edmund Blunden, written on Japanese paper.

Kikufuji Hotel
Hongo
Tokyo

25 Oct. 1925

My love Autumn

It is nine o'clock on Sunday evening and the day seems to have gone nowhere; walking out this morning, I felt very unsteady, but seem better tonight, & asthma much less troublesome – yet the day has been rather wasted. A Japanese picture Dealer came (unannounced) for advice this evening, and I have written an article on Buddhist paintings; but I feel very so-so. How are you, so many hours' journey away? your Sunday has been a working day which is not at all just. I have missed you!

I ordered the bed which was to have been 10 yen, ~~but~~ and is now only 12; it is a wooden frame, raised by the usual posts from the floor, with a rope mattress, and I understand that it serves very well. It's possible that it will be ready here by the time you next arrive. If I had been wise I could have come to Nagoya this week-end, for there's no lecture tomorrow nor Tuesday; but it might have been too much for my chest at present.

Once again there is nothing special to report. I see here on the table the pictures of my small son & daughter looking at me, but I am sure they have altered a good deal since the early spring of 1924. Some more news of them would be welcome, and I daresay I shall hear tomorrow. In England the principal subject seems to be Football, which develops into a kind of lunacy among the young men about this time – it dominates all the world's troubles, wars, seditions, famines, discoveries. I played every week before coming here, & on a frosty afternoon it's a cheerful exercise: but so is a walk round the farms, or a visit to the market town. Alas, our churches are in winter rather cold places, and we cannot well enjoy antiquarian rambles when the north-easter whistles through the shrivelled weeds. I daresay the Kyoto temples are rather bleak about January & February. Moral:– stay in the Kyoto Hotel.

Time for me to turn in; I shall read in bed, which seems to me one of the greatest pleasures of ordinary existence in Japan, Flanders, England or mid-ocean. Goodnight & great love.

Your affectionate
Edmund

Kikufuji Hotel
Hongo
Tokyo

10 Nov. 1925

My dearest Autumn

. . . wrote a few more pages of my book on war experiences, which had been left uninspected since March. There is much to be done with it and after all I cannot complete it until I once again have access to my letters and notebooks now in England.

You will see my 'Shelley & Keats' book[1] here when you come; it is at least very pretty, though not very startling inside. I am sorry I have only one copy, and it is very expensive.

You told me of a book of coloured pictures illustrating the Daimyo's[2] procession. I think you are right not to get it if the colours are too gaudy – it's the art value of those pictures which is congenial to me; their historical interest or curiosity is for somebody else. I can trust your eye and taste in this matter – presently you'll see something good at a few yen, and carry it away in triumph.

On returning from Kamakura I had just time to go to the library & borrow a Shakespeare. I'd have regretted buying one as I must have 6 old editions at home!

I had a letter from my wife who has been to see my old friends of this hotel, Prof. Whymant & his wife, & from them has received a sad story of my health last year & the discomfort in which I live. But she doesn't say she wishes she had come with me to help get things comfortable, which is perhaps only her forgetfulness. She has been in Scotland, but where exactly she doesn't say; & she disappointed my father & mother by not going to see them – she blames them for postponements. Well, this is dull gossip for Aki. I must look about for some reading matter to send you my dear. Meanwhile be patient & happy! eat & sleep well.

My kindest love
Eddie

Notes

1. See note 3 to the letter of 5 September 1925.
2. Feudal lords.

Kikufuji Hotel
Hongo
Tokyo

14 November 1925

My dearly loved Aki

I had yesterday afternoon your letter of Armistice Day and took it in my pocket, when I went out in the evening, in your place. By no means be ashamed of your prints,[1] although colours often seem different by daylight & the imperfect surface then reveals itself. They are sound and bright prints, and by no means look amiss among what I already had.

It is like your strong and active love to go to your Canadian friend's house & see how some things are done abroad. I shall not cause you a lot of trouble & difficulty, for I know you will do everything well. It will seem like liberty itself & delight with it to me, after almost two years of no-home –.

> 'What more felicity can fall to creature
> Than to enjoy delight with liberty?'[2]

You will be with me; that's enough, the words are powerful.

Yesterday it rained so heavily and blew so chillingly that I didn't go to Yokohama, but I am to do so next Friday, as the British Consul has invited me to visit him. That pleasant function done, perhaps I could come on in your train with you? As usual, I can't find my time-table, but you will be able to tell me what train you are likely to take & what time I should be on the look-out on Yokohama platform.

Alas for me, I have a busy week-end now. This afternoon I must finish a manuscript school-book which Mr Brady[3] & myself have prepared – it is a simple edition of some Poems by Bret Harte an American humorist,[4] and Mr Saito has arranged its publication. It's really Mr Brady's idea & his kind of book, but I very feebly let myself share the job. We have much to do in a hurry now, revising and amplifying the notes. Then I have promised special lectures at the Univ^{y} on Monday and Tuesday morning, and one at the American School[5] on Tuesday afternoon; these are as yet only hazy in my mind, and I must strike in and shape them. – After those engagements I think there is nothing much to worry me.

Tell me about money; am I to go to the Bank & draw some? at

present I have none in pocket money except my hotel charge. If you too are in that state I'll go to the Bank immediately on receiving your answer & send you a postal order. Be sure & tell me; in any case I think I must draw on my Bank.

My asthma has only threatened faintly, and I have had several excellent nights' rest. May this continue, particularly when you come.

I must get myself ready for my lecture; so now goodbye dear child

Your loving
Edmund

I've put down on paper a list of the books I want to produce here next year, and if they materialize, they'd add a trifle to our funds for England. *If*!

Notes

1. The *ukiyo-ye* prints Aki found, and bought for Blunden and herself in order to raise some funds for their travel to England.
2. Edmund Spenser, (1552?–1599), *Complaints* (1591); Muiopotmos, I.209.
3. Benjamin Brady, see note below.
4. *Bret Harte: Selected Poems*, edited with an Introduction and Notes by Edmund Blunden and Benjamin Brady (Tokyo: Kodo-Kwan, 1926). (Kirkpatrick B19.)
5. Established mainly for the purpose of educating the children of American and Western diplomats, missionaries, teachers and businessmen stationed in Tokyo.

Aki,
awaiting the happy day
when she explores
London for herself, from
Edmund.
23 Nov. 1925

So much love!

Kikufuji Hotel
Hongo
Tokyo

8 December 1925

My dear one

What an excellent letter you wrote to me on Sunday! I heartily enjoyed it. You seemed in somewhat better spirits. It surprised me that the Parcel had reached you so quickly; there is some mystery in the postal arrangements here, but I hope this change will continue. Do you write a card to this Hotel about your visit on Saturday? Perhaps best to do so. Today I missed my lecture as the University celebrated the arrival of the princess[1] with a day off; a student took me to Ueno to see the animals unfortunate enough to be exhibited there, and I was rewarded by a violent attack of asthma on the way back, which I fear will be followed by others. . . .

So you liked my small Poem; that's splendid, for you know how little I have written of late. I must hope for a real awakening one day. To have done what I have is only to have promised something, &, if nothing comes of it, I suppose it looks very foolish altogether.

Perhaps I shall not stay the full week in Sendai.[2] I don't want to; but it may be awkward to do otherwise. My plans in literature must be my general excuse for not being away long. Indeed time will be most precious if I am to produce the books I intend next year.

. . . so truly there is enough to keep me going for some time to come. I eagerly await your assistance, my dear Secretary. You have no cause to bewail your 'want of imagination' &c for you have great powers – how many people here could keep up this correspondence as you do?

Now I must get myself ready for the evening misery – but I shall see my friend Bernstein,[3] God bless him! he'll lighten the darkness of the occasion. With blessings & love to you my Aki

Yours always
Eddie

Notes

1. Princess Shigeko, the eldest daughter of the Emperor, was born on 6 December 1925.
2. The largest city in the Tohoku district, the north-eastern part of Japan,

where Blunden's friend Ralph Hodgson was teaching English Literature at Tohoku University.
3. Hans Bernstein, a Jewish businessman, a bachelor and a close friend of Blunden in Tokyo. See letter of 1 November 1953.

Kikufuji Hotel
Hongo
Tokyo

Dec. 20, 1925

My very dear Aki

I have your letter written last night & am not a little sorry that your headache has attacked you again; at least we can make sure that you sleep warmly here. You will soon be here. I think we shall be all right to go to Ikao[1] and I am posting the letter to the hotel at the same time as this. Will you come to this place from Tokyo station? I suppose that's best; and it will be quite good enough to catch the 12.25 from Ueno, if there's too much to do. The bank can be postponed, if we think fit: but probably I could fix all my business there in good time for the 12.25. – If you are not leaving Okazaki[2] till the 24th, will you telegraph to the Ikao hotel as from 'Blunden, Kikufuji Hotel' &c.? and say I arrive on the 25th instead.

Your face cream, the same as before, is already bought: handkerchiefs and pastilles I will get. And I will have your Kori brought to my room, and glad to have such an assurance of yourself, quickly following. Alas, I cannot obey your order about going out at night – tonight I have to go out to dinner, and yet I wish I was staying indoors. Miss Collie put another rug on my bed, so I am well fortified against the winter. I bought several quite good 'actor prints' at 15 sen each from a street dealer in the Ginza. What a miscellaneous letter I have written you! forgive it. I feel very slack, and will now have a good wash & see whether that will wake me up.

With my love to you, dear.
Eddie

I shall ask you to wear a little woollen coat, which I do not use; my wife has sent me a new one and altogether I have 4.

Notes

1. 'Ikao' is Blunden's spelling of 'Ikaho' (see p. 2).
2. City some 35km north-east of Nagoya.

Kikufuji Hotel
Hongo
Tokyo

Dec. 22, 1925

My dear one,

This is to say that your nimotsu[1] has come & is in my cupboard, & that I am just off to Mito[2] and shall be back tomorrow evening about 7. No reply from Ikao, but I did not ask for one. I expect you are more than busy, and I hope you have a very pleasant farewell meeting although you'll be tired afterwards. It is wretched that you have to travel in the night train but as soon as possible you must get a good rest. I forgot to say that on the 24th I must call at the University for my salary, besides any other jobs; but I can do that in half an hour or so. My packing shall all be done beforehand. – I have a Christmas pudding from my Mother, which will keep until we come back; whether it retains its virtues after such a long journey is to be seen. . . . We'll talk & laugh for hours when you are here. I shall be happy. Don't get into the train for Shimonoseki![3]

your ever affectionate
Eddie.

Bless you!

Notes

1. Luggage.
2. Capital of Ibaraki Prefecture, central Honshu, famous for plum blossom in early spring.
3. Furthest western city of Honshu on the Kanmon Strait and in the opposite direction by rail from Tokyo.

A Promise

To Aki Hayashi, of Kozu,[1] Japan.

You desire me to write down for your own satisfaction and assistance in planning your future the promise I have made. This I very gladly and hopefully do. I will take you to England as my secretary, and this will be about June 1927. You shall remain with me as long as you wish. If any circumstances at present unforeseen and unforseeable arise, I shall not myself withdraw from my promise; it will be in Aki's hands to decide her proper course of action. But I think the course is set, and you may look ahead with clear eyes and a quiet spirit.

March 4, 1926 Edmund Blunden

Note

1. North-eastern district of Sagami in Kanagawa Prefecture facing Sagami Bay.

16 Kotodaidori
Sendai

24 March 1926

My dear & ever kind Aki

I read your letter of yesterday with great emotion and warm affection, & shall be pleased indeed to be once more with you; but I am afraid you must wait until the 31st for that. It is not easy to tell you so when I know from every word you write to me that this will be a pain to you. I am hoping you find time goes a little quicker now than the first day of absence; do not count up the date too much, I ask you; let the clock take its course. If I feel I can leave here before the 31st I shall do it. It is not a case of what is, but what might be happening. The air is cold, but weather fine; Mr Hodgson[1] has to stay in his room, so I am not much inspired to go out, nor do I wish to do so – my time here must be applied in one particular way, – real conversation. I play the listener's part except where I feel it is better otherwise. . . . No letters ready for the foreign mail. I daresay I shall get busy soon. Thank you my dear for several envelopes & all your attention. As soon as the money arrives, provide yourself with something really good to eat. I am without a fire just now, so will stop,

my love to Aki
Eddie

Note

1. Ralph Hodgson (1871–1962), English poet. Blunden visited him there in order to assist in the solution of some undisclosed 'problems'.

16 Kotodaidori
Sendai

26 March 1926

My Aki

I am glad to tell you that Mr Saito succeeded in arranging the 'Hundred Poems'[1] matter, & the publisher will pay me 600 yen when I give him the manuscript. This is so unexpected and effective an assistance that I know it will brighten your spirits and make you brush aside the troubles of the moment. I have felt, really & truly, the pains of your heart since a week ago, & yet I could not do any thing different to what I have done. As it is I shall leave here by a night train on the 29th arriving on the 30th, but I am not certain of the actual hour. Do not take too seriously the rudeness or malice of the people in the hotel: their opinion is not worth a farthing now, and presently all vanishes. . . . That food question of yours is bad: please use your money & buy something good.

My love dear rogue.
Eddie

Note

1. *A Hundred English Poems from the Elizabethan Age to the Victorian: To Which Are Added Specimens of Sonnets, Ballads, Epigrams, &c.; and of the Principal American Poets*, selected by Edmund Blunden, with notes and illustrations (Tokyo: Kenkyusha, 1927). (Kirkpatrick B22.)

Aki asks me to write, –
That I would sooner live with her,
And be her love,
Than with anyone,
If I was not already married.[1]

E. B.

May 5, 1926

Why question so often?
Why rob me of my peace?
Have I not shown you my spirit,
made you the receiver of my intimate ideas,
entrusted to you the desires of my heart?

Note

1. Cf. 'The Passionate Shepherd to His Love' by Christopher Marlowe (1564–1593):

Come live with me and be my love,
And we will all the pleasures prove
That hills and valleys, dale and field,
And all the craggy mountains yield.

16 Kotodaidori
Sendai
8 September 1926

Kind and dear Aki

You must have answered me without losing a moment, for by 12 o'clock today your letter was here. Mr Hodgson will not come up to Tokyo, & I shall come alone by one of those two trains; the 10.00 I suppose. It would not be friendly to leave Mr Hodgson sooner, as the time I have spent with him is so short; but I am very much disturbed to hear of your illness & unhappiness, – It is not long now before I am back. When this is in your hands, you will soon be seeing me. I shall be very happy to see Aki. . . .

. . . The autumn hue begins to show & the afternoon is drowsy as it sh[d] be. You would much like the red, yellow and scarlet flowers in the garden here, & there is a remarkable black fork-winged butterfly which visits them with proud swiftness.

Why do you speak of typing & such things? I do not demand them unless you are in health & eager to do them. Your chief business is to go to the doctor and get right. Do not neglect this if you are still ill – but at any rate I shall see you first.

Now I must start off, & so come to a close,

with undiminished love & admiration
most affectionately yours
Eddie

Understanding that Aki will faithfully observe my wishes and study my needs and my difficulties, I promise her to take her to England with me, no matter what opposition is made by anybody.

Sep. 28, 1926 Eddie

Kikufuji Hotel
Hongo
Tokyo

6 December 1926

To whom it may concern.

This is to certify that I desire to employ Miss Aki Hayashi as my literary secretary after my return to England in 1927, and that I shall duly pay all her expenses, as long as she is willing to occupy the post, in England.

Edmund Blunden
Professor of English Literature
Imperial University: Tokyo.

17 January 1927

In case I should ever marry a second time I should in all { probability / likelihood } marry Aki.

Edmund Blunden

draft

Department of English
Imperial University
Tokyo

27 January 1927

Hiroyoshi Hiratsuka, Esq.
Governor, Tokyo-fu[1]

Sir,

In respect of the application for a passport to England made by Miss: AKI HAYASHI, at present my secretary, I have the honour to inform you that I wish to retain her services in that situation in England; and accordingly I hereby guarantee to provide all her travelling expenses and all necessary expenses in England; and further I personally undertake all legal responsibility affecting her, and guarantee to fulfil exactly and completely all official requirements concerning her. I beg therefore that Miss AKI HAYASHI's request for a passport to England may be granted.[2]

I am, Sir,
your obedient Servant
Edmund Blunden
Professor of English Literature in
the Imperial University of Tokyo.

Notes

1. City of Tokyo, now called Tokyo-to.
2. Blunden thus undertakes full responsibility for Aki on her arrival in England, both in legal and financial matters.

copied

13 Courtenay Street
Salcombe
S. Devon

27 August 1927

Sir

I have the honour to submit to you my request that Miss Aki Hayashi, a Japanese subject, my amanuensis, may be permitted to remain in this country. This lady, on landing at Plymouth on the 25th inst., duly presented her passport to the Immigration Officer, who allowed her to enter the U.K. for one month, and advised me to apply to you for an extension of that term.[1]

During the last two years of my appointment as Professor of English Literature in the Imperial University of Tokyo, from which I have just returned Miss Hayashi has acted as my assistant in the preparation and transcription of my literary works. Such assistance is indispensable to me. Miss Hayashi is of excellent character and ability.

With regard to my status and prospects, the following gentlemen can testify:

The Editors of the *Times Literary Supplement*, *London Mercury*, and *Nation*:[2]

or Sir Edmund Gosse C.B.,[3] 17 Hanover Terrace N.W.:

I may also be permitted to refer, for particulars of my career, to the biographical summary in *Who's Who*.

I am able, and shall continue to be able, to maintain and remunerate my amanuensis; who, as I know, is also in possession of a sum exceeding £200 in case of emergency.

I am, Sir,
your obedient Servant
Edmund Blunden

H. M. Chief Inspector
Aliens Branch
Home Office

Notes

1. It is clear from this document that Aki was granted a visa for one month only on her arrival in England.
2. The three most influential literary journals of the time. *The London Mercury*: see note 4 to the letter of 23 October 1925. *The Nation*: a weekly

review of literature and art; *The Athenaeum*, founded in 1828 was merged with *The Nation* in 1921, and the combined paper became one with *The New Statesman* in 1931.

3. Sir Edmund Gosse (1849–1928), one of Hardy's chief friends and one of the most distinguished and influential men of letters at the time. He knew everybody and everything in the literary world of the time. He was Clark lecturer at Trinity College, Cambridge, from 1884 to 1890. See also note 3 to the letter of 17 September 1942.

The Villa
Cowlinge
near Newmarket
Suffolk

4 October 1927

Dear A. H.[1]

I hope you have not lost yourself in London & that you have by now heard from Mr Cobden-Sanderson,[2] Mrs Lion[3] and again the Downings,[4] with invitations which you could accept. Do not hesitate to approach any of my friends. Would you like to write to Mrs Hodgson,[5] whose address is 115 Ebury Street, Victoria, London, S.W.1, and perhaps go and see her? And Mrs Jones[6] of the *Nation* office, 38 Great James Street, will welcome you & go out to lunch with you if you call there. Since I came here I have been very busy in sorting out and cleaning my books of which there are many, and the work was all the more exhausting because the shelves at my disposal are fixed and the books of all sizes. By the way, when you have copied the passages from 'The Indicator',[7] do not send the book here, as I have 2 copies, but return it to Mr Downing at 14 South Square, Grays Inn, W.C., adding my thanks to your own. I am in the middle of a bad cold, so take warning, as this climate plays tricks. There are here many books containing Fables, and I will look through and send some without delay. Much on my hands, but when I am settled I shall perhaps work at my former pace. This letter contains too much about work, but that can't be helped. All round are trees and fields, still excellently green, although so late in the year.

Have you been to the Japanese restaurant?[8] Take all

opportunities, for I know how I felt when I was alone in Tokyo, of getting some touch of your own original life and language. Best luck.

Yours sincerely
Edmund Blunden

Notes

1. This letter marks a remarkable change in tone in Blunden's letters to Aki. He now addresses her as 'Dear A. H.' and signs himself 'Yours sincerely, Edmund Blunden'. His tone becomes formal and detached for a short time. This may be a deliberate attempt to evade his wife's accusations of intimacy with Aki in Japan. (See p. 134: '. . . even if I am compelled to seem distant and severe'.)
2. Blunden's publisher.
3. Friend of Blunden at this time.
4. F. A. Downing and his wife, Maud. Blunden dedicated to Downing his book *Leigh Hunt*, and wrote: '*To The Secretary of the Elian Society*, F. A. Downing. This Life of his admired Friend of Elia is affectionately dedicated by his unalterable Brother E. Blunden.' (See also note 3 to the letter of 30 May 1941.)
5. The wife of Ralph Hodgson.
6. Friend of Blunden at this time.
7. *The Indicator*, a periodical published by Leigh Hunt, 1819–21.
8. *Tokiwa* in the West End.

The Villa
Cowlinge
nr Newmarket
Cambs.

9 October 1927

Dear A. H.

Many thanks for the corrections you made in the Oxford Press list of Japanese libraries – they seem to be just what was wanted. I am glad that you had the kind invitation of Mrs Lion for today & hope you have not found the London streets once more full of fog on your return. It is not only strangers who get lost on those occasions, but Londoners even. Curiously enough the weather here has been extraordinarily fine for a whole week. I am coming to London on Tuesday morning and shall arrive at Liverpool Street at 10.23, or by the train after that if I happened to miss the first. Could you meet me on the station, at the booking office? I will bring some work for you to go on with. I suppose you will have given the lecture to your friend's society by now. On Wednesday ~~Tuesday~~ night I shall dine (by present arrangements) with Mr Sassoon, and so if you will ask Mrs Griffith[1] to have a room ready for me that night I shall be grateful. If she is full up, never mind: but it w[d] suit me well seeing that Sassoon's flat is so near.

I could not find Mr Rose-Innes' letter, but fancy I sent it to my publisher.

If you cannot come to the station on Tuesday, please ask for me at the *Nation* office, & wait there if necessary.

yours sincerely
Edmund Blunden

Note

1. Aki's landlady at that time.

New Erringham House
Shoreham
Sussex

17 October 1927
7.30 a.m.

My dear Aki

I have been thinking over the matter of dear Siegfried's promise,[1] and how I might best use the gift, and during the night I decided when it comes to give you £50 of it so that you may feel no anxiety in the question of ready money during the next few months. I shall try to give you this sum in *cash*, in such a way that (except Siegfried) no one else knows of the transaction. (Of course I hope to keep the whole thing private and unknown.) At the same time I hope to send you small amounts from time to time, and if questioned I shall say you are living on these and your own small savings. – I make this arrangement (& long to see it all settled and done) chiefly because in any case I cannot receive much income for some months, and because I have been troubled by my own nervous and physical weakness, which *may* (by bad luck) prevent me from getting my work done for a time. Given health and happiness, I feel sure of the future, but I must take care meantime. My wife will see this.

Mrs Murray[2] here has suggested an address to me where, if you found a room to let still, the cost of bed and breakfast would not be more than 25s. a week. I will ask her again and let you know. I am sure however that you can find a place at some such price, though it might be necessary to go into the less convenient and showy districts.

No more now: I write in a hurry: my love to you, ever dear Aki.

Destroy this paper as soon as you have digested all it contains.

yours affectionately
E.

Notes

1. Sassoon's gift of money to Blunden. This letter is originally written in pencil, which seems to indicate that Blunden took steps to ensure that the secret agreement between Aki and himself was not revealed to his wife. He may have considered that a pencil-written letter would be less obvious. In any case he specifically instructs Aki to 'Destroy this paper . . .'.
2. Friend of Blunden at that time.

New Erringham House
Shoreham
Sussex

18 October 1927

Dear and noble A.

I have read with many strong emotions your splendid letter of yesterday and all your endeavours for me. I can only reply in a great hurry as I have to walk into Shoreham (some miles) and send some telegrams. You mustn't worry too much about Mrs Hodgson, she was equally inquisitive to my wife; but I hope she won't do any damage. I wish I c[d] make your life easier to bear under present circumstances, but I still think if you look steadily ahead that things will improve. Thank you again for the handkerchief, I am now well supplied, and thank you for the courageous act of hiring the typewriter, which is the best thing for my work but puts you to much inconvenience. I hope to get Mr Downing's assistance in buying a cheap one soon which will not be so troublesome to get and return as a hired machine.

Do not write any more after this comes as the post here is very slow and I am leaving early on the 20th – any letter on business c.^{d} go to me at 'The Nation' if you find it necessary. I shall try to arrange for my wife to meet you during her visit, and remember you are *always* in my mind and my eager sympathies, even if I am compelled to seem distant and severe. My love to you.

yours
E. B.

The Villa
Cowlinge
nr Newmarket
Suffolk

28 October 1927

Dear A. H.

I did not open your packet of typing until I arrived here, when I saw that you must have been working extraordinarily hard on the Clare papers.[1] Did you finish them? If so, you will need something more to do and I am posting something soon. I wonder what happened to your copies from Leigh Hunt's *Indicator*:[2] you showed them to me, but I think you must have kept them for I cannot find them at the moment. You must tell me whether you are changing your address, and if I can do anything for your benefit. I will see you when I am in London again, and will receive from you some books that I left in your charge. I hope you are very well and meeting friends, but it is a gloomy time of year in London now. Mr & Mrs Downing were speaking very kindly of you.

The Clare poems must have been difficult because of the hurried way in which they had been copied by me and the many provincial words. You did excellently and I am very grateful. One copy will go to Mr Kobayashi[3] and I will look through it before I send it to him, so do not pack it up yet.

If you have any notes on the Japanese educational system and other questions about student life, please let me have them, for I am to write some articles, and the sooner the better.[4] Kind regards.

yours sincerely
Edmund Blunden

Notes

1. John Clare (1793–1864), a rural poet who went insane in 1837. He published *Poems Descriptive of Rural Life* in 1820, *The Village Minstrel* in 1821, *The Shepherd's Calendar* in 1827, and *The Rural Muse* in 1835. Other poems of his were published after his death, and an edition of his poems by Blunden and Alan Porter appeared in 1920. An autobiography of his early years was edited by Blunden in 1931: *Sketches in the Life of John Clare, Written by Himself Now First Published*, With an Introduction, notes and additions by Edmund Blunden (London: Cobden-Sanderson, 1931). (Kirkpatrick B48.) Thus Aki's help with Blunden's work started in England.
2. See note 7 to the letter of 4 October 1927.
3. Tsuneo Kobayashi, author of the article 'Discovery of John Clare', in *Edmund Blunden: His Professorship and His Writings – Appreciations by Some of His Students and Friends* (Tokyo: Kenkyusha, 1927) pp. 47–9 (in Japanese).
4. It is not clear exactly to which articles Blunden was referring, for he wrote several reviews concerning education in Japan. The relevant article mentioned here may be the review article by Blunden discussing *Social Currents in Japan . . .* by Harry Emerson Wildes which appeared in *The Times Literary Supplement* 15 December 1927, p. 967 (unsigned). (Kirkpatrick C651.)

Cowlinge
Newmarket
Suffolk

22 December 1927

Dear A. H.

I have looked over your copies of the Bloomfield[1] papers and like them well; perhaps as you proceed some literary items of importance will come to light, so go ahead. I was urged by Mr Beaumont[2] to collect some articles on Lamb[3] for a book, and when I can think out the sources of these you shall have directions, so that you will be kept busy – and there's some Leigh Hunt business too,[4] but I can't attend to it yet. Tomorrow morning my family and I are going off to Salcombe,[5] where everybody will be glad to have some news of you. I admired your successful copying of 'R. Bloomfield's' signature. How are you? is your foot still giving trouble? I feared you would be half frozen by the unusually hard weather but today the air is gentle here and I hope it is the same in London. Mr Vines sent his book on modern English Literature,[6] published by the Okhayama Publishing C.º of Tokyo, whom I do not know otherwise; and I had for review another book of Lafcadio Hearn's lectures, published by Hokuseido.[7] Apart from these, I have had nothing from Japan, but have written to Mr Rose-Innes[8] and others – what a long correspondence I have, still many people cursing me for a lazy knave! . . .

Wishing you a happy Christmas, and that you may not spend it alone but with some pleasant friends

yours sincerely
E. Blunden

(13 Courtney St, Salcombe, if there is anything you wish to write about, until the New Year.)

Notes

1. Robert Bloomfield (1766–1823). Stricken with humiliating poverty he published the poem *The Farmer's Boy* in 1800. His circumstances were similar to those of John Clare.

   Blunden writes to Aki on 4 February 1928, 11 p.m.: 'Thank you for Leigh Hunt's memoir and more Bloomfield extracts: you help me greatly in this way, don't overtask your eyes.'
2. Cyril William Beaumont, the owner of the Beaumont Press, his major publications of Blunden's books are as follows:
   (1) *To Nature: New Poems by Edmund Blunden* (1923);
   (2) *Masks of Time: A New Collection of Poems Principally Meditative by Edmund Blunden* (1925);
   (3) *Japanese Garland* (1928);
   (4) *A Summer's Fancy* (1930);
   (5) *To Themis: Poems on Famous Trials with Other Pieces by Edmund Blunden* (1931).
3. Charles Lamb (1775–1834), essayist, educated at Christ's Hospital where he formed an enduring friendship with S. T. Coleridge. (Blunden was the President of the Charles Lamb Society at one time.) In November 1932 Blunden gave the Clark Lectures at Cambridge, which resulted in the publication of *Charles Lamb and his Contemporaries* (Cambridge: Cambridge University Press, 1933).
4. Leigh Hunt (1784–1859), editor of the *Examiner* and essayist. Blunden

published *Leigh Hunt's 'Examiner' Examined* (London: Cobden-Sanderson, 1928), and *Leigh Hunt: A Biography* (London: Cobden-Sanderson, 1930). See Appendix 3.
5. See note 7 to the letter of 23 October 1925.
6. See note 4 to the letter of 5 September 1925.
7. Blunden's review of *Some Strange English Literary Figures of the Eighteenth and Nineteenth Centuries in a Series of Lectures*, by Lafcadio Hearn, edited by R. Tanabé, appeared in *The Times Literary Supplement*, 5 January 1928, p. 14 (unsigned). (Kirkpatrick C656.)
8. See note 2 to the letter of 29 September 1925.

Cowlinge
Newmarket

27 March 1928

My dear A.

. . . I have been toiling without pause since Sunday morning first on reviews, then on L. Hunt's Life; will you keep note of any articles sent to Japan so that I may write the next as soon as they are due?

Nothing from the forwarding agent either: perhaps you know all about the matter & have paid him: I hope our books reached *him* safely at any rate, for I am not very clever at packing large boxes & sawing up the lids to the right size.

I am shamefully behindhand again with all letters, haven't written to Salcombe for months: but I'll try to do so soon. With my devoted love & thoughts every day

E

Ikao ni orimashita toki ni . . .[1]

Note

1. 'When we were staying in Ikao . . .'.

Cowlinge

3 April 1928

Dear A.

I think I shall come on Friday by the first train: will try to let you know *if not*. Be sure not to suffer if I fail? . . . I am worn out with writing, but it's healthy exhaustion I imagine. There are some things for you to do, – I wish you to examine the *Morning Chronicle* 1810–1813 for L. Hunt & Lamb articles or allusions of importance – & especially to copy a sonnet to Miss K or Kelly in this newspaper for 1813 – it's by Lamb, I think. I also want you to copy a poem welcoming Barron Field home – in the *New Monthly Magazine* 1824, or should be; and to look up the obituary notice of Isaac Hunt, father of L. H., in the *Gentleman's Mag.* (shelves of the Reading Room) for 1809. Enough for the present, poor Labourer; you must not overtask your eyes or your strength. I send you my love and constant thought. E. . . .

Dear A., God bless you. I received y^{r} copies & most gentle & fond message this morning, wish you could be *well* but know the difficulty – shall come on Wednesday as usual if all is well, must soon make a decision about the whole situation under which I am being crushed out of existence. L. Hunt at a standstill. Rec^{d} the 'Studies' edited by Saito with my 1st Letter from England in it, will bring it. Have been asked by a well-known painter to sit for my portrait!

This note, under difficulties; & yet all is sunshine, flowers, birds and bees outside.

Have asked P. T.[1] to fix for me on Wednesday night, & I hope Mrs L. will invite you to dine at Bushey. Love, my A.

E.

4 June 1928

Note

1. 'P. T.' is Philip Tomlinson.

Cowlinge
Newmarket

9 July 1928

Best & kindest A.

Once again I have to tell you that I have been in a melancholy state and unable to attend to anything. I hope you got your train and reached home safely; it was a most happy afternoon in the air and in the church too, though as you know so well England is not at her best in the present mood. I cycled from Cambridge through the dark, & was somewhat troubled by the speed and glaring lamps of the motor-buses and cars, but got home in a little more than 2 hours. The next day we went to Felixstowe:[1] it was a failure. M.[2] said she would send you a present, & that was almost the only kind thing she said all day. I have begun to treat her with coldness & silence, & if I can keep it up it may yet save the situation, which proves to be, on the evidence of her mother & brothers, much more deplorable than even I guessed. How all will end I can't tell. M. at any rate returns tomorrow. – I shall come, unless something unusual arrives, on Thursday as usual, but return that night as far as I know. Next week I come on Monday, stay Tuesday, leave Wednesday: have to see several people & on Tuesday evening appear at Mr Sitwell's[3] meeting. But more of that later. I hope you are getting some of this sunshine and bloom, and making yourself well.

With my love as always, dear A. E.

Your Sembei[4] are not all gone yet.

Miss A. Hayashi
c/o Mrs Horton
10 Mecklenburgh Sq.
London W.C.1[5]

Notes

1. In Suffolk, a port and resort on the coast between the Orwell and the Deben.
2. Mary Daines, Blunden's first wife. He finally left her (21 August 1928). She sent Sassoon a rude letter (3 November 1929). In 1930 Blunden was expecting instructions from his lawyers with regard to divorcing Mary Blunden (4 and 6 July). He mentions that the divorce case will be heard 'next week' (28 January 1931). The process was going to be delayed further. Aki was referred to in the case (31 January 1931).
3. Sir Osbert Sitwell (1892–1969), brother of Edith and Sacheverell Sitwell. A poet, who also published short stories, novels and an autobiography.

He praised Blunden in a tribute on his sixty-fifth birthday: 'Edmund Blunden, as well as being a very good poet, is free from the literary vices of jealousy and sharp sayings. By appearance, disposition and achievement, he could belong to no other country except England. There is no character whom I admire more' (see *Edmund Blunden, Sixty-Five* [Hong Kong: Hong Kong Cultural Enterprise Co. for the English Society, University of Hong Kong, 1961] p. 169).
4. Rice cracker.
5. Aki's address is recorded on the envelope which is with Blunden's letter.

30 July 1928
[Postcard stamped
on this date.]

Miss A. Hayashi
8 Newton Road
Bayswater
London W.2.

Suiyōbi. Itsu mo to onaji.
Sore kara Paddington e ikitai; C. E. B.[1]
to G. M. B.[2] to Salcombe kara 1.15 ni
tsukimas; yo ji goro Sussex e dekakemasu.

A. wa itsudemo { warui / suki } desu. E.
getsuyōbi.

Notes

[*Translation*:
Wednesday. Same as usual. Want to go to Paddington from there; C. E. B. and G. M. B. will arrive from Salcombe at 1.15; will leave for Sussex about 4 o'clock. A. is always naughty
Like (am fond of) A. always. E.
Monday.]

Blunden's knowledge of Japanese was limited, but he liked to use it as a sign of intimacy with Aki; cf. Swift's 'little language' when writing to Stella (see the complete *Journal*, ed. Harold Williams, 2 vols [Oxford: Clarendon Press, 1948]).
1. Charles Edmund Blunden, Blunden's father.
2. Georgia Margaret Blunden, Blunden's mother. Blunden called her 'Mug'.

at Mr Cobden-Sanderson's
Long Crendon

13 August 1928

Always my Aki

I have been so busily engaged in holiday-making that I have neglected all letters, and indeed all writing. Tomorrow I shall see you. Be in good spirits and endure the usual difficulties of my visits to town, my dear; I arrive at 10 at Paddington, & must then go on to the *Nation*. My father & mother reach Victoria at 11.53, but I think I shall be unable to go there; perhaps you will care to do so, and tell them how I am placed. . . . And on Wednesday afternoon let us go over the letter to the Home Office. I greatly wish, dear villain, that you could have been here, for the country is as fine as Sussex – all colours blended into a rich soft expanse of blue and green; there are fine hills too on all sides. The beer of the district is good too, and has been flowing. I wonder what you have been doing while I was among these pleasures – Rev. Campbell Morgan[1] I suppose! – I had no other letters of importance since arriving here, & really I *must* write to Ichikawa[2] & send my article to Saito[3] when I see you again. Insist on my doing so. . . . I hope your arrangement at Newton R^{d} is all right. My kindest love to Aki.

your affectionate
Eddie

over

I have now had your letter and am refreshed and strengthened by it. I understand A.'s deep and selfless love, and must always wish her to understand my devotion and unchanging faith. Thank you for this wonderful letter, which I hate to destroy as you request – yet I think it is necessary to do so. I am in that state of mind w^{h} prevents expression, so do not be disappointed, dear Aki, if my letter is quiet and plain – that is the case with all my faculties at present.

I find I can be at Paddington at 10, by starting from another station here, & I hope you can be there at that time. As the day will be one of the over-hurried sort, it is very lucky that I can gain ¾ of an hour with you in this way. Love once again. E. . . .

Notes

1. A well-known minister in London. Aki was a frequent church-goer and attended the City Temple regularly.

2. Sanki Ichikawa (1886–1970), Emeritus Professor of English at Tokyo University and a famous linguist. He was a senior, and rather strict, colleague of Blunden when he first taught at Tokyo Imperial University.
3. See note 3 to the letter of 9 October 1925.

at
Wilsford Manor
Salisbury

12 September 1929

My dear Aki

You had only gone a few yards down the road when Mr Sassoon and Mr Tennant[1] arrived in a very large car & off we started. I shall be back on Saturday, but am not sure of the hour. Perhaps you would look in on Sunday evening? . . .

I am writing on a seat inside a small circle of tall trees, with the light wind in the leaves, and a brook passing by. The calls of many birds, some inside an aviary and some on the branches above my head, often make me look about. There is a sunflower in view as big as a kuruma-puller's hat.[2] If this is autumn, what splendid flowers and bird-music must be here in spring? . . .

I hope you are less rheumatic & generally in good spirits. If you could have a day or two in a place like this, I think you would be enchanted out of all illness and trouble. With my love, dear Aki,

yours as always
Eddie

Notes

1. Stephen Tennant, Sassoon's friend.
2. A hat worn by a man who pulls a rickshaw (a small two-wheeled passenger vehicle); large and of triangular shape.

Hawstead
near Bury St. Edmunds

8 Decr. 1929

My dear Aki,

Post the enclosed for me like a good girl. I shan't be in London until Saturday, and if I do not write again (but I hope I can) will meet you at 1.30 at the British Museum entrance. Am still laboriously sorting out old papers & books. Bought a fine Shakespeare, printed 50 years ago or so, at Bury; it is in 3 volumes folio, large paper, and is printed in facsimile of the First Folio. Also, a new car is being bought, partly by selling the old one; it is of the closed kind, and will suit better for the long winter ride to London. I was pleased that you so quickly advanced to the subject of Coleridge's Letters & are allowed to take the 2 printed volumes into the MSS. room. Without doubt you'll find a number that are not in the volumes, and though parts may be dull or difficult much will be vivid. In turning out my papers I have found a good many press cuttings which will amuse you in y^{r} leisure moments, but those I will bring with me. Only one review of Saito has come along and I have put it in an envelope ready to dispatch, hoping to be able to include more in a day or two. I am delighted that you are attending lectures & concerts, & more & more I think you ought to be writing a London Letter for some Japanese magazine. Still a strong and loud wind blowing here. My window looks into the top boughs of several fine trees, & there is a further view of horses in their yard, a pond, a green, a thatched house, more horses feeding in a meadow, plough lands marked out with black hedges, and a ridge beyond with trees like crow's feathers. All this you will see presently. My love dear A. as ever.

Eddie.

Hawstead
nr Bury St Edmunds

27 January 1930

My dear Aki,

I am distressed to hear that you feel so unwell & unsettled, and if you get the chance to go to Bristol the change w^{d} probably do you good. I doubt if there is anything of much importance touching S. T. C.[1] there, although he was so closely associated with the town; but you could enquire. Chatterton[2] was even more a son of the place; but I have some recollection that the Public Library was burned down and much valuable manuscript, &c., lost. – Last night I dreamed that you were riding in a bus with me, when someone touched my shoulder, & it was Mrs M. Blunden, who made a 'scene'. This was no prophetic dream, but only history! I am tired, but haven't seemed to be doing anything very definite. The mild weather is bringing on the bulbs all round the garden. No incidents to report, except that the dog in trying to play cricket received a blow with the ball, & is now recovered. A payment for my Liverpool lectures arrived this morning and I am enabled to send you part of what is due to you. Please keep account of everything for I have many odds & ends to settle. Should you hear nothing further, I'll be coming up by train on Thursday, arriving either at 11.27 or ¼ of an hour later. There is a stain on the cheque, caused by the spilling of a flask of whisky! Mrs — of Cambridge would rejoice to know this! With my love & kindest wishes & especially wishing you will not become melancholy and ill, Eddie.

Notes

1. Samuel Taylor Coleridge (1772–1834), poet and philosopher. Lodged and lectured in Bristol; married in Bristol 1795; lived in Bristol (Kingsdown). Wordsworth first met Coleridge at 7 Great George Street, now the Georgian House Museum in Bristol.
2. Thomas Chatterton (1752–70). A lay clerk of Bristol Cathedral. While still at school wrote a notable satire *Apostate Will*, 1764, and other verses. He wrote a number of poems purporting to be the work of an imaginary fifteenth-century Bristol poet, Thomas Rowley. The fraud was exposed by T. Tyrwhett in his *Poems supposed to have been written . . . by Thomas Rowley* (1777–8); but the poems are usually thought to have remarkable qualities in their own right.

Hawstead
nr. Bury St. Edmunds

July 13, 1930

My dear Aki,

This is to say, Meet me at *Chancery Lane* station on Monday morning about 10.15. I hope you are well & a flourishing member of the City Temple. My father & mother were very pleased to see you once more & in such lively spirits. I am not quite well. Nothing to report. Must as usual attend to numerous uncalled-for letters.

I wonder if you remember the old Camel at Ueno Zoo, who used to thrust his head out of his stable with a very anxious expression when we came to give the animals a little to eat. We have a Cow here, shut up in a shed, who does exactly the same since I have been offering her a bit of bread now & then.

With my love.
E.

Hawstead
nr. Bury St. Edmunds

Oct. 2, 1930

My dear Aki,

Here is the Keats for you to mark where necessary according to K.'s original editions. It appears to be quite a convenient book for this purpose. No matter how small the difference between it & the original, please make a note of it. But I think it will be generally accurate.

And would you look up a magazine called 'Annals of the Fine Arts' 1816–1820, and see what poems by Keats occur there, and again compare the texts with those here given? You will find especially the Ode to the/a Nightingale, & Grecian Urn. You'll see that H. B. Forman in his footnotes mentions *some* of the points.

Am still in some pain, my ear & head worried me all night & still do. . . .

Tomorrow I am obliged to write a leading article for the Times Literary Supplement, but would much rather rest for once. However, I can't grumble. The sun is out & sky blue here today.

With my love.
Eddie.

Cleave's
Yalding
Kent

Saturday,
31 January 1931

My dear Aki

. . .

Tomorrow S. Sassoon comes to carry me off to his house for the day; so I have been really busy, endeavouring to finish my long essay on Churchill,[1] &c. For Churchill, your notes from the B. M. have been a great help. I am too tired however to write anything with spirit. . . .

Love
E.

Notes

1. Charles Churchill (1731–64), satirist. Edmund Blunden wrote a review entitled 'Charles Churchill' (*The Times Literary Supplement*, 5 February 1931, pp. 85–6) on the bicentenary of his birth. It was unsigned, and reprinted in *Votive Tablet: Studies Chiefly Appreciative of English Authors and Books* (London: Cobden-Sanderson, 1931). (Kirkpatrick C1095.)

Ipsden House
Ipsden,
Oxford.[1]

3 September 1931

My dear Aki

S. S.[2] brought me your letter just now which pleased me greatly. Obedient to yr. commands I am wearing the black tie, which it was a specially good action of yours to send; and I feel much more comfortable with it than with the more ornamental sort. Heavy rain so far has made excursions difficult, but S. has his car & so we shall be paying a visit some miles away today, & last evening we walked about in an old town called Abingdon[3] (full of curious houses). I think it will be Tuesday that I shall leave here, but will write again. Best thanks for the list of Lamb[4] papers at S. Kensington. I should like you to go into one matter closely. . . . Find in that Lamb's review of Hood's[5] 'Odes & Addresses' & compare with the 2 reviews which appear in your list. The point is that the review known as Lamb's comes from the *New Monthly*.[6] Perhaps these others are different (tho' also by Lamb?) – anyway, all the details you can. And with your 2-vol. edition of Lamb in hand you might compare all the items in your list, and make out a paper or two of notes; which I can easily use in my 2-vol. edition. – What especially is that proof called 'Variorum'? & the note on it? But I leave all to yr. usual diligent skill.

There's something also that I shd like you to look up for S. Sassoon. About 1913 there was a celebrated trial for murder or manslaughter called The Veronal Case. The dead man's name was Trevanion. S. S. wants a complete copy of the report of the trial. Not sure if it *was* 1913; but you can find the date of the case through the index to the *Times* & then the report in the *Times* itself. Or probably there is a more exact report in some legal publication (? *Law Reports* – you cd. ask the friendliest face at the supervising table of the Reading Room). When you have found & transcribed this curious trial, send yr. copy to S. Sassoon here. Now I must go downstairs & join him & bless me the sun is burning through the rain in intense brightness! what wild autumn it is! This country is hilly and the sun & cloud make romantic landscapes like Collin's Ode to Evening.

Love
Eddie

Notes

1. The address of Harold Owen (brother of Wilfred Owen and editor of Wilfred's letters). A small village on the Icknield Way, 3 miles south-east of Wallingford.
2. Siegfried Sassoon.
3. Old town on the Thames, once the county town of Berkshire, 7 miles south of Oxford.
4. See note 3 to the letter of 22 December 1927.
5. Thomas Hood (1799–1845), friend of Lamb, Hazlitt and De Quincey. He edited various periodicals at different times, such as *The New Monthly Magazine* (1841–3).
6. *The New Monthly Magazine*, a periodical founded in 1814, and continued, with various changes in its subtitle, until 1871, when it was continued without subtitle until 1881, and then until 1884 as *The New Monthly*.

Merton College[1]
Oxford

7 March 1932

My dear Aki, I am sorry that you were so worried about my catching my train the other night, & that you ran such a risk by waiting on Paddington station for the Oxford train. Indeed I arrived by the 5.50, and was met by my Miss Norman,[2] who took me up to Hampstead to dine with her father and mother; I had appointed that evening for her as you know & so did not look out for you. Some things in your letter trouble me, above all your feeling so down-hearted about your illness. The need is for you to take action and to go to Dr Macduff[3] as soon as you can. There can be no danger *then* of anything worse than your being sent away to a sanatorium and made well; but this long delay is not good, until we know what the matter is. I have the greatest wish to see you well and happy, and in steady good spirits, and continuing to work for me as you always have done; and although I may ask much of you in regard to letting me live my life as my new emotion & vision suggest it, yet you will know that I have a strong affection for you and your place in my world is yours always. If I do ask much, your calm judgment will I think tell you that I have not been selfish, at least; and your love for me will not for a moment wish to hurt me if I am naturally and honourably happy in any thing.[4] Nothing shall be allowed to deprive you of the best that I can ever give you – my trust and admiration and constant thought for your good. I particularly, dear Aki, implore you to put away black sad ideas, and to bind all your energies to the task of getting well. Your future is bright – you will be doing most valuable work, and honour and sympathy will be yours; whatever may be my lot, you will not be cut off from the essential fact that you will be helping me. – You would be surprised, perhaps, how often I bless you with words spoken to myself, sometimes to others, because I think of you as a pattern of courage and goodness. Woman or man makes little difference to me nowadays, apart from Sylva N. – and I am stirred by her not so much by feminine qualities as by general genius of which she has a share. – My tiredness does not disappear, indeed my late illness is not quite gone. I don't know at the moment when I shall see you, probably not before Saturday & Sunday, but shall be writing again. Do try to hear Mr de la Mare's reading,[5] it should be pleasant. And send me my dear Aki the account of what I owe you, and I will do my best – I have a cheque this morning from the *Times* – which will help me greatly, and I do not get easy until you are comfortable about money. With love from

Eddie.

Notes

1. Blunden became Fellow and Tutor in English there in 1931, remaining until 1942 when he resigned from Merton and returned to *The Times Literary Supplement*.
2. Sylva Norman (1906–71), a novelist of Armenian descent and Blunden's second wife. The marriage took place on 5 July 1933. Blunden wrote to Dr Takeshi Saito, 'I am to be married to Sylva Norman, a novelist, on 5 July, after a long courtship. We shall wander in Brittany for 3 weeks after the great day' (22 June 1933). Aki found it difficult to accept their marriage, ever mindful of Blunden's promise (17 January 1927). She tried to 'make things difficult for him' (9 March 1932). Though a little afraid of Sylva, perhaps due to her talent and success, Aki got on well with her and did some work for her book (25 January 1936). Blunden and Sylva lived in Oxford until their marriage was dissolved in 1942. Sylva seems to have been a lively, sociable woman, loving grand balls in Oxford, long walks and swimming (2 August 1937). She did military service during the War and was often away (13 and 18 October 1939). Even after their divorce, Sylva wanted to remain a 'friend' to Blunden. Blunden suggested that Aki should rely on her while he was away in Hong Kong (21 August 1953). Sylva wrote many letters and sent periodicals regularly to Blunden in Japan and Hong Kong (28 July 1949), and reported Aki's major illness (27 December 1949). Sylva's book on Shelley was published in America in 1954 (Sylva Norman, *Flight of the Skylark: The Development of Shelley's Reputation* [London: Reinhardt, 1954; Norman: University of Oklahoma Press, 1954]) (6 April 1954). Her obituaries were published in *The Times* on 14 May and 29 May 1971. In the latter I. A. Richards wrote the tribute (see note 1 to the letter of 15 February 1955).
3. A general practitioner in Hampstead.
4. An extreme egotism is revealed in these lines. See also his letter of 9 March 1932.
5. Walter de la Mare (1873–1956); a poet who wrote about dreams, fairies and the world of nature. He was a friend and contemporary of Blunden. When young, both poets were considered as belonging to the 'Georgian' school.

MERTON COLLEGE
TELE. 2259. OXFORD

9 March 1932

My dear Aki,

. . . But you are not really trying to *gain money* from me, I know that well; you are trying to make things difficult for me, I am afraid. I have noticed that tendency in you, and forgiven it; but try not to hurt me! . . . In short, should it become possible for me to marry Miss Norman, I ask you to show your gratitude to me, and your love for me, by treating that with the greatest reverence and good will. As you know, such a step on my part would ~~does~~ not mean that your living in London and serving me is to be altered. You have my promise and I mean it. . . .[1]

Love
from
Eddie.

Note

1. This is one letter which shows clearly how strained their relations were at this time, when Aki was distressed about his forthcoming marriage.

MERTON COLLEGE
TELE. 2259. OXFORD

9 June 1932

. . . You may hear again from Mr Graham Greene[1] about Japan, but he seems as yet uncertain what he wishes, or is obliged, to do; and I dare say Mr Kishimoto[2] has communicated with you. . . .

Love. Eddie.

Notes

1. Graham Greene (1904–), novelist and dramatist. Blunden described him as 'an admirable young man' (10 April 1932), who 'wanted to know about Japan' (9 June 1932). Greene was in Hong Kong (19 February 1954),

and his younger brother, now Sir Hugh Greene, was Blunden's pupil at Merton College. See Chapter 5, section (a).

2. Ichiro Kishimoto, a Japanese undergraduate at Oxford, a pupil of Blunden (7 June 1932). Kishimoto organised a Japanese Society in Oxford (5 October 1933). He had an excellent personal library and Blunden considered him a promising scholar (13 October 1933). Blunden promised a talk to his Japanese Society (19 January 1934); Kishimoto treated Blunden respectfully (23 January 1934), yet Blunden's assessment of his pupil's work became rather low; he noted that Kishimoto's paper on Leigh Hunt was full of mistakes, and wrote jokingly to Aki that when Kishimoto was baptised perhaps he would make fewer errors in his work! (4 March 1936). Kishimoto was baptised and confirmed (16 March 1936). He sent Blunden a Christmas card from Japan (2 January 1937), and he edited *The Face of England* (Tokyo: Kairyudo, 1938), the usefulness of which to the Japanese reader Blunden doubts (28 October 1937). One of Kishimoto's simple errors in *The Face of England* is that he mentions in the Biographical and Bibliographical Table of Mr E. C. Blunden: '1921 Went to South Africa in a tramp steamer the Bonadventure'. (It should be South *America*!)

Cleave's
Yalding

8 September 1932

There is something dear A which you can usefully do at once for me at the Museum.[1] I want to have by me while writing my new book with Sylva Norman[2] such passages from *Froissart's Chronicles*[3] as may serve. It is a famous old book but I have no copy. The passages I shall need are those relating to the English in Perigord, and especially their wars and so on in these places: Domme, Brive, Sarlat, Perigueux, Rocamadour[4] – all which we lately visited. . . .

Love E.

Notes

1. The British Museum
2. *We'll Shift Our Ground, or Two on a Tour, almost a Novel*, by Edmund Blunden and Sylva Norman (London: Cobden-Sanderson, 1933). (Kirkpatrick A47.)
3. Jean Froissart (1337?–c.1410), a French chronicler, of Hainault, Northern France, who spent most of his life at the courts of princes. His

'Chroniques' cover the period 1325–1400; they deal with the affairs of Flanders, France, Spain, Portugal and England.
4. All places in south-west France associated with the Hundred Years War between France and England recorded in *Froissart's Chronicles*.

Tues. 27 September 1932

Only to say I shall be at London Br. in the morning, S. Norman will probably be with me but you will not be alarmed. . . .

Love, great haste
E.

MERTON COLLEGE
TELE. 2259. OXFORD

24 October 1932

My dear Aki

I am very glad that you liked Sylva, & she likes you. You need not think you gave a bad account of yourself at the meeting; far from it. I intend coming to town on Thursday evening as I said, arriving at 5.50 & hope to see you then at Paddington. Unless something happens to prevent this I may not write again before Thursday. If I can I will bring a list of poems for you to transcribe, towards the great Work.[1] But many are my present disturbances and I am ashamed to have so little energy at the end of the day. This reminds me that I have not yet scribbled the unfortunate Kubota's article.[2] I must, and quickly. Curse these chiming clocks. Saw the Poet Laureate[3] again yesterday, once I was his neighbour and his humble hero-worshipper; he is the gentlest of men. Keep as dry & warm as you can;

love.
Eddie.[4]

Notes

1. It is not clear to what work Blunden is referring here; perhaps to his projected edition of his collected poems.
2. This was mentioned in Blunden's letters regularly, almost on a monthly basis, from 28 January 1929 to 8 March 1935. Mr Kubota was the editor of *Eigo Kenkyu* (The Study of English) published by Kenkyusha. It was a popular monthly journal containing articles on English literature and life. Apart from Blunden and a few others who wrote in English, articles were written in Japanese. It also contained some interesting photographs. The aim of Blunden's contribution from England, 'Literary England, Month by Month', seems to have been to relay up-to-date brief literary news and information to Japan. The series began with the issue of June 1928 (which was dated London, 16 March, 1928 by Blunden) and ended in March 1935. The headings of his articles (which were about 150 words in length) included 'The Exposure of a Number of 19th Century Pamphlets', 'Letters of Gerard Manley Hopkins', 'The Life of Robert Bridges' and 'The Autobiography of Mr H. G. Wells' (vol. 27, no. 3, June 1934, pp. 210–11); and 'B. T. in "The Observer"', 'The English Countryside', 'Marlowe's "Dr Faustus"' 'Life of Queen Elizabeth', '"The Modern Muse"' (vol. 27, no. 8, November 1934, pp. 712–14); 'The Codex Sinaiticas' (with a cutting of a photograph), 'Mr Loyd Haberly', 'The Completion of 900 Volumes in "Everyman's Library"', 'Mr John Sparrow's "Sense and Poetry"' (in which Blunden supports this young critic's view that the followers of T. S. Eliot and Ezra Pound are dealing in nonsense), and 'Self-satisfied New Age' (vol. 27, no. 2, May 1934, pp. 112–15). Blunden's feelings about writing these articles are clearly expressed in his letters to Aki. He always had some difficulty in completing articles by a given date, and tended to send them late (20 October 1930), even though he knew that each piece was to be sent before the 20th of each month (14 June 1930). He sometimes found it difficult to write (20 April 1931; 28 August 1934), and in consequence his pieces tended to be very short (24 September 1931) or 'thin' (29 December 1932). Kubota wanted to stop publishing the articles (5 May 1932) but they continued. Blunden determined to continue unless Kubota said 'stop' (29 June 1933). His main purpose in writing these articles was to gain some additional money and hence the motivation for writing was not particularly high – in fact, he not only sent the articles late, but sometimes forgot to write for Kubota! (3 March 1935). Blunden was indeed very concerned about his finances: 'The *yen* seems to be at 1*s*.3*d*. so our chances of a little money from K. are not good. Would it be better if he paid less, but more regularly?' (10 December 1932). Aki was helping with these articles, and Blunden mentions that she was copying one of the manuscripts neatly enough to 'get it off quickly' (26 August 1929).
3. John Masefield, O.M. (1878–1967).
4. This letter shows that the strained relationship between Blunden and Aki caused by his second marriage had by then been resolved and that a mood of reconciliation prevailed.

19 Woodstock R^{d} Close
Oxford
2 September 1933

My dear Aki

. . .

I will attempt the special article you wrote about. Not only the Japanese but I also don't know 'what tendency prevails' in recent English verse![1] There is a beautiful confusion – But I'll see what can be said, & without delay. . . .

Blessings ever
E.

Note

1. Blunden was very critical about the tendency of English poetry towards Modernism represented by T. S. Eliot, his fellow-Mertonian. On 19 October 1954 he expresses an adverse opinion more explicitly:

> I am asked to be at the Cathedral one Sunday evening when some records of modern English poems are being given, so that I may 'answer any questions' – I have said *yes* but requested that I might be allowed to choose the items. The public impression is that T. S. Eliot is the POET and that we should all be ready to worship and interpret him; but as I have never (in all simplicity) found much of my kind of Poetry (not what I write but what I love to read) in his pages, I am obliged to seem rather perverse. You have heard me defend the *variety* of even recent English poetry, & in any case no one man deserves *all* the attention.

MERTON COLLEGE
TELE. 2259. OXFORD

16 May 1935

My dear Aki

. . .

Lectured last night to the English Assoc^{n} here, on the After-Fame of Keats – the subject I knew fairly well but it took me days to work it into some shape. If you see *any* early references to Keats please let me have them, for I may enlarge my lecture into a little book. . . .[1]

Love.
E.

Note

1. Blunden is probably referring to his book on Keats: *Keats' Publisher: A Memoir of John Taylor (1781–1864)* (London: Jonathan Cape, 1936). (Kirkpatrick A58.)

POSTCARD

28 August 1935

But we left Frankfort a day or two ago and are now in Koblenz – or rather we are having our lunch in a village called Arenberg which overlooks the Rhine. And of course lunch here means incidentally a glass of wine, which costs next to nothing but if it got to England would be thought handsome! On *Saturday* I hope to be exploring the Farr. Rd. as usual,[1] from 12 – & if you can appear there I shall be delighted. Germany has not provided quite the kind of books I like, though the new books are very fine and are finely displayed. If you sent any newspapers they did not reach me – but we have still to call at Koblenz Post-office for anything that may be waiting. . . . Sylva sends her kind wishes, & says we must now rise from this table and walk down to Koblenz – I dare say I can manage it! E. Later – called for our letters, received y.r card & newspapers, much pleased with them.

Miss A. Hayashi
6 Worsley Rd
Hampstead
London N.W.3,
England

Note

1. See Chapter 5, section (d).

St Raphael,
Blue Bell Hill &c.

31 December 1935

. . . I am wondering about the Cowden Clarkes[1] as a possible job for Sylva after her Shelley is done, & if they come on you will be kept busy. E.
Annie's[2] Cake is still being eaten & looks like being there for weeks to come.

Notes

1. Charles Cowden-Clarke (1787–1877), a schoolmaster friend of Keats and author of *Recollections of Writers* (with Mary Cowden-Clarke, London: Sampson and Low, 1878). Mary Victoria Cowden-Clarke (1809–98), wife of Charles Cowden-Clarke, and the author of *The Complete Concordance to Shakespeare* (London: C. Knight, 1845), which she published in monthly parts (1844–5).
2. Annie, a German sister-in-law of Blunden, who married his brother, Gilbert. According to Claire Blunden, his widow, Blunden looked after Annie and Aki, somewhat in the spirit of Charles Lamb (of whom Blunden was an admirer) who devoted himself to caring for his insane sister, Mary. Annie and Aki formed a close relationship as Blunden's dependants. He suggested they support each other in their particular individual needs. Annie took Aki to tea (25 May 1930), and helped her to find a flat (4 January 1931). They spent Christmas together at Annie's (16 December 1935). During the Second World War Blunden had a difficult time keeping both Annie and Aki in his care, as they were regarded as enemy aliens. Annie was taken to hospital (15 June 1954) with an illness which turned out to be cancer (19 October 1954) and her condition became worse (10 November 1954). She died in the early part of the following year (15 February 1955).

9 Woodstock Close
Oxford

24 January 1936

My dear Aki,

Could you if necessary go down to Rochester,[1] and Blue Bell Hill, on Wednesday next? I understand Annie will be discharged from hospital that day, & taken by ambulance to her house. There seems nobody in prospect there, to see that things are comfortable for her.

I think you would have to call at the hospital (S[t] Bartholomew's Hospital, – Annexe Ward –, Rochester) fairly early in the day, get the key from Annie, & go on to S[t] Raphael & make fire & bed & so on. Stay the night, & next day take A. to London & see her on the Worthing train – from Victoria. – (This last part depends on my Aunt's being able to take Annie for her fortnight of convalescence.)

If you can manage this good deed, send me a postcard at once; for if not I must think again. I will tell Annie all about it as soon as I get your reply and my Aunt's. Will of course send you money to cover all the expense. The chief difficulty might be your finding the way to the Hospital, & then getting into touch with Annie – but I am sure you could manage that. I should *think* Chatham[2] station rather than Rochester would be the one, and I believe the Hospital is near the Chatham fire station. But you'd enquire.

Must now write other letters on this subject, so goodbye for the moment.

E.

Notes

1. A cathedral city on the Medway in Kent.
2. One of the Medway towns in Kent.

MERTON COLLEGE
TELE. 2259. OXFORD

4 February 1936

My dear Aki

. . . I notice that a book is announced with some such title as 'Japan Must Fight Britain', by a Japanese author:[1] if this author is right, it will keep me from thinking of going to Japan for some time. But presumably he is an Ass. . . .

Loud blessings.
E.

Note

1. At the time articles and books of a pugnacious kind were appearing in the Japanese press.

9 Woodstock Close
Oxford

4 March 1936

My dear Aki

. . . News from Tokyo appears to be still under censorship. I fear the Emperor has lost a chance of encouraging liberal minds, and yet who can say on the scanty information we have had? Much hoping your dentist is doing good, – with affectionate blessing

E.

MERTON COLLEGE
OXFORD

28 May 1936

My dear Aki

. . . Today a friend of Sylva's sent her a cutting from a *Sunday Pictorial*,[1] in which the Prince of Wales is stated to have been nearly arrested as a spy on the Canal Bank, Ypres[2] in 1917, and to have been brought to our Battalion H.Q. where Lieut. Edmund Blunden all alone received him! This is passing strange. I don't think I should have forgotten the episode, though Canal Bank in July 1917 was enough to make one forget anything! Mr Mottram has published a new book on the Western Front in which he several times mentions me very handsomely.[3] . . .

Love
E.

Notes

1. A popular Sunday newspaper of the time, specialising in photographs of the world of society and fashion.
2. A town in West Belgium, in the province of West Flanders near the border with France: scene of many sieges and battles, especially during the First World War, when it was completely destroyed.
3. R. H. Mottram (1883–1971), novelist whose most important work is *The Spanish Farm* (London: Chatto and Windus, 1952), for which he won the Hawthornden Prize in 1924. Blunden's review of Mottram's book *Journey to the Western Front Twenty Years After* (London: G. Bell and Sons, 1936) was published as 'Mr Mottram Returns', *Spectator*, 12 June 1936, pp. 1090, 1092. (Kirkpatrick C1535.)

12 Woodstock Close
Oxford

10 December 1938

My dear Aki

. . .

I am expecting to undertake the biography of Thomas Hardy[1] & then you will have to work on old *periodicals* for me, watching for little bits.

In haste,
E.

Note

1. Thomas Hardy (1840–1928). See note 2 to the letter of 14 December 1938.

12 Woodstock Close
Oxford

14 December 1938

My dear Aki

I was sorry you did not appear on the Farr. Road today, and hope it was not because of any illness. I hope that all the more, because it would be a very good idea if you could come here for the week-end; come on Friday evening or Saturday morning, and enjoy a little good food and clear sky. Our wireless set is not working so I can't promise much about that. I could not find Campbell's 'Pleasure of Hope'[1] on the bookstall and imagine you may have picked it up.

My Thomas Hardy volume,[2] at present under discussion, would be wanted in 1940, the centenary year; and I shall have plenty of work for you I am sure among memoirs and periodicals of the period. I shall begin to make a bibliography soon, for this purpose, and any notes you take of the B. M. catalogue will be useful. It was foolish of me not to collect the notices that appeared at the time of T. H.'s death, 1928; but I was then out of the way.

There are many bits of paper here for me to attend to, and incidentally I am to give Edgecumbe[3] a short introduction for the new Edition of his Keats House Catalogue. Should you by chance see him, please tell him I am not forgetting it.

Make up your mind now, and come for the week-end.

E.

Notes

1. Thomas Campbell (1777–1844) published *The Pleasures of Hope* in 1799.
2. *Thomas Hardy* (London: Macmillan, 1941). (Kirkpatrick A72.) Blunden began to conceive ideas for a book on Hardy (3 April 1940) and, once started, wrote quickly (14 July 1940). He was still at work on the Hardy book (9 April 1941), finishing the first draft (14 May 1941). The book was completed and sent to the editor (30 May 1941). Blunden writes that 'T. Hardy is in proof' (12 September 1941), and that it will eventually appear after the new year (17 December 1941). Blunden then planned to begin 'extensive work about less known poets' (25 April 1942) and also a biography of Coleridge (28 November 1947).
3. Fred Edgcumbe (1885–1941); curator of the Keats House, a generous and well-liked man. J. H. Pearson succeeded him.

HEYTESBURY HOUSE,
WILTSHIRE.

24 August 1939

My dear Aki,

I am here for a day or two with Mr Sassoon and shall not come to town this week, & – will there be a railway strike?? if not, I shall be up in town probably on Tuesday, and maybe I could in any case come by motor coach. This queer recurrence of the railway-strike goblin quite puzzles me, and I hope it will not happen, especially as these big strikes have a way of growing. The times are very odd & uncertain! But I am pretty sure we shall be spared an international disaster. People brood over the news and it looks worse to them the more they stare. I hope you are well and should like you to keep going at B. M. with the letters addressed to Leigh Hunt[1] & his family, unless indeed you are going for your holiday, but perhaps September will give you your best chance.

Nothing much to report otherwise. I feel very anxious about my getting ahead with my T. Hardy book.[2] Here has been Sir Sydney Cockerell[3] (of the Fitzwilliam Museum, Cambridge for many years) who has been talking much and well on M[r] Hardy and his life. It appears that T. H. was obedient to, 'dependent on' his mother all her days, & when he was 70 he was still, so to speak, a little boy to her.

With my blessings
E.

Notes

1. See note 4 to the letter of 22 December 1927.
2. See note 2 to the letter of 14 December 1938.
3. Sir Sydney Cockerell (1867–1962); Director of the Fitzwilliam Museum at Cambridge from 1908 to 1937, and Thomas Hardy's literary executor.

MERTON COLLEGE
TELE. 2259. OXFORD

5 September 1939

My dear Aki,

Sylva and I hope to pass through London on Thursday. I don't know just when. Will you try and meet us at Paddington – try and be there by 11? of course we may arrive later, and I hope you will wait patiently.

In the House yesterday, Sir J. Anderson[1] made an important statement which I should like you to consider, 'I am anxious that use shall be made of the help of friendly aliens in any direction in which their assistance may be advantageous to this country.' And so on. I think you would do well to report once again at Bow Street[2] and ask if there is any way in which you might be of use, under Sir J. Anderson's idea. Censorship of letters from Japan perhaps. Or ordinary national service. I am sure they would give you information, and in any case you may be expected to keep in touch with Bow St. Would your Bank know anything about all that?

As to your remaining in London, we have been thinking over that matter, and on that account as on others we hope we can see you on Thursday or before very long. There again you probably need to know if any official arrangements or recommendations exist.

Alas, alas for this dreary and ghastly business.[3]

But we must think that, as it has come on us so astonishingly, the way out may come with equal strangeness and surprise.

I shall anyway hope you are well & reasonably happy and hopeful, and looking forward to the Cricket Season.

N.B. try Beer,[4] it is likely to be our chief amusement if this affair drags on.

Blessings,
E.

Notes

1. Secretary of State for Home Defence and Minister of Home Security at that time.
2. All the 'enemy aliens' had to report their movements, etc. to the local police station.
3. The Second World War which began on 3 September 1939.
4. Blunden's optimistic view of the forthcoming war is revealed.

Merton Coll. Oxford

24 May 1940

My dear Aki,

. . . I dare say you have been quietly hunting old T. H.[1] through the newspaper files. 'Tess'[2] – now although you, and Sylva, have provided me with numerous reviews, there is one which I still want very much. . . .

All blessings
E.

Notes

1. Thomas Hardy. See note 2 to the letter of 14 December 1938.
2. *Tess of the D'Urbervilles*, 3 vols (London: James R. Osgood, McIlraine, 1891).

Merton College
Oxford

30 May 1941

My dear A.

Thank you for postcard just received. I was going to write, Yes, Victoria sta.ⁿ Kent side at 3 on June 5 will be right. I see in this morning's paper that Sir Hugh Walpole[1] is sent to bed for 2 months – heart trouble – which means our Book Society[2] meetings will lack a real chairman. – I am sorry your neighbour is so troublesome, and wish I knew how to protect you against such worries. You could perhaps get some rooms through one of my friends, – I'll try & hit on an idea. Mr Downing's[3] offices in Red Lion St. were quite burnt out on May 10, and he has removed the business to Edgware. I had only a printed circular about this, but that is something. – At present *all* the active A. R. P.[4] for this College is falling on me and I never get to bed till early morning, at least to sleep; then most days I am in uniform for the Cadets, and am now on the point of going along to lecture to them. In fact life is very crowded, and tobacco is very rare! – *The Japan Times*[5] arrives at very odd times, but I will bring the latest received, & anything else interesting. The bill enclosed will show the sort of small jobs which are constantly being forced upon me. Still, I do not lose hope of pleasanter and quieter times for everybody. – Yesterday I was suddenly fetched out to practise cricket at the Nets with one of our team, at present in the Navy, and he was preparing for other such occasions, but last night his leave was interrupted and he had to return. – T. Hardy is almost complete & ready to go to Macmillan's office.[6] Indeed I may get you to deliver him there. – Well then, I hope to arrive at Victoria quite by 3 on June 5 –

our constant kind thought
E.

Notes

1. Sir Hugh Walpole (1884–1941), novelist.
2. Commercial institution, the aim of which was to promote book selling by providing its readers with good reviews. Some of Blunden's academic colleagues at Oxford did not approve of his association with such a commercial society.
3. See note 4 to the letter of 4 October 1927.
4. Air Raid Precautions.

5. The first English-language newspaper in Japan to be put out by Japanese publishers, started in 1897 with the backing of government leader Hirobumi Ito. *The Japan Times* absorbed *The Japan Mail* in 1918 and then in 1940 consolidated two other English-language papers being published by foreigners, the *Japan Chronicle* and the *Japan Advertizer*. It was for many years the sole foreign-language news publication in Japan. The paper's new format was modelled on that of *The Times* in London, and aimed at explaining Japan's position on international affairs and at fostering mutual understanding between the Japanese and foreigners living in Japan.
6. See note 2 to the letter of 14 December 1938.

Merton College
Oxford

29 July 1941

Mr dear Aki,

I asked to meet Claire Poynting[1] in London on Thursday, and think it will be best to bring her along to Hampstead & all meet for a little airing on the Heath. But we shall arrive at the end of Worsley Rd.[2] a little later than I mentioned – let us say 3.45; & I can catch a rather later train back to Oxford. . . .

Best blessings – & Sylva's –
E.

Notes

1. Claire Poynting (1918–). Blunden's third wife, who was educated at Withington Girls' School in Manchester and went up to Oxford (St Hilda's) at the same time as his daughter Clare (13 October 1939). His second wife, Sylva Norman, was often away then for military duties (13 October 1939: 'Sylva is in uniform'). Claire read English and was given a tutorial by Blunden. She got to know him well in 1940 (through cricket) and married him on 29 May 1945. They had four daughters. Blunden's comment on her to Aki was 'Claire *likes* doing things when somebody is in a difficulty' (11 October 1946). She is said to have been attracted to Blunden because he looked so sad (see Caroline Moorehead, 'The Poets We Nearly Forgot', in 'Women at War', *The Times*, 9 November 1981, p. 8).
2. Aki lived at no. 6 Worsley Road, Hampstead, London N.W.3. (Now it is 34 Pilgrim's Lane.)

MERTON COLLEGE,
OXFORD.

8 December 1941

My dear Aki,

. . .

Sylva suggests, and I agree, that you might possibly offer your services, if the opportunity arises, to the British Government – for example, there would be translating of the Japanese newspapers needed I imagine. . . .

Affection*ate* blessings
Edmund

The Two Books[1]
A New Poem by Edmund Blunden

Come, tell me: of these two books lying here,
Which most moves mind and heart to tenderness –
The one approaching its three-hundredth year,
The other a recruit, fresh from the press?
The one well honoured down the years, and still
Trusty to light our pathway, pose our view;
The other quite unknown, which may fulfil
As great a task through centuries strange and new?
In both you find one nature, one appeal,
And that antiquity and this young birth
Share the same glory, equally reveal
Man in his wisest, luckiest hours on earth.
Man the inventor with his ceaseless power
Of shaping engine, fabric, instrument,
Never was happier than in the early hour
Which gave him books; and to his short span lent
Almost eternity, to his local speech
Almost unbounded range. Thus from the tomb
Unseen romancers charm, and magi teach,
The white truths conquer and the kind loves bloom.
A world so opens on us by this key,
We may not count its continents; we may glide

Over a myriad-times extended sea
And land of life triumphant, time denied.
And this, like roses in the year's decline,
This blest invention grows much sweeter now;
Things of the spirit thus arise and shine
From far and near through cloud and wind-stript bough.

Christmas, 1941

Best greetings to
Aki from E.

Note

1. First published in the *Book Society Annual*, December 1941; and reprinted in *Shells by a Stream* (London: Macmillan, 1944) and *Poems of Many Years* (London: Collins, 1957). (Kirkpatrick A71.)

MERTON COLLEGE
TELE. 2259. OXFORD

6 April 1942

My dear Aki,

. . . Sylva means to try for some bean sauce[1] to help your cookery problem, when she is in London. I wondered if beer or stout might be a substitute. . . .

Hoping then to see you,
our best wishes always
Edmund

Note

1. *Soyu* (*shoyu*) sauce. Aki writes to Blunden that soyu sauce is indispensable in her cooking, particularly because she suffered from diabetes after 1946 and had to follow a strict diet (11 October 1946, 26 December 1953, 6 April 1954, 1 January 1955).

Merton College
Oxford

29 May 1942

My dear Aki

In the busy state of affairs lately I had forgotten to send you the enclosed (as from May 18th).[1] I am afraid you may have had some trouble because of the delay, but I hope not. We should like a word from you, – I don't know when I am to be in London next, but will soon tell you. If Sylva[2] comes up she would like to see you. We have been for a few walks and that is almost all there is to do outside daily business. Book-hunting is not so good as in the old days. I should like a good dinner in Tokyo style, and so would you – well, even wars come to an end, so be cheerful and keep as well as you can. Did I give you 'T. Hardy'[3] or not? I have forgotten.

Affectionate blessings –
E

Just had your card: I am still uncertain about my dates. Best luck. We meet soon.

Notes

1. Aki's wages. Both Blunden and Aki referred to them in Japanese as *okane* meaning 'money', possibly because they wanted to avoid the embarrassment of formality.
2. See note 2 to the letter of 7 March 1932.
3. See note 2 to the letter of 14 December 1938.

Merton Coll:
Oxford

17 September 1942

My dear Aki

. . .

General news I have not. Miss Poynting[1] has been called up, and though this was due to some official confusion I don't know if she will be released from the Army till everyone is. When will that be? Mr Sassoon has a new book in the press,[2] – more Memories of his life up to 1914, and how he became an Author and a friend of Sir Edmund Gosse[3] and others.

Affectionate blessings
E.

Notes

1. See note 1 to the letter of 29 July 1941.
2. Siegfried Sassoon, *The Weald of Youth* (London: Faber and Faber, 1942). See Blunden's review of it: 'Progress of Poesy', *The Spectator*, 6 November 1942, p. 436. (Kirkpatrick C1939.)
3. See note 4 to the letter of 27 August 1927.

Merton College
Oxford.

15 April 1943

My dear Aki,

. . . Yesterday's performance was not bad. We were presented to the Queen & Princesses & I had quite a long conversation with the Queen, who is really the most admirable woman. Your old friend Edith Sitwell[1] was wearing a green turban & was thought to be impersonating Dante.

Best luck, & better health –
E.

Mr Orwell[2] may get you to call; don't be afraid of it, you will find him and others very friendly.

Notes

1. Dame Edith Sitwell (1887–1964), poet, critic and eccentric. She exploited the musical qualities of language, sometimes at the expense of any clear meaning.
2. George Orwell (1903–50), the pen name of Eric Blair, a novelist who considered himself a democratic socialist. He worked for the BBC at that time and considered the possibility that Aki might assist their foreign broadcasting service.

7 Earl's Court Square
London S.W. 5

17 January 1946[1]

My dear Aki

I am afraid you must find this cold snap very trying – especially if your gas company is as mean as ours. Hoping to hear from you or have a visit I did not send the enclosed;[2] it runs to February 25 I believe but correct me if necessary. Perhaps you would be able to telephone to Claire one morning* (Flaxman 8832) and make an arrangement for coming along; especially if the frost yields to kinder weather. We do not go away this week end. I have been really more than busy & partly on things which are quite unprofitable to us. – Mr Preston[3] is disturbed, or else Mr Bailey,[4] at the discovery of an American that some marginal notes in books at Keats House are not by Keats as supposed but by W.m Hazlitt,[5] and I am to go & give an opinion shortly –

Our blessings
E.

*Not next week (the house will be full of people) – But can you join us for supper on *Monday evening*?

Notes

1. By then Blunden had married his third wife, Claire, and settled down in London.
2. Aki's wages.
3. J. H. Preston, Curator of the Keats House.
4. Mr Bailey worked for the Hampstead Public Library.
5. William Hazlitt (1778–1830), essayist and friend of S. T. Coleridge, Wordsworth and Lamb.

Times Lit.y Suppt
Printing house square
London E.C.4

13 March 1946

My dear Aki

. . . You may have noticed in the *Times* yesterday that Claire's long wait was over; & at 1.30 or so on Monday morning she had a daughter,[1] whom you will like. They are both well and enjoying life. I look forward to your soon meeting the young lady. . . .

Blessings, & Claire's too –
E.

C. says the Infant looks Japanese – about the eyes –

Note

1. Margaret, who was duly baptised (12 July 1946). Blunden sent contented accounts to Aki about how Margaret was growing. There was plenty for Margaret to do to amuse herself; she *'roared'* so loud that Blunden expected a complaint from next door! (Why she 'roared' Blunden doesn't say.) Blunden describes Margaret at the seaside in Scotland (22 May 1947); Margaret playing in a stream at the Sassoons (22 July 1947); Margaret walking (26 August 1947); and her love of toys (24 September 1947). The Blunden family arrived in Tokyo December 1947. Margaret spoke Japanese (20 February 1948); preferred Japanese to English (11 April 1948); and wanted to go to school (24 June 1948). Margaret's Japanese was improving (7 September 1948), and she did not approve of Blunden's Japanese (9 October 1948). She liked *sembei* (rice-crackers) (12 November 1949). The Blundens were in Hong Kong from September 1953. She had her own opinions – her verdict on a play they went to see was that it was 'super!' (19 February 1954). Blunden's second daughter, Lucy, and third daughter, Frances, were born in Japan in 1948 and 1950 respectively. Claire expected a boy (19 May 1956), but gave birth to a fourth daughter (28 September 1956). On 15 October of the same year, Blunden's first wife, Mary, died (3 November 1956). After the divorce, Blunden had been on friendly terms with her for over 20 years.

c/o Foreign Office
S.W.1.
[letters marked Tokyo, top left corner]

28 December 1947

Mr dear Aki,

. . . As yet no plans are finally agreed, but no doubt I shall be sent at times to places far from Tokyo;[1] and I expect to begin at the old Imperial Univ.[2] here in mid January. So now I am, as usual, writing a series of criticism on great authors. . . .

our love & blessings.
Edmund

Notes

1. As arranged by Vere Redman, cultural attaché to the United Kingdom Liaison Mission in Tokyo, Blunden delivered about 600 lectures from January 1948 to March 1950 in many places (January and February 1948) including Kyoto, Osaka (11 April 1948), and again to an audience of 1000 on 20 May 1948; at Waseda University in Tokyo (17 June 1948), where he gave two lectures a day (24 June 1948); in Hokkaido and Sendai (7 September 1948); at Tsuda College, International Christian University, where he 'instructed the next generation' (9 October 1948); in Hiroshima, Kure and Osaka (12 December 1948). The following year his busy lecture tours continued, with lectures in West Japan (29 January 1949) where he gave twenty lectures (14 February 1949) and many more in the autumn (13 June 1949); in Kyushu (9 September 1949); and then a lecture tour to Okayama and Takamatsu (4 March 1950). In the letter of 14 February 1949 he writes in humorous tone: 'plenty of hard work and of hospitality. We shall go from here to Kumamoto and that will see the close of *these* lectures – back then to Tokyo and the two little girls a week hence.'
2. Tokyo University. See note 4 to the letter of 9 October 1925.

Tokyo

c/o Foreign Office
London S.W.1.

11 April 1948

My dear Aki

. . .

Today I was invited to lunch with a party, French, English, Japanese, at a Mr Kato's[1] country house, and I wish you had had this excursion. The cherry flowers are falling already, but the light green all round and many blossoms now at their best (the purple magnolia, the yuki-yanagi,[2] and violets below) make the picture. Mr Kato's house is thatched, and has such pleasant novelties within as a fine open hearth and there (as it was chilly today) a log fire was blazing. We had our lunch in his 'restaurant',[3] over the garden, and it was tempura;[4] but I cannot send you a bit of ebi[5] or whitebait or I would at once. I shall not go to Kyoto until May 15 but am expected in Osaka on April 25 for one or two lectures, and T. Saito[6] is going there with me; he also will give a lecture or two. For the first half of May, many lectures are arranged in Tokyo, some at a girls' school

(The Sacred Heart).[7] On Friday I paid a visit to another such school where T. Sone, I. Nishizaki and Y. Sakai[8] teach (Women's Higher Normal).[9] My trouble is that I have such a wretched memory, and names soon escape me. . . .

With our united love, Edmund

Notes

1. A Japanese scholar who had become a friend of Blunden.
2. Snow-willow with small white flowers on its branches.
3. Mr Kato might have meant his dining-room, but called it a restaurant because of his limited English vocabulary.
4. Deep-fried vegetables (onions, mushrooms, a cluster of sliced carrots and burdocks, sweet potatoes) and fish such as prawns or flatfish fried in light Japanese batter.
5. Prawns.
6. See note 3 to the letter of 9 October 1925.
7. The Sacred Heart University in Tokyo. A Catholic university for women; the Crown Princess Michiko studied English Literature there and took a BA degree.
8. Tamotsu Sone, Ichiro Nishizaki and Yoshitaka Sakai were all Blunden's students.
9. Ochanomizu Women's College in Tokyo.

Matsushima[1]

Melodious is that name Matsushima;
Men love the place before they travel there,
And when they see those islands and their pines,
Still more and more amid those waterways,
Perhaps the melody excels the scene,
Singing in silence to the inward ear;
A dreaming song, in which each island gives
Its own true note, the largest and the least,
Between the temple and the ocean foam.

Christmas Greetings to Aki
from Lucy, Margaret, Claire & E.
1948 Tokyo

Note

1. Matsushima, on a famous archipelago in Miyagi Prefecture, north-eastern part of Japan. A memorial stone on which this poem has been carved is to be found at the scenic site of Zuiganji Temple in Matsushima. Matsushima is one of the three most beautiful areas in Japan. Many small islands (*shima*) with pine trees (*matsu*) are scattered here and there in Matsushima Bay. A boat trip can enable one to catch glimpses of these islands and appreciate their beauty. Other stones commemorating Blunden stand in Itoh, Yashima, Matsuyama and Hiroshima. This poem was reprinted in *Eastward: A Selection of Verses, Original and Translated by Edmund Blunden* (1950); in *The Shikai*, no. 1 (October 1950) p. 1; and in *Contemporary Verse: An Anthology* (Japan Poets' Club, 1955). (Kirkpatrick A86.)

Tokyo

E. Blunden
c/o Foreign Office
London S.W.1.

14 February 1949

My dear Aki,

. . .

It is a pity that we can get so much Japanese fruit, vegetables & fish without being able to send you some. We are not often defeated by what is offered. But Claire was a little uncertain when nama-ko[1] appeared. I ate almost all her share. . . .

E.

Note

1. A trepang (a sea-cucumber), a Japanese delicacy, which goes well with *sake* (rice wine).

Tokyo

E. Blunden
c/o Foreign Office
London S.W.1.

21 September 1949

My dear Aki

. . . *The Times* want me back as early as possible but we can't make the voyage before the end of March.[1]

Love from us all
Edmund

Note

1. Blunden was initially to stay in Japan until March 1949 (13 March 1948), but the Foreign Office, that is, the British Embassy in Tokyo, who were greatly impressed by Blunden's successful mission, wanted him to stay for one more year (26 July 1948). Subsequently his appointment was extended until March 1950 (9 August 1948). *The Times*, on the other hand, awaited Blunden's return (9 September 1949). In the archives of *The Times* there is some correspondence between the Foreign Office and *The Times* concerning Blunden's extended stay in Japan.

326 Stroude Rd.
Virginia Water, Surrey

5 May 1951

My dear Aki

You have sent me some very useful notes on the photographs of the queer Japanese Weddings which I suppose may now be popular; no doubt when there is more money about the old arrangements will be usual again. The last Wedding I attended was a church wedding, Makoto Saito's,[1] and I had to make a speech. I have been thinking of Japan this morning rather particularly, for in the newspaper there is a short paragraph saying that Mr Fraser[2] who took over from me has been found on the railway line injured. It is as yet impossible to know if this is a serious accident, but I hope not for everybody's sake: he has been doing splendidly as a lecturer &c., & he has just had a second child. Like you I have been bothered with dizziness for some time, and shall welcome a bit of a rest: we are all to stay for a few days from 11 May with Mr and Mrs Finzi[3] at Ashmansworth near Newbury. He is a musician who composed the music for my poem on St Cecilia's Day,[4] & dedicated his songs from Thomas Hardy to me. I lately sent congratulations to Mrs Hani's School[5] on the 30th anniversary which still finds the old lady full of enthusiasm & ready to make her appearance on the platform & talk away though she can scarcely see. I wish you felt better & could travel here. You will hardly recognize our youngest, who now plays quite capably with the others indoors and out. I took Margaret yesterday, since Claire could not go, to the opening of the Festival Book Exhibition at the Victoria and Albert Museum; the only child in the large audience! She bore it cheerfully even if the speechifying was rather a strain.

Plans for Tonbridge go on.[6] I believe I can borrow money enough now, with what publishers may pay me, to buy 67 Pembury Road & we shall probably move in July.

All send their love.

E.

8 May I thought this had gone off. Hope you are *much* better, but it is wintry enough to prevent that.

Notes

1. The eldest son of Dr Takeshi Saito. See note 3 to the letter of 9 October 1925.
2. G. S. Fraser (1915–80), a poet and critic, who was Blunden's successor to the post of cultural liaison officer in the British Embassy, Tokyo, in 1950 and 1951. He was the author of *The Modern Writer and his World* (London: Derek Verschoyle, 1953; rev. edn London: André Deutsch, 1964), which was originally written for Japanese students. On his way back from a lecture tour in Fukushima, he attempted suicide by jumping out of the train between Utsunomiya and Tokyo, narrowly escaping death. He was believed to have been suffering from a nervous breakdown caused by strains associated with his work. US Occupying Forces took him into their care, and he returned to England. It was said that Fraser was much frustrated because he felt it impossible to maintain the standard Blunden had set by giving 600 lectures, and by working from 7 am to 10 pm, never refusing requests from the Japanese people.
3. Gerald Finzi (1901–56) and his wife Joy. A composer, who set many of Thomas Hardy's poems and also some of Blunden's poems to music. The Finzis collected Ivor Gurney's songs. Finzi and Blunden met each other in 1947 in order to collaborate over Blunden's poem 'St Cecilia's Day'. Blunden's poem 'The White Flowering Days', which Finzi set to music, was published in *A Garland for the Queen* in 1953.

4. 'An Ode for St Cecilia's Day', first published in *St Cecilia's Day Festival Concert* in 1947, then reprinted in *Eastward* in 1950, and *A Hong Kong House* in 1962. It is also reprinted in the programme for *St Cecilia's Festival Concert* on 22 November 1950, p. 11. (Kirkpatrick B121.)
5. Jiyu (meaning freedom and liberty) Gakuen, in Tokyo. Motoko Hani (1873–1957), Japan's first woman newspaper reporter and co-founder of the liberal private school, Jiyu Gakuen, with her husband. They also started the 'serious' magazine for women, *Fujin-no-tomo* (Woman's Friend). The school pursued educational goals that emphasised the students' ability to reason, to make their own decisions, and to master basic skills. Their daughter Keiko stayed with Blunden's family in London.
6. Plans to move house.

P. & O. Carthage

6 September 1953[1]

My dear Aki

. . .

You will perhaps like a little account of the voyage. Some rough weather at the beginning was over when we passed close to the coast of Portugal, and the children could then enjoy life. (There are many others travelling, especially girls.) The usual day of Sports and Races excited them and they didn't do badly. At Port Said a conjurer came to the ship and his tricks with coins that vanished and chicks that suddenly appeared were much applauded. The Suez Canal, though to me & Claire highly interesting and beautiful at sunset & in moonlight, did not impress them specially! and in the Red Sea great heat began. Frances[2] was asked to explain 'Red' Sea and she said that the name was used because the mountains along it are red. F. is in Claire's cabin and Margaret and Lucy[3] share the next one. I am with a gentleman who goes to Tokyo on business. I have met three Japanese professors who are travelling Tourist class, and there is one Japanese woman student of English literature they tell me. They all seem happy and comfortable. My cabin companion is very sensible about Japan and Japanese trade and should do very well in that country. . . .

I had a letter from a friend who is not an Old Blue[4] but attended the 'Dede of Pittie';[5] he says as an experienced theatre-goer that I have the touch for writing for the theatre, and urges me to try a play. But it would depend on 'a bright idea'. Some adaptation of the life of

John Clare[6] might do – and sympathy would be an advantage there. But I dare say before I make any dramatic attempt I ought to send Messrs. Collins[7] an ordinary Book. . . .

All send you their love.

E.

Miss A. Hayashi
6 Worsley Road
Hampstead
London N.W.3
England

E. Blunden
The University
Hong Kong[8]

Notes

1. The Blundens were on their way to Hong Kong.
2. Blunden's daughter.
3. Blunden's daughters.
4. An alumnus of Christ's Hospital.
5. Blunden's play on the history of Christ's Hospital, *The Dede of Pittie: Dramatic Scenes Reflecting the History of Christ's Hospital, and Offered in Celebration of the Quatercentenary 1953 at the Fortune Theatre* (London: Christ's Hospital, 1953). (Kirkpatrick A118.)
6. See note 3 to the letter of 29 August 1925.
7. William Collins, Sons & Co. Ltd, Blunden's publisher.
8. This is an air-letter and the addresses of Aki and Blunden are written on the outside.

1 November 1953

My dear Aki, It seems quite a few days since I wrote to you, & time runs away even here. Plenty for me to do but of course less travelling. We are at the moment getting ready for our Sunday morning at the Cathedral, where there is always a large congregation and a good choir, and a Sunday school takes off our children. They have just put up a ring of bells given by the Hong Kong & Shanghai bank, but I fancy these will not be *rung* in the old style but by some chiming apparatus. It has been raining hard & that was wanted: but the sultry heavy air is much as before, and makes me slower with my work than I like. Claire has been invited to take some classes at a school not far off and will soon begin there. No doubt it will not be very different from teaching in Japan. We begin work in good time, 8.30 a.m. is usual, and not much is done in the afternoons in classrooms. The University Library and many of the teaching departments are together in one big building, a pleasant place: there is a Great Hall, and on 10 Novr I give a public lecture there as Professor. The fact is, that this University is still in an experimental stage, and to build up its academic reputation is one of the ideas. I must request your prayers therefore for the success of this particular lecture! We hope you are getting the better of your illnesses, and not being drenched or frozen by the approaching winter. I have a postcard from Mr Bernstein[1] ending 'I am more than ever attached to the East, and, of course, to E. B.' He is indeed one of my oldest friends. . . . The British Council has a reading room here and I am booked to give a lecture there; I mean often to look in and see the English newspapers, but it hasn't happened yet.

Our garden is almost flowerless at present, but there are bright yellow and purple and white and rosy blooms on some of the shrubs near us. Great rocks lie about the grounds, such as at Kyoto I think, and there is a lily-pond but nothing as interesting to me as the Daimyo's Pond at Tokyo University, even if the carp have been mostly eaten which used to be so majestic in those shadowed waters.[2]

This letter can stay open a little longer, in case there is anything special to tell you.

2 Novr 1953 The Peking Opera we saw was not unlike a mixture of the various Japanese theatre styles, – the stories of the plays were not much & went very slowly, but the acting was rich and the groups on the stage wonderfully well directed. An orchestra went on most of the time, especially a man with a gong which almost battered our hearing into permanent deafness, but I missed the singing or intoning which goes with say the Bunraku[3] performance. I think the women's parts were acted by men, much as in Japan of old. – The audience was very smart, and I think dressmakers in Hong Kong must be pretty busy. There may be a trade depression but there is money about, – though God knows there are multitudes of poor & needy, who do not appear at Operas. . . . Now I will attend to some letters just received from England & America, and once again they are mainly from people who *request* something of a literary veteran. If they would send me a Cheque too, I might feel

better! We are hoping that here we can save a little money, and I shall look forward to the day when I can send you enough for a holiday. Hastings? I think you could well try the Lake District presently, but it is a matter of getting things quite arranged first. T. Cook & Son?

If you should pick up any picture-postcard of Hampstead or Highgate,[4] use it for a message to us. Or any B. M. card relating to art/or literature; you know the kind of thing.

Love from all of us.
E.

Miss A. Hayashi
6 Worsley Road
London N.W.3
England

E. Blunden
University of Hong Kong

Notes

1. See note 3 to the letter of 8 December 1925.
2. See Blunden's poem 'The Daimyo's Pond', which was first published in *The Augustan Books of Modern Poetry* (London: Ernest Benn, 1925). (Kirkpatrick A18.)
3. A Japanese form of puppet theatre in which each puppet is manipulated by three puppeteers.
4. Hampstead: a district of London to the north-west of Hampstead Heath where many writers and artists lived. Highgate: a district to the north-east of Hampstead Heath. Coleridge lived for 19 years in Highgate.

1 January 1955

My dear Aki,

. . .

I mean to write an article on George Sewell, MD.[1] of Hampstead, who died in 1726, – he translated Ovid's Metamorphoses and wrote many things. Can you send me the list of those in the B. M. Catalogue? and also look at some of these books and tell me what is in them. Sewell for instance published, or rather his friends published in 1728, a volume containing 'Richard the First' and several poems, and these may be pleasing. But also his posthumous essay 'On the Usefulness of Snails in Medicine' and copy for me any poems in it. I know there is one, beginning 'Why, Damon, with the forward day,' written at Hampstead. There may be some remarks in prose on it. Can you also look him up in a book called Alumni Cantabrigienses by Venn[2] and copy for me the memoir there? – I have one or two other eighteenth-century poets in mind, & so shall keep you a little busy. . . .

Our love
E.

Notes

1. George Sewell, MC (d. 1796), educated at Peterhouse, Cambridge, and studied medicine at Leyden. Practised in London for a time. Afterwards a political pamphleteer. Author of many miscellaneous pieces. Died at Hampstead in great poverty.
2. J. A. Venn (compiler), *Alumni Cantabrigienses*. Blunden's review of Venn's *Alumni Cantabrigienses*, Pt 2: *From 1752 to 1900*, vol. 5 (University of Cambridge, Official Documents – Lists, 1922), appeared as an unsigned review entitled 'Cambridge Men', in *The Times Literary Supplement*, 5 June 1953, p. 367. (Kirkpatrick C3035.)

15 February 1955

My dear Aki,

. . .

Sylva continues to write long letters full of literary news; her book on Shelley[1] though it has been greatly praised in reviews may not be selling rapidly, but that is not unexpected with things as they are. She should take a holiday, and so should you, but you do not care to go out of England which is *my* idea of a holiday, even if only as far as North France[2]. . . .

With our love, best luck,
E.

Miss A. Hayashi
c/o The British Museum
London W.C.1
England

E. Blunden
The University
Hong Kong

Notes

1. *Flight of the Skylark: The Development of Shelley's Reputation* (London: Reinhardt, 1954; Norman: University of Oklahoma Press, 1954). I. A. Richards writes in her obituary in *The Times* of 29 May 1971: 'Her *Flight of the Skylark: The Development of Shelley's Reputation* (1954) took the story in detail to 1900 and sketched the sequel through the next 50 years. It is in many ways a type-specimen account of the diverse sources of fame and of the interplay of literary and biographic concerns.'
2. Having hardly ever been on holiday from when she came to England in 1927 until her death in 1962, Aki had managed to save a considerable sum of money (approximately £2000) which she left to Blunden in her will.

24 June 1955

My dear Aki,

. . . We have gone on much as usual, and last night entertained the Chinese author of 'Lady Precious Stream'[1] . . . and this went on till morning nearly; when I was alone I tried for the Test Match news[2] but got little – the Far East broadcast was still devoted to higher themes. . . .

Love from us all,
do get better quickly.
E.

Miss A. Hayashi
c/o The British Museum
London W.C.1
England

E. Blunden
The University
Hong Kong

Notes

1. S. I. Hsiung (1902–), popular Chinese dramatist.
2. Blunden was said to be 'mad' about cricket, together with his other enthusiasm – beer. He played cricket wherever he went to live – Sussex, Kent, the West Country (Salcombe), Oxford (12 June 1936) and Hong Kong (13 January 1954) – and even played the day before leaving for Hong Kong (21 August 1953). His father was also a cricketer and Blunden played for a longer time than he did (25 November 1958). He loved to go to cricket matches, and often took Aki (24 July, 5 August and 9 August 1933 and 6 August 1936), and he took Aki to Lords (16 May 1935, 2 July 1946). He came to London for the Test Match (19 August and 28 August 1934). He asked Aki to send him cricket scores (18 August 1935); strained his leg playing cricket (3 June 1936) and even went on a cricket tour (13 July 1937). Blunden's social circle through cricket was indeed wide – he belonged to the Keats and Shelley Association which organised cricket matches (3 September 1952) and his friends Sassoon and Rupert Hart-Davis were also cricket fans. In Hong Kong he wrote that he hoped Aki would attend cricket matches in London (15 April 1954). He himself listened to Australian Test Matches on the radio (26 April 1955), staying up quite late (17 June 1956). Although still keen, Blunden started to feel too old to play (13 October 1955) and now played infrequently (13 November 1955). Yet, he still played a match in mud and rain (28 February 1959). He planned to be at a cricket match in London (25 April 1961) and was president of the cricket club in Hong Kong (10 March 1962). He published *Cricket County* (London: Collins, 1944). (Kirkpatrick A76.)

15 February 1956

My dear Aki

Perhaps I mentioned that I had a letter from A. Pryce-Jones[1] of the *Times Literary S.* in which he asked me to say if I would be a candidate for the Oxford Professorship of Poetry.[2] I replied that *if* some things could be arranged, e.g. a rather better paid job at *T.L.S.* than I had, I was willing. The Professorship itself is worth perhaps only £300 a year. But in fact A. P.–J. had written too late. So nothing comes of that. . . .

Our love,
E.

Miss A. Hayashi
c/o The British Museum
London W.C.1
England

E. Blunden
The University
Hong Kong

Notes

1. Alan Pryce-Jones (1908–), then editor of *The Times Literary Supplement*. He came to Japan in April 1964 for the Festival commemorating Shakespeare's Quartercentenary. He participated in the symposium 'Shakespeare in the Modern World' held at Sophia University, chaired by Professor Joseph Roggendorf and formed by Edmund Blunden, Junzaburo Nishiwaki and Peter Milward, published in *Sophia: Studies in Western Civilization and the Cultural Interaction of East and West*, vol. 13, no. 2 (Summer 1964) pp. 117–41 (in Japanese).
2. Ten years after this letter, in 1966, Blunden was elected Professor of Poetry at Oxford, in succession to Robert Graves. He resigned two years later because of ill-health and because he decided this would prevent him giving the required lectures. All his supporters very much regretted his decision.

27 June 1958

My dear Aki

. . . S. Sassoon sends me a long Meditation on his conversion to the Church of Rome, and I am wondering how I can reply to him for he wants me to announce that it's one of his masterpieces. I must read it on our lonely Island[1]. . . .

With love from us all,

E.

Miss A. Hayashi
c/o British Museum
London W.C.1
England

E. Blunden
The University
Hong Kong

Note

1. During the summer the Blunden family went on holiday to an island, Cheung Chau.

UNIVERSITY OF HONG KONG
DEPARTMENT OF ENGLISH

15 August 1958

My dear Aki

. . .

I think S. Sassoon's[1] conversion was due partly to a Nun who on reading his poems 'Sequences' sent him some comments on his spiritual condition, and a correspondence arose; & then he lives near Downside[2] which is a great abbey & a public school together, & his great friend Ronald Knox[3] was his neighbour (dead, alas), a great example of R. Catholic inspiration.

No news of my Mother yet.

Here comes your *okane*.

We sent our love, & wishes for your sunny holiday.

E.

Notes

1. See note 1 to the letter of 31 August 1925.
2. A Roman Catholic abbey and public school in the west of England.
3. Ronald Knox (1888–1957). The Right Reverend Monsignor Ronald Arbuthnott Knox was Roman Catholic chaplain at the University of Oxford from 1926 to 1939. Apart from his books on theology, he also wrote six detective stories.

UNIVERSITY OF HONG KONG
DEPARTMENT OF ENGLISH

17 November 1958
(now 25th! so fast days go.
Too busy, or drowsy; see back)

My dear Aki

. . .

I must end my letter up here. We have you in mind while the months go by. It was nice of L. Brander[1] to send the War Poets but he is that sort of being. Soon I am to write on Lafcadio Hearn for an American mag. published in Tokyo[2] – and a charming one. Did you see *Geographical Magazine* for Oct^{r}? much about Japan[3] (text and illustrations) and partly by me. Our love

E

Notes

1. Laurence Brander is an English scholar associated with the British Council. See his article 'Edmund Blunden, Book-Collector', *Today's Japan*, vol. 5, no. 3 (1960) pp. 49–50. This article is not mentioned in *A Bibliography of Edmund Blunden* by B. J. Kirkpatrick.
2. 'Lafacadio [*sic*] Hearn, Teacher', *Today's Japan*, vol. 4, no. 1 (January 1959) pp. 63–5. (Kirkpatrick C3221.)
3. 'Japan's Cultural Traditions', *Geographical Magazine*, vol. 31, no. 6 (October 1958), pp. 277–89. (Kirkpatrick C3216.)

POSTCARD

The University,
Hong Kong

28 January 1960

. . . A copy will be sent before long. Thank you too for several transcriptions from R. Flecknoe's[1] poetry. I have sent several other names of 17th century poets & you will be coming to those, when it is less wintry. . . .

Love from all
E. B.

by air 0.65 [these words are written in pencil]

Miss A. Hayashi
c/o the British Museum
London W.C.1
England

Note

1. Richard Flecknoe (d. 1678?). A legendary figure of letters, said to have been an Irish poet who privately printed several poems and prose works. He was the subject of a lampoon by Andrew Marvell, which gave Dryden the idea for his satire on Shadwell, *Mac Flecknoe*.

UNIVERSITY OF HONG KONG
DEPARTMENT OF ENGLISH

17 April 1960

My dear Aki,

. . .

We are much as usual, and the girls are having their Easter vacation. All went to the Cathedral for this morning's early family service, which was well appreciated. The youngest looked round at the beginning for God, but could not quite catch Him. She is a merry and bright child, Catherine, and goes to school next door as long as Mrs Stock[1] keeps one. The main education is much the same as yours or mine at that stage – they beat tambourines &c. . . .

Our love
E.

Note

1. Mrs Stock ran a nursery school for under fives, and was the wife of the Professor of Surgery at Hong Kong University.

15 February 1961

My dear Aki

If only I could help with this problem of your lodgings[1] – perhaps somehow I can in the summer when we have our short leave. If we were enriched by Hong Kong it would be simpler, but we are in truth always worried lately by money matters; here as everywhere prices go up, and we are only able to save 'superannuation' money, which is good but would only buy us a modest house in England & pay a few expenses, for a year or so. . . .

No more today except our love.

E.

Note

1. In her letters to Blunden, Aki would express her worries about her lodgings. She was now 72 years old and had to prepare for her approaching old age or possible invalidity. Her present lodgings were far from ideal, because she had only one room and constantly had to worry about being unable to invite any of her friends or Japanese visitors there. She was ashamed of being unable to hide her bed from visitors' eyes. She wrote to Blunden:

> My dear E.
>
> My happiest place is B. M. [British Museum], but so many visitors even in the Reading Room & in MS room are occupying seats. (19 August 1959)
>
> After considerations I had better stay somewhere nearer London, so that I can go to B. M. often, for apart from B. M. I shall be miserable. (22 February 1960)

UNIVERSITY OF HONG KONG
DEPARTMENT OF ENGLISH
PROF. E. C. BLUNDEN, C.B.E.,
M.C., M.A., F.R.S.L.

24 November 1961

My dear Aki

. . . *26th*. Sunday is almost an English day, bleak and colourless. I think I had better send you a cheque; whether it is already due I don't remember. Please tell me presently. There is one piece of news, but you will do me the favour of keeping it to yourself: I am to receive an honorary degree from the University of Leeds; in May next, and Claire and I hope we shall be able to give you lunch at least in London on our way back from the ceremony. Messrs. Collins are preparing the new volume of poems, 'A Hong Kong House'[1] &c. for about the same date. Alas I can't feel very poetical lately. Like you I am too often, in Chas. Lamb's[2] phrase, 'ratherish unwell.' But must run about as if all was well. . . .

Our love.
E.

Notes

1. *A Hong Kong House: Poems 1951–1961* (London: Collins, 1962). (Kirkpatrick A156.)
2. See note 3 to the letter of 22 December 1927.

The University
Hong Kong

6 November 1962[1]

My dear Aki

Sorry to have left you without a letter, but thank you for yours. I have been lazy and nervous. The house at Long Melford[2] seems to be practically ours, thanks mainly to my daughter Clare and her husband Philip Ross,[3] and the generosity of S. Sassoon.[4] You will have read of the death of R. Hodgson[5]. . . . I hope you will not find the winter horrible. Here it begins to be cooler. I enclose a cheque & you must work out how far it takes us & let me know. . . . Lucy[6] appeared on T.V. here & will again – she looked quite cheerful &

ready. We shall find Christmas on us before we know. Thank you for commemorating my birthday.[7] All send love. I await the Test Match commentaries.

E.

Notes

1. This is the last letter sent by Blunden to Aki before her death on 14 December 1962.
2. Long Melford, near Sudbury, Suffolk. Blunden lived at Hall Mill from his return from Hong Kong in 1965 to his death in 1974, and is buried in the churchyard.
3. Philip Ross worked for the Treasury. He told me that he had met his wife in Oxford. He died in 1983.
4. See note 1 to the letter of 31 August 1925.
5. See note 1 to the letter of 24 March 1926.
6. Blunden's daughter. See note 3 to the letter of 6 September 1953.
7. 1st November 1896.

Undated Letters

Some of the undated letters are significantly more intimate in tone. The reason may be that Blunden left them at Aki's lodgings.

218 Karuizawa

My dear child,

Tomorrow I'll meet you at the Post Office at 9.50; or a moment or two later. If you're unwell, don't come: I'm much distrest to find that your throat is still bad. I loved yesterday: & it's only so that I shan't seem an unkind guest that I am staying in today. I walked down the street with Mr Carey[1] but was back again, (to my present sorrow) before you can have come. Let's meet tomorrow: if you're not at the P. O. I'll know you're ill, & shall call at Ichidaya.[2] How I see you all the time, but would much rather the reality than the imagination!

Love & love again to you; your
Edmund

Notes

1. An English friend he had made in Japan.
2. The inn where Aki was staying at that time.

Merton College
Oxford

Tuesday morn[g]

Ever dear Aki

Incidentally I am joining a large Choir here, which is well known, and called the Bach Choir. It is likely to be pleasant on winter evenings & may do my chest good. I went last night to see what it would be like, & found I was very *rusty* inside; c[d] hardly keep up my mild noise for 2 beats together after long absences from the Musical World.

Love
Eddie

17 August

My Aki, I write in haste, being overwhelmed with delayed correspondence. I wish you would not spend so much of your time and mine in foolish complaints against me; I do, & I feel, all I can, and I never forsake you or fail you – why then this exhausting impatience of yours? Please be better and wiser.

On Tuesday I shall come up by the 1st train if I can, then to the *Nation*, & it is possible I may have to lunch with the Bradys but I don't know yet.

Mr K.[1] wrote me an insolent and menacing kind of letter; it is impossible to negotiate with such a young ruffian, and the position otherwise is the same, so I feel more & more compelled to move away. I have told M.[2] that I am going. She seems ashamed, and aware of her gentleman's inferiority, but 'is in love with him', & evidently intends to sacrifice everything except 'her children' to that. You are not mentioned nowadays, I notice.

Meanwhile, look at the enclosed cutting, 'Lee Nichols'. I believe

Vines told me this was the man who would succeed him at Keio. If so, would not Keio have a vacancy?[3]

I have written another article for Kubota,[4] & I think it is time he had my original manuscript, don't you? he'll perhaps appreciate it; so, if you agree, send it directly.

Now I must tackle other things, so I end, with my constant love – my devotion.

Eddie.

Notes

1. Mr C. Keeble, Mary's lover, and later her husband.
2. Mary.
3. T. Saito hoped Blunden would come to Japan again (6 February 1930), and Blunden himself was interested in that possibility, because he was so distressed and disturbed by the affairs of his first wife. He wanted friends who would heal his 'wounds' by treating him with love and care. Japan seemed to offer that balm. Later Saito sent a letter to Blunden concerning prospects for a visit to Japan (19 August, 4, 9 and 20 September 1934).
4. See note 2 to the letter of 24 October 1932.

. . . You will have been as surprised as every one else by the announcement that S. Sassoon[1] is to marry. I am rather waiting for the official statement but as he has not denied it I suppose we must take the newspaper paragraph to be correct. Yesterday the *Telegraph* called me up to get my views on the King's poetry medals.[2] I was very unwilling to say much, for I am feeling quite bitter at the fact that others use my name while I can't quite make a living. . . .

Love,
E.

Notes

1. See note 1 to the letter of 31 August 1925.
2. Blunden was awarded the Queen's Gold Medal for Poetry in 1956 (14 July 1956).

T. L. S.

27 June

My dear Aki

In one of the enclosed Papers you will find the Night Sky for August.[1] I am sorry I was out when you telephoned. . . . Best luck. E.

Note

1. This 'map' of the Night Sky for August is left among Blunden's letters to Aki which she kept together with her diary and the letters from her mother and friends.

5

Interviews

Interviews with and letters from persons who met Blunden and Aki Hayashi

---

(a) INTERVIEW WITH SIR HUGH GREENE

Sir Hugh Greene, who was a pupil of Blunden at Merton College, Oxford, recollected in my interview with him (9 February 1984) that he was very fond of his tutor, who was a kind and conscientious teacher. For example, when Blunden wanted to cancel his tutorial in order to go to London, he set some examination questions for his pupil to complete in his absence. Sir Hugh still possessed some of these letters. Sir Hugh Greene died on 19 February 1987. His obituary was published in *The Times* of 21 February 1987.

Merton College
Oxford

May 21, 1933

Dear H. C. G.

I am sorry to trouble the programme, but would you be able to come this week on Thurs. 11 (instead of the usual time), or maybe you w^{d} not mind having the week undisturbed?

EB

(b) EDMUND BLUNDEN AS AN ENGLISH TUTOR: REMINISCENCES OF PROFESSOR RICHARD STORRY

This is based on my interview with him on 7 December 1981 at St Antony's College, Oxford

It was at the end of 1936 that the late Richard Storry, Professor Emeritus of Oriental Studies, Oxford, saw the advertisement of a vacancy at Otaru Kotoshogyo (College of Commerce and Economics). He was then an undergraduate at Merton College, Oxford. He was attracted to the idea of going to Japan, but at the same time undecided, because of the country's rather militaristic and totalitarian image. He was a scholar of history but he knew nothing about Japan. What he knew then were on the one hand such 'clichés' as Mt Fuji, the kimono and delicate art; and on the other the soldiers in Manchuria and the Stock Exchange in Osaka. So he consulted Blunden, his English tutor at Merton, who had taught at Tokyo Imperial University for three years. Blunden urged him to go, predicting that he would enjoy it. Richard Storry felt sure that war was drawing near and wanted to see the country before then out of sheer curiosity. Further, the attraction of a high salary was one of the factors which induced him to go to Otaru, a relatively unknown town on Hokkaido, the northernmost island of Japan.

On Storry's departure Blunden gave him three pieces of advice. First, not to get involved in politics. This advice was wise when one remembers Japan's militarist and imperialist behaviour in Indo-China at that time. Secondly, let the students be your guide in the classroom as well as in the street. Thirdly, remember that though there are many mean streets, the people are kind and well-mannered. Richard Storry found these tips valuable when he arrived in Japan. Of course, his appointment was much less prestigious than that of Blunden as a Professor of English at Tokyo University. Tokyo was then, and still is now (perhaps even more so) the centre of politics, economics and culture, and the University of Tokyo retains its dominant influence on the power structure of the country, as most of the top-class politicians, industrialists and academics were and are graduates of the University.

In the less sophisticated environment of Otaru Kosho, Storry nevertheless found the standard of English spoken among the senior professors to be quite high. In fact, their desire to become proficient in spoken English seemed to be so ardent that the Japanese teachers were determined to speak only in English, not only in the classroom, but also in the senior common room. This tradition was kept unchanged until the outbreak of the Pacific War. Professor Storry, praising this rather strenuous effort, attributed his 'insufficient' command of Japanese to it. His claim was that he had been forbidden to speak Japanese in the classrooms by his contract with the Japanese Ministry of Education. Apart from that contract – and his so-called laziness – it was probable that the political atmosphere of the time deterred him from learning Japanese more fully. He suspected that the Japanese government had a strong fear that any foreigner acquiring a full command of the language would use his access to people and places to spy against Japan.

Professor Storry also noticed that political and ideological restrictions deeply permeated Japanese education. For instance, even in his college library all the books by Communist writers such as Lenin, Kropotkin and Trotsky were banned from the reading room and kept on special shelves under stricter surveillance. In short, compared with the Taisho Era when Blunden taught at Teidai – which was often called the Period of Taisho Democracy, and which encouraged a much greater openness to western thoughts and ideas – Storry's time (the beginning of the Showa Era) showed signs of the paranoia which preceded the catastrophic war.

In daily life, however, Storry had similar experiences to those Blunden might have had. He had a maid and her mother living with him in the official residence of the university. He was waited upon by them, which left him free to concentrate on his teaching and work. Through his students he gradually became familiar with the lifestyle of the Japanese family. For instance, he was surprised to find that the people went to bed early, that every one of them took a bath every night, and that there was an order as to who took it first. Discovering that even in such a trivial matter as taking a bath, the people created a quasi-feudal hierarchy, Storry was much amused. In that hierarchy a guest and the head of the family took first priority, and the women the modest last! There were also the formalities associated with leaving and returning to the house – ritual greetings from the maid and her mother.

Apart from the language barrier and the loneliness which might afflict any foreigner going to Japan, there occurred in Storry's case the serious problem of 'deciphering' the people's mind. The trouble with the Japanese, he felt, was that every person behaved politely and nicely to foreigners; it was difficult to penetrate to the reality underneath the mask. He had to distinguish between sincerity and the possible duplicity concealed by the 'mask'. He learned a lot from this experience. So later, returning home to teach at Oxford, he used to say to the Japanese visiting scholars that they should try for at least six months to endure the 'rudeness' of the English people who speak their minds much more directly than the Japanese.

During his stay in Japan, which lasted until 1940, Storry received several letters from Blunden, but they did not meet each other for another ten years until in 1949 they dined together in Kakinokizaka, in the Meguro Ward of Tokyo. Blunden was married to his third wife, Claire, and worked energetically as a cultural attaché of the British Embassy, giving 600 lectures in all. Blunden was steadfast in his pursuit of reconciliation. He went all over Japan encouraging the people, who were hurt and had lost confidence due to the defeat of 1945. The war had destroyed not only visible objects – towers, bridges, theatres, domes – but also to some extent the will of the distressed people. Again Blunden tried to help people turn their thoughts away from their own misery towards the world at large, promoting peace and a larger perspective through the appreciation of English literature, Western arts, ideas and traditions. He introduced these as a potent source of spiritual recovery.

To Storry, Edmund Blunden was a genius. He was a good tutor and a widely read scholar. When the undergraduate Storry first met him, Blunden had a great reputation as a poet, and was already famous through his book *Undertones of War*. Storry met his tutor quite frequently in his fourth year at Merton College where he was reading English. He started as a history scholar, but as he had four years' grant, after having taken a History degree, he tried to obtain an English degree in his remaining *one* year. Of course, it was an impossible task. Hearing about this, Blunden tried to discourage him. But realising that Storry was adamant, Blunden, 'out of the kindness of his heart', said merely, 'Speed the plough.' But in the end, though he 'took up the plough', Storry failed the examination, fulfilling the prediction.

As a tutor, Blunden was a very sympathetic, kind-hearted and quiet man. Storry remembered him often playing cricket, and his face reminded one of a bird, possibly because of his enormous nose. There might have been a vigorous character behind the gentle mask, but as a student Storry was not able to get on very intimate terms with Blunden, who often used to say that nothing seemed real to him after his sad experiences during the First World War.

In conclusion Richard Storry summed up Blunden's personality as that of a man who had about him a vulnerability which attracted the maternal instincts of women.

Professor Storry died on 19 February 1982. His obituary was published in *The Times* of 25 February.

(c) PERSONAL REMINISCENCES OF EDMUND BLUNDEN RELATED BY DR TAKESHI SAITO

This is based on my interview with him on 5 January 1982 at his home, in Minamienoki-cho, Shinjuku-ku, Tokyo.

Dr Takeshi Saito, Emeritus Professor of English Literature at Tokyo University, and the closest Japanese friend of Blunden, told me in my interview with him on 5th January 1982 that he had been unaware of Blunden's intimate relationship with Aki Hayashi in Japan during 1925–7. Dr Saito died in July 1982; his obituary and a tribute to him were published in *The Times*, 16 and 21 July 1982.

1. Aki Hayashi

After coming back from England in June or July 1925, Dr Saito first chanced to meet Aki Hayashi in Karuizawa. There every year the 'Summer College' for the junior school teachers all over Japan took place under the sponsorship of the Education Committee of Nagano Prefecture. A number of distinguished lecturers assembled there, including Inazo Nitobe (1862–1933), a Christian educationalist and cultural interpreter of the Western world. T. Saito was one of those lecturers – the youngest, perhaps – who together with Edmund Blunden taught at the Summer College two years running.

One day after the sessions were over, Saito invited Blunden for lunch at his grand villa, which had been built by his teacher, John Lawrence. On their way to it, they saw Miss Hayashi sitting on the bank of the small river which ran through the town. Blunden introduced her to Saito, who, however, did not invite her to lunch, as he knew nothing about the romance developing between her and Blunden. Blunden had never confided to Saito about his love for Aki, who appeared to be a commonplace woman, unremarkable either in her features or in her manners. Saito was much surprised to learn about Blunden's love letters and his proposal to her, which were disclosed in my article in the *Times Literary Supplement*.

Dr Saito met Aki Hayashi for the second time in 1947, when he was making a tour of the world starting from America. In England he intended to read as many rare books as possible in the British Museum, where Miss Hayashi was also working as a copyist for Blunden. She met Saito in the small tea-room near the foyer of the

British Museum, and treated him to tea despite his attempts to insist on paying. It was the last time he saw her. When Blunden took her to England on his way home in 1927, Ralph Hodgson was also with them. None of Blunden's friends or pupils understood the real meaning of Aki's embarkation. The pupils might have had vague intimations of their relationship, but nothing certain had been revealed during this time. Above all, most of Blunden's English friends, such as Sir John Pilcher, former Ambassador to Japan, and the late Professor Richard Storry, wrote to me that they knew nothing about Aki in relation to Blunden. Aki herself seemed to prefer to remain obscure, as is shown in her insistence that only her initials should be attached to her article on the visits to Elia's graveyard, published in the *Rising Generation* by Kenkyusha in August 1948.

2. On Inviting Blunden to Japan

Dr Saito told me how he chose Blunden as a successor to Robert Nichols, then Professor of English at Tokyo Imperial University. Nichols, though his three years' contract was incomplete, tendered his resignation to Dr Sanki Ichikawa, a famous linguist and the Chairman of the English Faculty, on the grounds of poor health. Dr Ichikawa wrote to Saito, who had been in England on sabbatical, asking him to find a suitable person for the vacant post. At that time Saito was on friendly terms with three English poets – Sassoon, Hodgson and Blunden. It was Siegfried Sassoon who introduced Saito to Ralph Hodgson, who was already about fifty years old. Through Hodgson, Saito first met Blunden and his wife, Mary. Blunden was the literary editor of the *Nation* in London, and though not yet very famous, was already regarded as one of the most promising young poets. He was only twenty-seven, but Saito was impressed by Blunden's wide learning and knowledge in every field of English literature. On the other hand, Hodgson's qualifications were insufficient for the Teidai post, as he possessed no university degrees. Although Hodgson was clearly very talented as a poet, Saito feared that as a teacher he might be less able. So, though he had met Blunden through Hodgson, Saito sent a telegram straight to Blunden asking him whether he might accept the teaching post as Nichols's successor. Hodgson might have been hurt by this direct method which bypassed him; but Saito none the less decided to write to Blunden again after his first telegram – he had obviously found his man.

Towards the end of 1923, possibly in November or December, Blunden wrote back to Saito accepting the invitation. The arrangement of the contract proceeded rapidly and smoothly. Though all went well, Blunden was obviously unable to leave the *Nation* without giving adequate notice, so it was decided that he should sail to Japan in April 1924. Mary Blunden clearly showed concern for her husband's welfare in Japan, asking Saito about the living conditions in Tokyo, particularly about the effects of the Great Earthquake of 1 September 1923.

One London newspaper reported that the Enoshima (Eno Island) near Tokyo had collapsed and sunk under the sea as a result of the earthquake. Though this article soon turned out to be mistaken, Saito was only too well aware how severe the damage must have been, and he feared being called back to Tokyo. About the aftermath of the disaster he had nothing but the second-hand information reported in the English newspapers, and consequently he could not assure Mary Blunden that there would be enough milk for her young children if they were taken to Japan. Mary Blunden decided to remain in England with the children. Saito presumes that she may in fact have had other reasons for refusing to come with her husband.

3. On Blunden's Friends, Early Life in Tokyo, Letters and Books

Dr Saito commented on Alec Hardie's book *Edmund Blunden* (London: Longmans, 1958; published for the British Council and the National Book League). He criticised Hardie's inaccurate account of how Blunden came to Japan. Though Hardie interviewed Saito, gathering information for his future book, he misrepresents Blunden's appointment by attributing it to Hodgson's desire to bring Blunden to Japan and hardly mentions Dr Saito's role. Hardie presents the story something like this: 'En route to Japan to take up his appointment as Professor of English at Tohoku University, Hodgson thought how nice it would be if Blunden came to Japan, too. So he soon tried to make this wish come true.'

Vere (later Sir Vere) Redman, whom Blunden knew well during 1947–50, was originally an English teacher at Hitotsubashi Kotoshogyo (now University). He subsequently became a diplomat and worked for the British Embassy in Tokyo. He returned home during the Second World War, but afterwards resumed his diplomatic career in Japan, and was in fact instrumental in arranging Blunden's second visit. He telephoned Dr Saito at his office in Tokyo University to consult him about Blunden's appointment as a cultural attaché to the British Embassy from December 1947. Redman suggested that Blunden should give his lectures mostly at Tokyo University, which delighted Saito. Edmund and Claire Blunden with their baby daughter, Margaret, called on him at home one December evening in 1947.

In 1925 when Blunden first arrived in Japan, Dr Sanki Ichikawa, Chairman of the English Faculty, an austere and quiet man who often surprised his colleagues by the seriousness of his discussions, put him in a vacant house in his compound in Ushigome. Claire Blunden told me that Edmund had not got on well with Ichikawa, whom he found too spartan, and that this was the main reason for the unhappiness of his first year. Incidentally, the house was also used to accommodate Doi Kochi, a famous Professor of English at Tohoku University and a great friend of Saito. There Blunden lived with Crick, who came with him from England as a sort of batman. Neither he nor Blunden could speak Japanese well enough to communicate with the people or even to go shopping. In fact, Blunden might have learned some Japanese on board ship to Japan, but it was not good enough to deal with practical things. In despair Blunden asked Mrs Saito (Dr Saito was then in Oxford) to find a middle-aged and useful woman to help him with domestic matters. Mrs Saito very willingly started to search for the right person, and asked the Young Women's Christian Association for help. They sent a woman to Blunden's household, but for reasons unknown she did not stay long. Crick turned out to be less than helpful, too: the housekeeper told Mrs Saito that he was given to drinking while Blunden was out; he subsequently left, either of his own accord or at Blunden's request. Losing all domestic help, Blunden chose to move into the Kikufuji Hotel, which would provide him with meals and, if required, would run small errands and so on. In these circumstances Aki's appearance on the scene was clearly that of a *deus* – or rather *dea* – *ex machina*.

As soon as he returned from England in 1925, Saito called on Blunden at Kikufuji Hotel in Hongo, and was struck by the strange appearance of the room: an alcove – a recess in the main wall of the main room and traditionally kept as a special corner, sacred and respected, for decorations such as flowers and scrolls – had been transformed into a bed. Given some ingenuity, such an alcove can indeed be adapted in this way, as it is set about three inches higher than the *tatami* (straw mat floor). What Blunden did was to hang two strong plaited straw ropes diagonally from the four corners of the alcove, to hold a mat or bed pad (also made of straw) and a couple of quilts (*futon*) (see p. 116). Thus he impressed his students with an originality perhaps lacking in Japanese society. Blunden had only one room which he used as a bedroom, study and living room.

Blunden was most kind to Saito, giving him many books from his collection. One of them was the American edition of his famous book *Undertones of War* (Garden City, N.Y.: Doubleday, Doran, 1929), which Blunden recommended to Saito as a better edition than the original because of its extensive revisions. The others included some collections of French poetry in the original. Among these poems, particularly in the nineteenth- and twentieth-century volumes, Blunden had made comments in the margins. It was apparently Blunden's habit to annotate his books in this manner.

Dr Saito kept Blunden's letters, and about 330 of them have been transcribed. He gave a copy of each letter to Claire Blunden. Some of them are long enough to count as literary essays. Originally he wanted to publish some in *English Studies*, a journal for the English Literary Society of Japan of which he had been an editor, but regretted that he had not been able to do so.

Ralph Hodgson and Edmund Blunden formed a good contrast in their character and manners. Hodgson, an extrovert, loved to make people laugh with his big gestures. He seldom wrote occasional or impromptu poems for his friends, but when he did, he produced much better poems than Blunden. Being shy, quiet and yet friendly, Blunden was always reluctant to disturb his friends in any way, but offered numerous pieces for various special occasions. In Saito's opinion the quality of those poems is not always high.

Saito recollects that every time he met Blunden, he was presented with some sort of book. He was told that Charles Lamb behaved similarly. Of course, Lamb was an old graduate of Christ's Hospital, and one of the few literary men whom Blunden admired and with whom he felt a strong affinity. Saito fears, however, that despite his many virtues Blunden was prone to one weakness, which was drink. This became excessive in his later years, particularly in the company of his friends. It was probably due to his suffering from asthma and to his appalling experiences in the First World War.

Dr Saito heard that Blunden had a very difficult time with his first and second wives. Blunden, who hardly ever criticised or complained about people, did at that time send Saito very detailed accounts of his strained relationship with Mary. (Otherwise, most of the letters concern literary subjects.)

Sylva Norman, who was married to Blunden for two or three years in Saito's recollection [in reality it lasted for thirteen years], sent her book on Shelley to Saito. In it she mentions that it was Saito himself who first introduced and wrote about the poet in Japan. But this is not correct, because some other scholar, whose name escaped him, in fact did the first work on Shelley.

Saito remembered I. Kishimoto, who studied at Merton College, Oxford, in the early 1930s, coming to see him for advice. This happened both before Kishimoto went to England and again after his return. But Saito had no idea about Kishimoto's whereabouts at the time of my interview with him.

Dr Saito was very proud of the books in his study – the 'Blunden collection' – which were the books either written by Blunden himself or given by him. He believes that it is the largest collection of Blunden's books in Japan.

(d) LETTER FROM SIR RUPERT HART-DAVIS

A letter sent to me by Sir Rupert Hart-Davis in June 1982.

I first met Edmund Blunden in 1932, and Aki Hayashi soon after that. She was by then fat and very giggly. [Rupert Hart-Davis may not have realised that giggling is a form of politeness practised by Japanese ladies when in contact with strangers and men.] Edmund and I made frequent journeys to the book-barrows on the Farringdon Road, taking small suitcases, which we filled with the treasures we so often found there for sixpence or a shilling (many of them now cost £40).

When we could carry no more we walked up to the pub on the corner of Caledonian Road, where Hayashi met us. As we examined our finds, she sat happily giggling over a half-pint of beer.

After the war, whenever Edmund came home on leave from Hong Kong, he usually stayed in my flat in Soho Square. Hayashi visited him daily, bringing buns, sandwiches and other small comestibles, which Edmund never ate. She also did all his laundry, and hung it all over the flat on bits of string.

She clearly adored Edmund and would do anything for him. He was fond of her too, but in a more reserved and less demonstrative way. He worried about her too, feeling responsible, and she had been a financial burden on him ever since he brought her to England in the Twenties.

I never had more than small talk and a few jokes with her, but we got along splendidly.

(signed) Rupert Hart-Davis
June 1982

Epilogue

Among Blunden's impressions of Japan and the Japanese written in his book *A Wanderer in Japan*, his sympathy was strongest with the plight of young Japanese women who remained unmarried. This may also help to explain why he was so sympathetic to Aki who was one of those unfortunate women in Japan during the late 1920s. Blunden describes the social pressure tacitly imposed upon them in his essay on Japan, written during his second visit to the country in 1950.

> Yet, in farm, factory and everywhere else, the life of Japan, the outlook, the wisdom, the achievement, will certainly be modified by one thing especially which the New Constitution has introduced. If a visitor may form impressions without hopeless error, I see that modification as a thing already happening. It was never my view that the women of Japan, when I spent some years here under the old state of affairs, were all as oppressed and deprived of personal fulfilment as we were often told. I could enlarge on this matter. But there were bitterness and blind alleys enough for Japanese women especially for those who lost or rejected the opportunity of marriage.[1]

The tone of his writing is so modest and unpretentious here, that one may easily miss his point. Yet his sharp observation continues in his comments on women after the New Constitution has been inaugurated.

> Today, surely a new confidence reveals itself in the outward appearance and style of the young women of the country – a confidence springing from the assurance that life will not lack opportunities for them to do well, whether they marry or not. Here as elsewhere (I know that there are still obstacles which there should not be) a woman may now choose her career – and that alone (strengthened with new university admission) is creating a liveliness in the whole Japanese scene, and undoubtedly increasing the true power of the nation.[2]

His deep sympathy with Japanese women who had to endure a hostile society with submissiveness is well depicted in his poem 'Ainu Child'. Here an Ainu girl – the Ainu is a primitive tribe living in the northern island of Japan, Hokkaido – elicits his compassion as symbolising a woman doomed to accept her fate to live in the world of brutality – of the killing of bears by men. She is shut behind the 'locked gates' crying for help; possibly looking for help to Blunden's wife who is a symbol of liberated western society. At least, Blunden must have regarded himself as a liberator who challenged Aki Hayashi's fate and took her out of the 'locked gates' of the older Japan. In fact there is some truth in this.

In the same book Blunden views Madame Butterfly, the heroine of Puccini's opera, who fell in love with an American naval officer but eventually killed herself in despair over her husband's betrayal, as an example of unremarkable deeds – a common occurrence. He mentions that hundreds of thousands of lives like hers had probably been lived in Japan – and there are shades here of his own relationship with Aki.

> Is it China, or is it Rome, that is nearest? I am trying to account for that peculiar gusto, that special colour of life, which met us in Nagasaki as we went about. Madame Butterfly had nothing to do with it. There may have been many young women who fell in love with, or were beloved by, all sorts of unauthorized heroes; but the same thing might happen anywhere and the town might not be different by a particle. May I deduce altogether that Rome and the personalities and her missionaries have given to Nagasaki the curious, free and cordial energy of her daily occupations?[3]

Blunden is also shrewd, though again modest in his expressions, in his observations on what was lacking (and is still lacking) in English studies in Japan.

> I might be disconsolate over such a view of the existing state of things, seeing that I was when a young man, and have been in the past year or two, one of the many who came to Japan with the object of assisting in the English Studies so widespread here. After all these exertions by a host of people, Japanese and foreign, in the explanation and interpretation of English literature (and by that term, let me signify literatures written in English) – after all these seemingly productive courses in a myriad classrooms and

> lecture-halls, – after all these publications either of books or of periodicals illustrative of English literature, the chief thing apparently has not been accomplished.[4]

Commenting on what his friend, a Japanese professor, said criticising his own colleague for taking an anti-lyrical and materialistic approach to English literature, Blunden voices his own view.

> Hearing this, I was again moved by the amount of truth in what he said. Let us grant that the pursuit of knowledge is the duty of the scholar. It is unnecessary for a great scientist, for example, to have a *practical* object in view while he is looking into the properties of physical nature. He is there to find what composes the universe and in what manner and by what laws the whole great work is carried on. The *application* of what he ascertains as the truth does not interest him in his scientific character, though it may in the details of his ordinary life as a citizen. Now, the scholar of literature is also a seeker after truth, and I do not think we can condemn him because of some particular study, the results of which seem unlikely to matter to anybody. However, literature is not so much a material as a spiritual phenomenon. The first justification of an exponent of it is that he should show it to others as one of the delights and the blessings of human life. Walt Whitman gave the word for this. Literature is life-blood.[5]

He also noticed the clinical and orthodox style of the Japanese appreciation of English literature, which is often regarded as a subject to be pursued mainly by women; being engaged in literature carries the taint of effeminacy in Japan.

> I am sure, too, that Japan follows the conventional opinion in many questions.[6]

Then Blunden tries to give some advice on how to improve not only English studies but also the general cultural climate in Japan, which has tended to be rather negative in its pursuit of spiritual wealth.

> I think the new age in Japan requires both a lyrical joy or awareness in life, and at the same time a steady, clear and courageous kind of thinking. If English literature becomes the cultured man's interest here, I foretell a general gain.[7]

According to her sister-in-law, who still lives in Yokohama, Aki had a chance of marriage once, but hardly in favourable circumstances. One of her high school classmates died young, leaving her husband with young children to care for, so someone suggested to Aki that she might marry him, out of the kindness of her heart. But of course Aki refused and chose to go to England with Blunden. At that time, any woman over twenty eight could expect enormous difficulty in meeting an ideal partner, because in the unemotional and mechanical 'marriage-market', where women counted as objects, her quality (in terms of youth and naiveté) was presumed to lessen as she grew older!

Blunden had a great respect for Charles Lamb's work and life, as well as for Coleridge. They were all old 'Blues' and alumni of Christ's Hospital where Blunden himself studied as a young boy. Lamb's relationship with his tragically insane sister, Mary, seems to have influenced Blunden's attitude to the support and befriending of women in difficult personal circumstances. A similar pattern is clear in his relationship with Aki Hayashi. In the following passage we may see one of Blunden's ideal patterns of love, where he expresses great admiration for Charles Lamb's lifelong commitment to his sister.

> But the event which was to shape his life most of all was now near. One day in September 1796, his sister Mary, in a fit of insanity, killed her mother. Lamb, intensely agonized, for a time declared himself to have passed beyond poetry and such former enthusiasm. Mary was taken to an asylum; but Charles determined that she should not remain there. His comfortably situated brother John did nothing; Charles, with his narrow income, arranged with the authorities that he would take Mary under his care for life. So it happened; so Charles and Mary Lamb stand in our literature as an inimitable collaboration of brother and sister.[8]

A Wanderer in Japan is specially written for Japanese readers, and Blunden must have been well aware of this; but his previous book, *The Mind's Eye*, reveals much more candid opinions on the traits of the Japanese mind. For instance, Blunden observes:

> Mr Laurence Binyon will have done much of his expedition to

reveal our own paintings to the Japanese, whose habit of mind is to credit to each nation a monopoly of one form of achievement.

For, if I read aright, there is firmly rooted in the Japanese character a belief in the beauty of vagueness, and, arising out of that, a cherished formula that Japan has a spiritual secret so fine and rare as to be quite incommunicable to people of any other blood. Or it may be a still more primitive proposition than that; namely, that Japan must seem to be hiding something from the world. To be understood – to be degraded?[9] The 'wrapt in mystery' strain becomes a little monotonous at times. . . . Even at the Imperial University one is aware of this doleful esotericism in small matters such as the division of duties, or selection of books for a reference shelf, or a colleague's intentions for next year's course. Indeed in education vagueness goes so far that many students, encouraged by tradition, lodge themselves behind some dark term like 'aesthetics' or 'psychology' and live there illustriously but ignorantly ever after.[10] But no matter how ill-drawn and spiritless a hanging picture may be, the Japanese still retain some faith in its having a 'mystery', while usually they ignore the bright curious secrets of style and pattern, even of interpretation of nature, found in hundreds of colour-prints.

I often wonder whether the strong retention of the Chinese-Japanese writing characters, of which nobody seems able to give the number of thousands, is not due finally to the same creed of the superiority of the incomprehensible.[11]

Indeed, 'the creed of the superiority of the incomprehensible' exists in Japan, and that is the chief reason why Blunden has been so idolised there. The students at Tokyo Imperial University were immensely impressed by his courteous politeness and conscientious teaching as a foreign teacher. This might be quite common in England, but in Japan teachers were supposed to be strict, arrogant and a firm symbol of absolute authority. Blunden's pupils never changed their respectful image of him, and rather enjoyed creating around him an aura of near-sacred untouchability. In Japan the ultimate ideal is always one and single. Japanese single-mindedness is such that if a person, especially a famous foreigner, is revered as extremely personable and deferential, his image tends to become inviolable. Such values do not change by reasoning but according to an intuitive sense of incomprehensible worth. Inevitably but very ironically, Blunden has been enshrined in the 'superiority of the incomprehensible', though he himself criticised its enigma and extravagance.

A student of Blunden and also of Dr Saito who later became a Professor of English Literature at Tokyo University, the late Yoshio Nakano, attacked my article on Blunden and Aki (*The Times Literary Supplement*, 30 October 1981) in his review in the *Rising Generation* (May 1982) published by Kenkyusha. The emotions behind his review clearly indicate that many Japanese students or friends of Blunden still tend to prefer to 'put him on a pedestal' and are unable to perceive the true personality behind his gentle mask. These students are both jealous of and annoyed at a fairly unknown woman writer challenging their innocently and proudly held opinions of their idol/teacher.

On the other hand, a younger scholar of Tokyo University, Dr H. Yamanouchi, wrote a favourable review of my article in the same journal of March 1982. He summarised my description of Blunden's relationship with Aki objectively, and expressed appreciation of my contribution to the journal.

Thus the narrative ends: one of the closest human relationships in Anglo-Japanese history. Blunden seemed to take advantage of Aki by relying upon his natural charm, like children who knew how to appeal to their parents. Aki herself was a victim of Japanese education and culture. On the one hand she was struggling with her own ego awakened by her 'Western' and Christian education, and on the other trapped by the traditional concept and training of the Japanese woman which limited her idea of love and marriage, even when her partner was a Western man. For her, the physical ties born out of her relationship with Blunden could never be regarded as a casual love, but bound her to the man over the rest of her life, and that was the reason why she dedicated her love, service and everything to Blunden so faithfully. Above all, the human ties in Japanese society were, and still are, very strong, and a life-long commitment – represented by the word *giri* – binds people tightly. Aki tried to sustain her pride and sense of self-respect and independence in the belief that she had been helping a famous literary man with his valuable work. She stayed isolated, having hardly any friends apart from Blunden and his family, because she never became assimilated into English society, nor was the latter opened up to her.

The only revenge Aki managed to inflict upon Blunden seems to have been to ask him to send her wages promptly; and if he delayed – which in fact repeatedly occurred – she reminded him of it persistently! At the end of her life she had managed to save about £2000 which – ironically – was all returned to Blunden by the instructions in her will. Behind her persistence there was Aki's mother's constant advice to her that since she was single she should save as much money as possible in order to cover the cost of any crisis or contingency. Many of her letters to Aki which survive, show that she worried about her daughter's unstable future, but she paid due tribute to Blunden by calling him 'sensei-professor'. It is not certain how much she knew about Aki's relationship with him – she might have imagined that her daughter had been helping the professor to translate the *Tale of Genji* into English (her younger brother's reminiscences suggest this).

How would a British woman have reacted in Aki's situation? On hearing about my research topic, various reactions were expressed by such women. Mostly they showed sympathy for Aki and indignation against Blunden who had virtually 'ruined' her life. Many British women wondered why Aki had not returned to Japan when Blunden made a second marriage to Sylva Norman. To them it seemed humiliating to be tied to a man who beguiled a woman in this way and betrayed his promises.

On the other hand, most of the Japanese women who heard this story *understood* Aki's devotion, self-sacrifice and readiness for humiliation. They labelled such dedication as typical of a 'woman of the Meiji Era', trained to sacrifice herself and everything for the sake of her husband and family, even if they did not deserve it! The younger generation of Japanese women know, of course, that they are in a different situation from Aki, and will no longer tolerate such a life-style. They have been trained by the ideas of democracy and liberalisation of the post-Second World War period to Westernisation and increasing equality and individualism. They firmly believe that man and woman should stand equal in every respect.

The living standards of Japan are far higher now than in Aki's time in the 1920s, and life there is consequently much more interesting and meaningful for Japanese women. Furthermore, the cultural interchanges between England and Japan are extremely active, and the distance between the two seems to be shorter, thanks to developments in the media and technology. Younger Japanese women also feel pity for Aki's life and for the results of her 'blind' love. At the same time, they admire her for living with such an impossibly 'sacrificial' love: after all, for Aki it was her *own* way of fulfilling her love and life, as a married woman would attain fulfilment with children and the routines of marital life. They also understand the guilt, shame and disappointment that Aki experienced in her relationship with Blunden, and comprehend that she dared not return to Japan because she was not married to Blunden, which was the only way in which she could have 'saved face'.

Even the 'Hiroshima maidens' of today are reluctant to blame anyone for their plight, but prefer to live quietly to hide the shame of their appearance. Aki hid her shame too, but it seems fitting now to record her strange story, and so redeem her memory in the world.

Notes

1. Edmund Blunden, *A Wanderer in Japan: Sketches and Reflections, in Prose and Verse* (Tokyo: Asahi-shimbun-sha, 1950) p. 22 (Japanese translation by Shigeru Toyama).
2. Ibid., pp. 22–3.
3. Ibid., p. 66.
4. Ibid., p. 10.
5. Ibid., pp. 11–12.
6. Ibid., p. 13.
7. Ibid., p. 15.
8. Edmund Blunden, *Essayist of the Romantic Period*, edited with notes by Ichiro Nishizaki (Tokyo: Kodokwan Press, 1952) pp. 49–50.
9. Has Blunden realised that this is another manifestation of the 'Children of Heaven' complex?
10. Compared with such vagueness, Aki's responses to Blunden must have struck him as much more direct – nearer and appealing to his English sense of what was blunt and simple.
11. Edmund Blunden, *The Mind's Eye* (London: Jonathan Cape, 1934) pp. 95, 135–7.

Appendix: Chronology of Aki Hayashi's Work for Edmund Blunden

(a) AKI'S WORK FOR BLUNDEN

Aki did a considerable amount of work for Blunden in the British Museum, which included some discoveries of previously unknown literary material; for example, about Coleridge (17 April 1930), a letter from Woodhouse to Clare (27 June 1931), an unknown Shelley article (16 June 1934), an article on Leigh Hunt in *True Sun* (21 June 1934) and some of Shelley's papers (24 June 1934).

During the War, the British Museum was closed and Aki was saddened that she could do hardly any work for Blunden (13 September 1940). 'No work possible at B. M.' (6 January 1940), 'B. M. out of order' (13 December 1941); she had 'no work for' Blunden (3 and 12 January 1943). She was then able to copy sonnets of Charles Lloyd (11 February 1943), but after that again there was no work for Aki (16 February 1944). It was June 1945 before her really substantial work started again when she began hunting for Shelley's articles (29 June 1945).

While Blunden was in Japan, Aki sent him Coleridge letters (20 February 1948); and work on Coleridge again and Lamb (7 May 1948). Blunden found the Coleridge articles from Aki useful (9 and 13 October 1950). Aki also discovered Boyer's 'Album' (25 April 1952).

Blunden thought about Aki during his Hong Kong absence (4 March 1953). Aki copied Latin and Greek quotations accurately and well (28 April 1953). She copied John Clare's poems (8 March 1954), reported on Clare's death (17 June 1956), and found Milton's poems annotated by Lamb in the British Museum (14 May 1958).

Blunden suggested to Aki that she should write about 'Blunden at Hongo' (during 1924–7) for *Today's Japan* (29 November 1959), and accordingly she sent them her 'Reminiscences' (28 January 1960).

(b) AKI'S WORK FOR BLUNDEN ON LEIGH HUNT

Blunden's biography of Leigh Hunt (*Leigh Hunt: A Biography* [Hamden, Conn.: Archon Books, 1970; originally published 1930]) is written in descriptive narrative style, full of quotations from the original books of Hunt and his friends – Shelley, Keats, Lamb, Byron, etc. Blunden himself was aware of this tendency to quote rather often, and was apologetic about it: '"It wants," he wrote in his preface, making me run the risk of quoting him too often, "the crust of the old barks . . ."' (p. 151). In this circumstance Aki's assistance in copying out pieces from these authors must have been invaluable. The following is a list made by Blunden of the excerpts from Leigh Hunt's work which she copied for him.

Leigh Hunt

Monthly Mirror, 1810, April. Memoir by himself
St James's Magazine, 1875, vol. 14 p. 387 L. H. and Chas Ollier
People's Journal, 1846, pp. 268–270 L. H., by Mary Howitt
Grundy, Francis H. 'Pictures of the Past' 1879
L. H. and his Family pp. 162–170
Pitman, J. R. 'Excerpta ex variis Romanis Poetis'. 1808
Thomas, Capt. G. P. 'Poems'. 1847
verses to L. H. or his family
Whiting, Sydney 'Literary Melange.' 1847.
Jerrold, Douglas Life of
Hunt, Leigh 'Religion of the Heart.' 1854. [There is a special copy, marked by L. H. for 2nd edition. *Alterations and additions*.] Any other marked books by L. H. in the Catalogue, for example 'Ju-Kiao-Li', a Chinese novel.
Gentleman's Magazine
John Keats House Hampstead. *South Kensington Museum*
Buy a Catalogue *Dyce & Forster Collection.*
Ask about L. Hunt items, & if anything good may you take a note?
Leigh Hunt items. Presentation copies &c.

Guildhall Library
Leigh Hunt cat.
1846. Obituary notice of John Hunt, L. H.'s brother
1873 d^o^ d^o^ of Thornton L. Hunt, L. H.'s son

B.M.

L. Hunt in *Mrs E. B. Browning's Letters to R. H. Horne* 2 vols.

L. Hunt in Life of Chas Mathews by Mrs M. (actor) 4 vols.

[Same book, C. Lamb: copy *personal details.*]

Gent. Mag. 1838. C. V. Le Grice, – on Lamb. ⎤ copy
and ? 1851 d.º d.º a Sonnet. ⎦ all

Aki wrote in her diary:

> On Oct. 16/30 I started to copy all the publications of L. Hunt and T. Hunt on a special notebook, and finished it on 18 October and straightway I sent the notebook to E. These were 168 publications of L. H. & 10 of Thornton H.

One of the most striking character-sketches in this mediocre biography is of Hunt's mischievous son, John Hunt, who was the 'black sheep' of the family:

> Presently Brown moved from this 'pleasant lair' into Florence, and he appears to have taken with him, in an optimistic firmness, one of Leigh Hunt's troubles, as yet not come to full size but quite active – the urchin John Hunt Junr. Of this boy's psychological abnormality – a collection of brilliance, good-nature, savage temper and criminal subtlety – Thornton Hunt gives some account. In childhood 'he attacked his brothers with knives' more than once, and 'in order to extort some indulgence from his mother, whose state of health has already been mentioned, he held the carving knife over the soft part of the head of an infant brother'. (p. 209)

Aki found it difficult to decipher the handwriting of this John (or perhaps it was Leigh Hunt's brother John).

> Thank you for the John Hunt letter &c., which I think most valuable. . . . I could easily correct the errors in yr copy of

J. Hunt's puzzling hand: e.g. 'Mr Waylott' is Mr Hazlitt. The whole letter is just what I wanted.

(28 April 1928)

This biography seems to show some of the limitations of Blunden's ability as a literary critic and biographer – a lack of sharp observation and dry analysis of human character with less comprehension of philosophical ideas – he is so sympathetic toward Leigh Hunt and his friends, always prepared to defend them. (Blunden himself admits his distaste for abstraction: 'Metaphysicians are a trying kind of men' (p. 348).)

> Here we see in a sharp light the worse or weaker side of Hunt's personality, and the foppery that we regret in Hunt's writings is marked out in indelible black by an intense observer. The only objection to be made, since Hunt's natural predominance of fine qualities reasserted itself with Keats and must arise from his biography without rhetorical cultivation, is that Hunt was not given the chance to know what Keats was feeling towards him. (p. 143)

Yet, on the other hand, much has been revealed of Blunden's own personality through his accounts and descriptions of Leigh Hunt. For instance, Hunt was one of the Christ's Hospital band (p. 16) like Blunden, and both of them were keen advocates of liberal thinking. Hunt's *The Examiner* was described by Blunden as a 'keen instrument of liberty' (p. 81) and was strongly supported by Shelley and Hazlitt. The group then aspired to 'flexibility of style in verse' (p. 102), challenging Pope's metrical tyranny. They also popularised the use of the 'heroic couplet', and supported Keats's sensuality which was still regarded as 'foreign' by the public. Even Cardinal Wiseman attacked Keats's *Endymion* as blasphemy – the admiration of 'Nature' rather than the creator – omitting God, unlike Dante in his work (p. 335). In answer to this criticism Leigh Hunt defended Keats's work as 'affectionate and warm'.

Blunden and Hunt had some important similarities in other matters. Like Blunden's, Hunt's hand-writing was 'as beautiful as Tennyson's' (p. 333), and according to Nathaniel Hawthorne, 'he (Hunt) desired sympathy as a flower seeks sunshine' (p. 325) which may strike echoes in Blunden's own character. Also both men were attractive to women; and as Hawthorne said about Hunt, 'Women are the fit ministers at such a shrine.'

> 'Leigh Hunt loved dearly to be praised. . . . he never had been conscious of anything wonderful in his own person. And then he smiled, making himself and all the little parlour about him beautiful thereby. . . . Women are the fit ministers at such a shrine. (p. 325)

(c) CHRONOLOGICAL LIST OF WORK DONE BY AKI FOR BLUNDEN BETWEEN 1925 AND 1961

1925	29 August	'I need a secretary'.
	31 August	'We begin the secretaryship'.
	3 September	The plan to take Aki to England.
	5 September	Aki appointed secretary.
	7 September	A book on *Ukiyo-ye* [Japanese painting].
	13 October	Work in the British Museum.
1926	7 January	Sorting letters.
		Copying poems.
	24 March	Transcribing Keats.
1927	4 October	Copying from 'The Indicator'.
	5 October	Hopkins's list of Japanese libraries.
	18 October	Work for Mrs Murray for half a day to make savings.
	28 October	Copying Clare poems.
	1 November	Notes about University in Japan.
		Letter in Japanese from Kodokhan.
	15 November	Making a copy of the Essays.
1928	4 February	Leigh Hunt's memoirs.
		Bloomfield extracts.
	18 February	Copies of Leigh Hunt (Hunt's life).
	19 March	Leigh Hunt copies.
	27 March	Hunt's life.
	3 April	Old newspapers.

	21 April	All day in British Museum.
	5 May	Copying letters.
1929	29 April	Visa application: literary assistant.
	13 May	Cashes a cheque.
	26 August	Visa renewed by Home Office.
	3 November	Cashes a cheque for travel.
		Work on Coleridge manuscripts.
	11 November	British Museum search.
	8 December	Meet Blunden at British Museum.
		Work on Coleridge in Manuscript Room.
1930	6 February	Coleridge notebook.
		Proofs of Leigh Hunt.
	1 March	Check dates in British Museum.
	17 April	Discoveries at British Museum about Coleridge.
	14 June	Completion of Leigh Hunt and heavier work later.
	21 June	Transcript of manuscript; buy a typewriter.
		Clare's autobiography to be published.
	4 July	Editor will pay £8.00 for copy of it.
		Aki has to send Kubota's article regularly.
	6 September	Oxford 'Keats' made ready.
	2 October	Mark Keats for differences from original edition.
	20 October	Leigh Hunt queries.
	30 December	'Aki my literary assistant since 1925 in Japan and England'.
1931	9 January, 23 January	Blunden's need for a *TLS* study on Charles Churchill.
	31 January	Notes on Churchill helpful.
	2 March	Notes for Keats and Lamb.
	9 March	Work at British Museum continues.
	31 March	Work at Defoe's poems.
	15 May	Article sought about C. Lamb.
	4 June	Copying article on Shelley.
	18 June	Copying Leigh Hunt's poems.

	27 June	Discovery of letter from Woodhouse to Clare.
	2 July	Letters to J. Clare.
	10 July	Obituary notices of literary figures from *Gentleman's Magazine*.
	12 July	Keats's friends.
	14 July	Obituary notices from *Gentleman's Magazine* on Bailey – on Lamb.
	23 August	Examine *Morning Journal*.
	3 September	Copying a criminal report for Sassoon. C. Lamb's reviews.
	10 September	Copying the names of Christ's Hospital worthies.
	15 October	Work finished for Sassoon.
	21 October	Not paid by Sassoon.
1932	5 January	British Museum about or by Geo. Crabbe.
	3 February	Copying Blunden's lectures.
	8 September	At British Museum, Froissart memoirs.
	11 October	Gather poems for literary history.
	18 October	Southey's third volume. Poems for literary history.
1933	12 January	'Aki must make index of Lamb's book'.
	19 January	Index finished.
	25 January	Have Blunden's shoes repaired. Look for sonnet in old magazine.
	1 February	Shoes repaired.
	14 February	Medicine bought.
	19 March	Copying Lamb's work in Hazlitt, *Annual Biography*.
	29 March	Looking for material on Lamb.
	12 April	Sent Lamb's material to Blunden. Must look for more in *The Task*.
	22 April	Work on Lamb.
	24 May	Aki keeps hat for Blunden.
	21 August 28 August 2 September 7 September	Look for Hogg's material.
	17 September	Work on Taylor and Heney.

	20 September	Hogg in *Monthly Chronicle*.
	30 September	Taylor letters and Hogg.
	5 October	Start of work about Clare.
	13 October	Letter from Leigh Hunt.
		Hessey's letter.
		Two *London Magazines*.
	16 October	Letters to Clare.
1934	16 January	Lamb's proof reading.
		Works of Thomas Wade.
	31 January	Coleridge–Lamb relationship.
	2 February 4 February	To send Annual notice on Lamb.
	8 February	Leigh Hunt on Shelley.
	18 February	Plans articles on Coleridge: all notices about his death.
	21 February	Poem on Coleridge found.
	27 February	Conversation between Coleridge and Kenyon.
	10 April	To enroll at Ashridge, weekend course.
	12 April	Leigh Hunt material.
	18 April	Material about Lamb.
	25 April	Gutch and Lamb material.
	30 April	Notes on Ainsworth
	22 May 4 June	Taylor letters to Clare
		Copying from *True Sun* [early nineteenth-century magazine].
	16 June	Found an unknown Shelley article.
	21 June	Discover pieces by Leigh Hunt in *True Sun*.
	24 June	Discover some of Shelley's papers.
	6 July	Details about Coleridge.
		To buy Phyllis Coleridge pamphlet.
	19 August	Notes on Shelley and Hunt.
	9 September	Work at Manuscript Room of British Museum about Shelley.
	7 October	Obituary notice of Charles Lamb.
		M. Shelley's letters.
	3 November	Shelley's letters.

1935	12 February	Stead (publisher) asks for references on Southwell.
	16 April	Southwell references.
	26 April	Copying poems for literary history.
	20 May	Look for Southwell petition.
	30 May	Excerpts of De Quincey.
	8 July	Aki 'sometimes hires a typewriter'.
	19 July 23 July	Work at British Museum.
	1 August	References at British Museum (Collins).
	2 October 13 October	References in *True Sun* about Leigh Hunt.
		Work on Taylor, Hessey.
	10 November	Hessey's transcripts.
	25 November	Pictures of Taylor.
	12 December	Work on Taylor.
1936	8 January 23 January	Work on Shelley.
	10 February	Letters from De Quincey to Taylor.
	22 February	Coryll papers.
	13 April	Publications list of Hommers.
	27 April	Copying Moore's memoirs
	5 June	Shelley in *Oxford Magazine*.
	17 July	On Shelley in *London Weekly Review*.
	23 August	Index on Keats 'under Blunden's eyes'.
	29 August	Various notices on authors.
1937	12 June	Aki 'must check references' to Kensington Museum.
1938	14 February	Copying articles by Hunt on Pickering.
	10 December	British Museum manuscripts.
1939	16 January 26 January	To look through old magazines.
	3 April	Material on Shelley.
	21 July	On Coleridge.
	13 September	British Museum closed.
	20 September	Leigh Hunt's material; still at British Museum.

	18 October 3 December	To look for Hardy's material.
1940	6 January	No work possible at British Museum.
	24 February 13 April 12 May 9 July	All work on Hardy
1941	3 March	British Museum work.
	13 December	British Museum 'out of order'.
1942	16 April	Material about Keats in British Museum.
1943	3 January 12 January	Aki has no work for Blunden.
	11 February	Copying sonnets of Charles Lloyd.
1944	16 February	No work for Aki.
1945	29 June	Hunting for Shelley's articles.
	19 November	Works on John Bramsen. Shelley and Keats.
1946	17 April	Shelley work in local newspapers.
1947	4 February	Works on the difficult manuscript diary.
	18 August 26 August	Shelley work at British Museum.
	28 November	Help on Coleridge manuscript.
	4 December	Coleridge work.
1948	20 February	Sends Coleridge letters to Blunden in Tokyo.
	7 May	Sends Coleridge and Lamb work to Blunden.
	9 June	Work on Shelley at British Museum.
	24 June	Work at British Museum.
	9 August	Writes for *Eigo Seinen* (The Rising Generation). Work on Shelley.

	7 September	Aki's article published in *Eigo Seinen*.
	16 November	Coleridge material.
1949	14 February	Work in British Museum on Coleridge.
	4 May	Extracts from Edmund Oliver.
	25 June	Work on Lamb and Coleridge.
	12 November	Work at British Museum.
1950	22 July 16 August	Manuscript of James Thomson.
	9 October 13 October	Coleridge article – useful.
1951	10 January	Articles in the *British Critic* on Coleridge, Shelley, etc.
	27 January	Diary of Danvers. Entries on Coleridge.
	19 March	Explore the *Court Journal* 1830 for Shelley.
	3 September 19 September	Explore *Stamford Mercury* about John Clare and John Keats.
	5 November	Look in *Morning Chronicle* for Lamb.
1952	16 January	*Brighton Herald* to study.
	12 March 17 March	Much to do about Le Grice.
	25 April	Discovery of Boyer's 'Album'.
1953	4 March	Blunden thinks about Aki during his Hong Kong absence.
	2 April	Copying Coleridge essays.
	28 April	Good copy of Latin and Greek quotations.
	21 August	Work at British Museum on Leigh Hunt.
	22 September	Work at British Museum on Montgomery, Sotheby.
	7 October	Sotheby – Robinson.
	8 November	Look in British Museum for John Sterling.
	4 December	Books by Arthur Brooke.
	26 December	William Cole at British Museum.
1954	8 March	John Clare's poems.
	15 June	Material on Clare.

	24 June	Poems by Duncan or Pentycross.
	29 August	List of works by nineteenth-century writers.
	10 September	About engravings by Blake.
	28 September	All about Le Grice's poems.
	20 December	Material on Keats or Shelley in British Museum.
1955	1 January	List of works by Sewell (1726).
	21 January	Leigh Hunt's novel.
	15 February	Books of Thomas Crosby.
	26 April	Book on Farrer.
	25 May	Material on Bellasis and Hamilton. Material on Le Grice.
	7 July	William Wales, Harris.
	29 August	About Lewis Hind and Gilly.
	23 September	Dyer's autobiography.
	28 September	Paul Wright, Collins.
	21 October	Dyer's autobiography.
	3 December	John Upton.
1956	24 February	William Dodd.
	16 April	Brydges.
	19 May	Dodd poems.
	17 June	Report on Clare's death.
	28 September	Mathilda Betham.
	3 November	Mathilda Betham and Lamb.
1957	21 January	Looking for poems by Loveling and Gilbert.
	9 February	Call at Christ's Hospital offices.
1958	31 January	Dyer's letters.
	10 February	Milton's poems annotated by Lamb.
	17/25 November	Thomas Maurice.
1959	29 March	Dalmon/Dilke materials in British Museum. Other writers.
	23 April	Material on White.
	19 August	Material on Webbe and Smith.

	25 October	Material about Bowring.
	31 October	Jeremy Taylor
	29 November	Writing about Blunden at Hongo for *Today's Japan*.
		Material on Ayres.
	28 December	Material on Billingsley.
1960	28 January	Aki sends her 'Reminiscences'.
	8 February	Material on Sir Frances Hubert.
	10 April	Seventeenth-century poets, Sherburne.
	17 April	Material on Procter.
	28 June	Material on Procter, *Ann Collins*.
	12 December	Material on Claris ('Arthur Brooke').
1961	3 March	Material on Arthur Brooke.
	17 September	Material on Thomas Vaughan.

There are in addition eleven exercise books still in existence containing Aki's careful copies of quotations from *Henry White's Diary* (two exercise books) and *The Garden Kalendar* by Gilbert White (nine exercise books). She also copied out three notebooks which she entitled *Mary Leapor's Poems*, II, III, IV, for Blunden. All of these are in the possession of Mrs Claire Blunden.

Bibliography

NOTE: Only major books and articles in English are included in this bibliography. Place of publication is London, unless otherwise stated.

UNPUBLISHED SOURCES

Probate of Wills, Somerset House

An entry of death of Aki Hayashi, 14 December 1962, at 6 Worsley Road, Hampstead.
An entry of death of Edmund Charles Blunden, 20 January 1974, at Hall Mill, Long Melford.
Will of Aki Hayashi.
Will of Edmund Blunden.

Merton College Library, Oxford

A letter from Blunden to N. H. Gibbs, 6 October 1943 (D.1.41A).
A letter from Blunden to Roger Highfield, the Librarian, Merton College, Oxford, 22 April 1963 (D.1.41).
'HRH The Duke of Windsor in 1936' (Blunden's verse) (E.2.30).
Moore, Sir John Henry, *Poetical Trifles* (1778); this book was given to the Merton College Library by Blunden.

The Humanities Research Center, Texas University, Austin

TL Hayashi Jiro to Edmund Blunden, 1963.
8 ALS, 1 TLS Hayashi Shigeru to Edmund Blunden, 1949–56. Enclosed with ALS (27 February 1956) 3 poems AmsS (1 p. each), 1955–6.
4 AL/copies Blunden to Hayashi Shigeru, 1939–52.
Hayashi, Shigeru, *Endless Wandering: A Selection of Verses*, Ams/notebook S (68 pp.).
87 ALS, 30 ALI, 2 ANS, 1 ANI, 4 APCS, 15 ACPI Aki Hayashi to Blunden, 1927–62 (17 n.d., 17 inc. d.).
Hayashi, Aki, excerpts from diary, n.d. Ams/Copies (7 pp.).

Hayashi, Aki, a visit to Elia's grave. Ams/draft 1 (6 pp. on back of *Endless Wandering* folder); Ams/draft (4 pp.); Tccms (2 pp.).
2 ALS Aki Hayashi to Claire Blunden, 1950, 1955.

Christ's Hospital Library, Horsham

(a) Blunden edited *The Blue* from October 1914 to July 1915. Volume XLII (pp. 90–3) contains a review of *Poems by ECB* by a fellow Grecian. Volume LXII (p. 81) contains an account of the Christmas Concert of 1915, which included a Japanese Song and March.
(b) Grecians' Reading Society Minutes Book: May 1913–July 1915.

(i) Blunden read a paper on *John Masefield's Poetry* on 14 December 1913.
(ii) Blunden became Honorary Secretary in July 1914. (Therefore it would become his duty to write the minutes from that date?)
(iii) 'The discovery of a hitherto unsuspected dramatic talent in Blunden' recorded in minutes for 4 October 1914 (reading of Goldsmith's *Good-Natured Man*).
(iv) Minutes on a talk by Blunden about Coleridge, 31 January 1914(5?).

(c) Manuscript Notebook, *John Masefield*, a paper read to the Grecians' Reading Society, Christ's Hospital, 14 December 1913.
(d) Fragments of Blunden's correspondence:

(i) To Mrs Rheam;
(ii) To H. S. Goodwin (his old Housemaster) and others in the 1920s;
(iii) To A. C. W. Edwards, master at C. H., mostly after the 1939–45 War.

(e) Copy of *Poems 1913 and 14*, inscribed by Blunden to Mrs Rheam, 1915.
(f) Copy of *Nature in Literature*, inscribed by Blunden to Mr and Mrs H. S. Goodwin, 1929.
(g) Copy of *The Outlook*, July 1921, with a Blunden contribution.
(h) Two folders of Blunden fragments (newspaper cuttings, etc.).
(i) The Christ's Hospital Papers II: proofs of an edition of unpublished Blunden poems in the Christ's Hospital Archives.

(j) Blunden's poems in manuscript: with the Archivist, N. M. Plumley.

PRIMARY SOURCES

Selections

Edmund Blunden: A Selection of His Poetry and Prose, made by Kenneth Hopkins (1950).

Edmund Blunden: Selected Poems, edited by Robyn Marsack (Manchester, 1982).

Blunden's Books and Pamphlets

Poems, 1913 and 1914 (Horsham, 1914).

Poems, Translated from the French, July 1913 to January 1914 (Horsham, 1914).

The Barn, With Certain Other Poems (Uckfield, 1916).

Three Poems (Uckfield, 1916). Contains 'The Silver Bird of Herndyke Mill', 'Stane Street', 'The Gods of the World Beneath'.

The Harbingers: Poems (Uckfield, 1916).

Pastorals: A Book of Verses (1916).

The Waggoner, and Other Poems (1920).

The Appreciation of Literary Prose: Being One of the Special Courses of the Art of Life (1921).

The Shepherd, and Other Poems of Peace and War (1922).

Old Homes: A Poem (Clare, 1922).

The Bonadventure: A Random Journal of an Atlantic Holiday (1922).

Dead Letters (1923).

To Nature: New Poems (1923).

Christ's Hospital: A Retrospect (1923).

The Doomed Oak, From the French of Anatole France (1925).

Masks of Time: A New Collection of Poems, Principally Meditative (1925).

The Augustan Books of Modern Poetry (1925).

Far East (Tokyo, 1925).

English Poems (1926).

More Footnotes to Literary History (Tokyo, 1926; repr. 1950).

On the Poems of Henry Vaughan: Characteristics and Intimations: With his Principal Latin Poems Carefully Translated into English Verse (1927).

Lectures in English Literature (Tokyo, 1927; 1952, enlarged).
Retreat (1928).
Japanese Garland (1928).
Winter Nights: A Reminiscence (1928). (No. 17 of the Ariel Poems.)
Undertones of War (1928; 1930 [rev.]; 1956 in *The World's Classics*, vol. 553; 1964 [with new introd.]).
Nature in English Literature (1929). (Hogarth Lectures on Literature, no. 9.)
Shakespeare's Significances: A paper read before the Shakespeare Association (1929; 1934, 1936 [repr.]).
Near and Far: New Poems (1929).
Leigh Hunt: A Biography (1930; repr. 1970).
De Bello Germanico: A Fragment of Trench History, Written in 1918 by the Author of 'Undertones of War' (Hawstead, 1930).
A Summer's Fancy (1930).
The Poems of Edmund Blunden (1930).
A Poet on the Oxford Poets (1930).
Keats's Letters, 1931; marginalia by Edmund Blunden (Tokyo, 1931). (From *Studies in English Literature*, vol. XI, no. 4, October 1931.)
Votive Tablets: Studies Chiefly Appreciative of English Authors and Books (1931). 39 essays reprinted with some adjustment from *The Times Literary Supplement* and *The Times*.
To Themis: Poems on Famous Trials; with Other Pieces (1931).
Constantia and Francis: An Autumn Evening (Edinburgh, 1931).
In Summer: The Rotunda of the Bishop of Derry (1931).
The Face of England, in a Series of Occasional Sketches (1932). Essays and 8 poems, with introduction and notes by G. S. I. Kishimoto; Japanese edition in English (Tokyo, 1938).
Fall in, Ghosts: An Essay on a Battalion Reunion (1932).
Halfway House: A Miscellany of New Poems (1932).
We'll Shift Our Ground: or Two on a Tour, almost a Novel; with Sylva Norman (1933).
Charles Lamb and his Contemporaries (Cambridge, 1933). (Clark Lectures.)
The Mind's Eye: Essays (1934). Contains pt 1, 'Flanders'; pt 2, 'Japan'; pt 3, 'England'; pt 4, 'The World of Books'.
Choice or Chance: New Poems (1934).
Edward Gibbon and his Age (Bristol, 1935). (Arthur Skemp Memorial Lecture.)
A Northamptonshire Poetess: Mary Leapor (Northampton, 1936).

Keats's Publisher: A Memoir of John Taylor, 1781–1864 (1936).
Verses to HRH The Duke of Windsor (Oxford, 1936 for 1937; repr. 1950).
An Elegy, and Other Poems (1937).
On Several Occasions, By 'A Fellow of Merton College' (1939).
Poems, 1930–1940 (1940 for 1941).
English Villages (1941). (Britain in Pictures.)
Thomas Hardy (1941 for 1942).
Leigh Hunt's Eldest Son (1942). (Read before the Royal Society of Literature on 29 October 1941.)
Romantic Poetry and the Fine Arts (1942). (Warton Lecture on English Poetry.)
Cricket Country (1944).
Shells by a Stream: New Poems (1944).
Shelley: A Life Story (1946).
Shakespeare to Hardy: Short Studies of Characteristic English Authors (Tokyo, 1948).
Two Lectures on English Literature (Osaka, 1948). Contains 4 poems.
After the Bombing, and Other Short Poems (1949).
Addresses on General Subjects connected with English Literature (Tokyo, 1949).
Sons of Light: A Series of Lectures on English Writers (Tokyo, 1949).
Poetry and Science, and Other Lectures (Osaka, 1949).
Hamlet, and Other Studies (Tokyo, 1950).
Eastward: A Selection of Verses Original and Translated (Tokyo, 1950).
College Song, For Tokyo Joshi Daigaku (Tokyo, 1950).
Influential Books: Lectures given at Waseda University in 1948 and 1949 (Tokyo, 1950).
Favourite Studies in English Literature: Lectures given at Keio University in 1948 and 1950 (Tokyo, 1950).
A Wanderer in Japan: Sketches and Reflections in Prose and Verse (Tokyo, 1950; 1951 without Japanese translation).
Some Women Writers: Three Lectures given at Tokyo Woman's Christian College, 1949 (Tokyo, 1950).
Reprinted Papers, Partly concerning Some English Romantic Poets, with a few Postscripts (Tokyo, 1950).
Records of Friendship: Occasional and Epistolary Poems Written during Visits to Kyushu (Fukuoka, 1950).
John Keats (1950, 1954; rev. edn 1959). (British Council Pamphlet.)
Chaucer to 'B. V.'; with an Additional Paper on Herman Melville: A Selection of Lectures given chiefly at Tokyo University (Tokyo, 1950).

Sketches and Reflections: with notes by S. Tomiyama (Tokyo, 1951). (*Today and Tomorrow Series*, vol. 2.)

Essayists of The Romantic Period, ed. Ichiro Nishizaki (Tokyo, 1952).

The Dede of Pittie: Dramatic Scenes Reflecting the History of Christ's Hospital and Offered in Celebration of the Quatercentenary 1953, at the Fortune Theatre (1953).

Charles Lamb (1954; rev. edn 1964). (British Council Pamphlet.)

Poems of Many Years (1957).

War Poets, 1914–1918 (1958; rev. edn 1964). (British Council Pamphlet.)

Three Young Poets: Critical Sketches of Byron, Shelley and Keats (Tokyo, 1959).

A Wessex Worthy: Thomas Russell (Beaminster, 1960).

English Scientists as Men of Letters (Hong Kong, 1961). (Jubilee Congress Lecture, University of Hong Kong.)

A Hong Kong House: Poems 1951–1961 (1962).

William Crowe, 1745–1829 (Beaminster, 1963).

A Corscombe Inhabitant (Beaminster, 1963).

Guest of Thomas Hardy (Beaminster, 1964).

A Brief Guide to The Great Church of the Holy Trinity, Long Melford (Ipswich, 1965; rev. edn 1966).

Eleven Poems (Cambridge, 1965 for 1966).

A Selection of The Shorter Poems (Long Melford, 1966).

Poems on Japan, Hitherto Uncollected and Mostly Unprinted, ed. T. Saito (Tokyo, 1967).

A Few Not Quite Forgotten Writers? (1967). The English Association Presidential Address.

The Midnight Skaters: Poems for Young Readers, chosen and introduced by C. Day Lewis (1968).

A Selection from the Poems of Edmund Blunden (Long Melford, 1969).

John Clare: Beginner's Luck (Chatham, 1971).

Some English Women Writers, annotated by Yoshitaka Sakai (Tokyo, 1976).

Blunden's Contributions to Books and Pamphlets

The Oxford and Cambridge Miscellany, ed. Herbert Baxter, Alan Porter, L. de G. Sieveking and Alec MacDonald (1920).

A Queen's College Miscellany (Oxford, 1920).

Poems Chiefly from Manuscript by John Clare, ed. E. Blunden and A. Porter (1920).

Georgian Poetry, 1920–1922 (1922).
A Song to David, with Other Poems, by Christopher Smart, chosen with biographical and critical preface and notes by Edmund Blunden (1924).
The Birth, Life and Death of Scaramouch, by Master Angelo Constantini; trans. C. W. Beaumont, together with Mezzetin's dedicatory Poems and Loret's rhymed News-letters concerning Scaramouch, now first rendered into English Verse by Edmund Blunden (1924).
Madrigals & Chronicles: Being Newly Found Poems Written by John Clare, ed. with a preface and commentary by Edmund Blunden (1924).
Shelley and Keats as They Struck Their Contemporaries: Notes partly from Manuscript Sources, ed. Edmund Blunden (1925).
Bret Harte: Selected Poems, ed. with an introduction and notes by Edmund Blunden and Benjamin Brady (Tokyo, 1926).
The Pyramid, by Sherard Vines, with prefatory verses by Edmund Blunden and Yone Noguchi (1926).
The Actor: A Poem, by Robert Lloyd; to which is prefixed an essay by Edmund Blunden (1926).
A Hundred English Poems from the Elizabethan Age to the Victorian; to which are added specimens of sonnets, ballads, epigrams, etc.; and of the principal American poets, selected by Edmund Blunden, with notes and illustrations (Tokyo, 1927; rev. edn 1949).
Edmund Blunden, His Professorship and His Writings: Appreciations by Some of His Students and Friends (Tokyo, 1927).
Autobiography of Benjamin Robert Haydon, with an introduction by Edmund Blunden (1927). (*World Classics*, vol. 314.)
Leigh Hunt's 'Examiner' Examined: Comprising Some Account of that Celebrated Newspaper's Contents, &c. 1808–25 (1928).
The Autobiography of Leigh Hunt, with an introduction by Edmund Blunden (1928). (*World Classics*, vol. 329.)
The Poems of William Collins, edited with an introductory study by Edmund Blunden (1929).
The Last Essays of Elia, by Charles Lamb, edited with an introduction by Edmund Blunden and notes by Frederick Page (1929).
Keats' View of Poetry, by Takeshi Saito; to which is prefixed an essay on English literature in Japan by Edmund Blunden (1929).
The War, 1914–1918: A Booklist, compiled by Edmund Blunden and others (1930).

A Book of Narrative Verse, compiled by V. H. Collins, with an introduction by Edmund Blunden (1930). (*World Classics*, vol. 350.)

Great Short Stories of the War: England, France, Germany, America, with an introduction by Edmund Blunden (1930).

An Anthology of War Poems, compiled by Frederick Brereton, introduction by Edmund Blunden (1930).

The Poems of Wilfred Owen, with memoir by Edmund Blunden (1931); also reprinted in Owen's *Collected Poems* (1963).

Sketches in the Life of John Clare, Written by Himself, with an introduction, notes and additions by Edmund Blunden (1931).

The Rime of the Ancient Mariner by Samuel Taylor Coleridge, introduction by Edmund Blunden (New York, 1931).

Tragical Consequences, or A Disaster at Deal: being an unpublished letter of William Godwin, preface by Edmund Blunden (1931).

The City of Dreadful Night, and Other Poems, by James Thomson ('B. V.'), with an introduction by Edmund Blunden (1932).

Charles Lamb: His Life Recorded by His Contemporaries, compiled by Edmund Blunden (1934).

Coleridge: Studies by Several Hands on the Hundredth Anniversary of His Death, ed. Edmund Blunden and Earl Leslie Griggs (1934).

The Legacy of England: An Illustrated Survey of the Works of Man in the English Country, with contributions by A. Bell, G. A. Birmingham [i.e. J. O. Hannay], E. Blunden, etc. (1935). (Pilgrim's Library.)

The War of the Guns: Western Front, 1917 and 1918, by Aubrey Wade, with an introduction by Edmund Blunden (1936).

The Immortal Heritage: An Account of the Work and Policy of the Imperial War Graves Commission, 1917–37, by Sir Fabian Arthur Goulstone Ware, with an introduction by Edmund Blunden (Cambridge, 1937).

On Shelley, preface signed E. B., G[avin] de B[eer], and S[ylva] N[orman] (1938).

Poems of This War by Younger Poets, ed. P. Ledward and C. Strong, with an introduction by Edmund Blunden (Cambridge, 1942).

Return to Husbandry: An Annotated List of Books dealing with the History, Philosophy and Craftsmanship of Rural England, and Intended to Suggest Alternatives to Commercialism and Mechanization. With four Preliminary Essays, ed. Edmund Blunden (1943).

Poems, by C. W. Brodribb, with an introduction by Edmund Blunden (1946).

The Life of George Crabbe, by His Son, with an introduction by Edmund Blunden (1947).

St Cecilia's Day Festival Concert (1947).

Hymns for the Amusement of Children, by Christopher Smart, ed. Edmund Blunden (Oxford, 1947). (Luttrell Society Reprint, no. 5.)

Shelley's Defence of Poetry, ed. with introduction and notes by Edmund Blunden (Tokyo, 1948).

Culture Through English, Book II, compiled by the Christian Education Association in Japan (Tokyo, 1948) pp. 49–53: 'An Impression of Thomas Hardy', by Edmund Blunden.

The Christ's Hospital Book, ed. Edmund Blunden (1953).

Selected Poems of Percy Bysshe Shelley, ed. with an introduction and notes by Edmund Blunden (1954).

Poems, by Ivor Gurney, principally selected from unpublished manuscripts, with a memoir by Edmund Blunden (1954).

Selected Poems of John Keats, ed. with an introduction and notes by Edmund Blunden (1955).

The Castle of Indolence, by James Thomson, introduction by Edmund Blunden; ed. with notes by Alec M. Hardie (Hong Kong, 1956).

The Genesis of Wuthering Heights, by Mary Visick, introduction by Edmund Blunden (Hong Kong, 1958).

Selected Poems of Tennyson, ed. with an introduction and notes by Edmund Blunden (1960).

'Homage to Edmund Blunden', *Today's Japan*, vol. 5, no. 3 (March–April 1960) pp. 29–32.

Memoir of Thomas Bewick, Written by Himself, 1822–1828, introduction by Edmund Blunden (1961).

Lee Lan Flies the Dragon Kite, by Ralph Herrmanns, English version by Edmund Blunden (1962). Photographs with text.

Wayside Poems of the Seventeenth and Early Eighteenth Centuries: An Anthology, gathered by Edmund Blunden and B. Mellor, 2 vols (Hong Kong, 1963–4).

The Unending Vigil: A History of the Commonwealth War Graves Commission, 1917–67, by Edmund Blunden and Philip Longworth, with an introduction by Edmund Blunden (1967).

Twelve Poems, by Ralph Hale Mottram, with a dedicatory poem by Edmund Blunden and illustrations by R. Graham (Stoke Ferry, 1968).

Wayside Sonnets, 1750–1850: An Anthology, gathered by Edmund Blunden and B. Mellor (Hong Kong, 1971).

Edmund Blunden: A Tribute from Japan, ed. Masao Hirai and Peter Milward (Tokyo, 1974).

Tribute to Walter de la Mare, by Edmund Blunden and Leonard Clark (1974).

Blunden also edited, with Neville Whymant, all six numbers of *Oriental Literary Times*, published by *Japan Times* (Tokyo, 1925).

Aki Hayashi's Articles

'A Visit to Elia's Grave on 27 May 1948', *The Rising Generation*, vol. 94 (1948) p. 239.

'The St. Matthew's Day Service of Christ's Hopsital', *The Rising Generation*, vol. 94 (1948) p. 359.

SECONDARY SOURCES

Bibliographies

Fung, Sydney S. K. and Grace H. L. Chu, *Edmund Blunden: A Bibliography of Criticism* (Hong Kong, 1983).

Kirkpatrick, B. J., *A Bibliography of Edmund Blunden*, with a Personal Introduction by Rupert Hart-Davis (1979).

Midzunoe, Yuichi, *Edmund Blunden in Japan*, bibliographical documents and 2 unpublished poems (Tokyo, 1981).

Muir, Percy H., *Points, Second Series 1866–1934* (1934).

Saito, T., 'A Blunden Bibliography', *Today's Japan*, vol. 5 (1960).

Watson, George (ed.), *The Concise Cambridge Bibliography of English Literature 600–1950* (Cambridge, 1966).

Willison, I. R. (ed.), *The New Cambridge Bibliography of English Literature*, vol. 4: *1900–1950* (Cambridge, 1972) pp. 234–8.

Reference Books

The BBC Year-Book 1930 (1930).

Dictionary of National Biography.

Kodansha Encyclopaedia of Japan (1983).

MLA International Bibliography of Books and Articles on the Modern Languages and Literatures, compiled by Paul A. Brown (New York).
The Oxford Companion to English Literature, compiled and edited by Sir Paul Harvey (1981); 4th edn rev. by D. Eagle.
The Oxford Illustrated Literary Guide to Great Britain and Ireland, compiled and edited by D. Eagle and H. Carnell; rev. by D. Eagle (1981).
The Times obituaries.
The Year's Work in English Studies, 1929, ed. F. S. Boas (London: Oxford University Press, 1931).
The Year's Work in English Studies, 1981, ed. Laurel Brake and others (London: John Murray, 1983).

Books and Articles about Blunden, or of Related Interest

Aaronson, L., 'Edmund Blunden', *Nineteenth Century and After*, vol. 129 (1941) pp. 580–5.
Allott, Kenneth (ed.), *The Penguin Book of Contemporary Verse* (Harmondsworth, 1962).
Barker, F. E., 'The Poetry of Blunden', *Nineteenth Century*, vol. 109 (1931) pp. 115–24.
Bayley, John, *An Essay on Hardy* (Cambridge, 1978).
——, *Selected Essays* (Cambridge, 1984).
——, 'The Undercover Poet', *The Times Literary Supplement*, 25 January 1985, pp. 79–80.
Bliss, W., 'Blunden's Poetry', *London Mercury*, vol. 23 (1930) pp. 257–64.
The Blue, vol. 42, October 1914–July 1915.
Blunden, Claire, 'Edmund Blunden Memorial Window' (letter), *The Times Literary Supplement*, 2 June 1978, p. 614. (The photograph is printed in *The Sunday Times*, 16 July 1978, p. 33.)
Edmund Blunden Sixty-Five (Hong Kong, 1961). Tributes.
Blythe, Ronald, *From the Headlands* (1982).
Bridges, R., 'The Dialectical Words in Blunden's Poems', *Society for Pure English Tract*, no. 5 (1921).
Buck, A. H., 'Edmund Blunden: Some Memories', *The Blue*, vol. CI, no. 2 (June 1974) pp. 93–7.
Church, R., 'Edmund Blunden: Agonist', *Fortnightly Review*, vol. 148, pp. 377–84; reprinted in his *Eight for Immortality* (1941).
Clare, John, *John Clare*, ed. Eric Robinson and David Powell (Oxford, 1984).

Corrigan, D. Felicitas, *Siegfried Sassoon: Poet's Pilgrimage* (1973).
Dunn, W. H., 'Blunden and his Poetry', *London Quarterly Review*, vol. 150 (1928) pp. 74–82.
Eigo Seinen, The Rising Generation, Edmund Blunden Number, 1 April 1950.
Fraser, G. S., *Impressions of Japan and Other Essays* (Tokyo, 1952).
——, 'Edmund Blunden', *London Magazine*, vol. 6 (1966).
Gathorne-Hardy, Robert (ed.), *Ottoline at Garsington: Memoirs of Lady Ottoline Morrell, 1915–1918* (1974).
Gittings, Robert, and Manton, Jo, *The Second Mrs Hardy* (1979).
Glendinning, Victoria, *Edith Sitwell: A Unicorn Among Lions* (1981).
Graves, Robert, *Goodbye to All That* (Harmondsworth, 1982).
——, *In Broken Images: Selected Letters of Robert Graves, 1914–1946*, ed. with a commentary by Paul O'Prey (1982).
Hankin, C. A. (ed.), *The Letters of John Middleton Murry to Katherine Mansfield* (1983).
Hardie, A. M., *Edmund Blunden* (1958). (British Council Pamphlet.)
Hardy, Thomas, *Selected Poems*, ed. Walford Davies (1982). (Everyman's Library.)
Hart-Davis, Rupert (ed.), *The Lyttelton Hart-Davis Letters: Correspondence of George Lyttelton and Rupert Hart-Davis*, 6 vols (1978–84).
Hassall, Christopher, *Edward Marsh: Patron of the Arts, a Biography* (1959).
Hibberd, Dominic (ed.), *Poetry of the First World War* (1981). (Macmillan Casebook Series.)
Hurd, Michael, *The Ordeal of Ivor Gurney* (Oxford, 1984).
Hynes, Samuel, 'The Irony and the Pity', *The Times Literary Supplement*, no. 4107, 18 December 1981, p. 1469.
Keynes, Sir Geoffrey, *The Gates of Memory* (Oxford, 1981).
Leavis, F. R., *New Bearings in English Poetry* (1982).
Lehmann, John, *The English Poets of the First World War* (1982). With 58 illustrations.
Mallon, Thomas, *Edmund Blunden* (Boston, Mass., 1983). (English Authors Series.)
Millgate, Michael, *Thomas Hardy* (1982). (New Oxford Books.)
Moorehead, Caroline, 'Women at War', *The Times*, 9 November 1981, p. 9.
Morpurge, J. E., 'Edmund Blunden: Poet of Community', *Contemporary Review*, vol. 225 (1974) pp. 192–8.

Motion, Andrew, 'A Spirit above Wars', *The Times Literary Supplement*, 29 January 1982, p. 114.
Okada, Sumie, 'Edmund Blunden and his "Dearest Autumn"', *The Times Literary Supplement*, 30 October 1981, pp. 1271–2.
The Oxford Book of Twentieth-Century English Verse, chosen by Philip Larkin (Oxford, 1978).
The Oxford Book of War Poetry, ed. John Stallworthy (Oxford, 1984).
The Penguin Book of First World War Poetry, ed. Jon Silkin (1981).
'Professor Edmund Blunden' (obituary), *Charles Lamb Bulletin* (1974) pp. 121–4.
Reilly, Catherine W. (ed.), *Scars Upon My Heart: Women's Poetry and Verse of the First World War* (1981).
Sassoon, Siegfried, *The Weald of Youth* (1942).
——, *Memoirs of a Fox-Hunting Man* (1945).
——, *Siegfried Sassoon Diaries, 1920–1922*, edited and introduced by Rupert Hart-Davis (1981).
——, *Siegfried Sassoon Diaries, 1915–1918*, edited and introduced by Rupert Hart-Davis (1983).
——, *Siegfried's Journey, 1916–1920* (1983).
Seymour-Smith, Martin, *Robert Graves: His Life and Work* (1982).
Shaw, Loretta L., *Japan in Transition* (1922).
Sisson, C. H., *English Poetry 1900–1950: An Assessment* (Manchester, 1981).
Symons, Julian, *The Thirties: A Dream Revolved* (1960).
Tennyson, Alfred, *'In Memoriam', 'Maud', and Other Poems*, ed. John D. Jump (1977). (Everyman's University Library, vol. 44.)
Thomas, Edward, *The Collected Poems of Edward Thomas*, ed. R. George Thomas (Oxford, 1983).
Thorpe, M., 'The Poetry of Edmund Blunden', *English Studies*, vol. 48 (1967) pp. 122–33.
——, 'Blunden's Joy Poems', *English*, vol. 17 (1968) pp. 9–14.
——, *The Poetry of Edmund Blunden* (1971). (Bridge Books.)
Thwaite, Ann, *Edmund Gosse: A Literary Landscape, 1849–1928* (1984).
Tracey, Michael, *A Variety of Lives: A Biography of Sir Hugh Greene* (1983).
Twitchett, E. G., 'The Poetry of Edmund Blunden', *London Mercury*, vol. 14 (1926) pp. 621–31.
Van der Post, Sir Laurens, *Yet Being Someone Other* (1982).
Vansittart, Peter, *Voices from the Great War* (1981).

Weatherhead, Leslie D., *Key Next Door, and Other City Temple Sermons* (1960).
Willy, M., 'The Poetry of Edmund Blunden', *English*, vol. 11 (1956–7) pp. 213–17.
Wood, F. T., 'On the Poetry of Edmund Blunden', *Poetry Review*, vol. 23 (1932) pp. 255–74.
Yeats, W. B., *The Collected Poems of W. B. Yeats* (1965).

Index